It's finally here—the clear, graciou...  ...n.
If you've been confused about what ... ...ts
happening—or if you want to help ... ...are questioning their
faith—then get this book.

> **JOHN L. COOPER,** front man of the Christian rock band Skillet, author of
> *Awake and Alive to Truth,* and host of the *Cooper Stuff Podcast*

With sharp minds for the issue but soft hearts for those beguiled by
it, Alisa Childers and Tim Barnett skillfully clarify the chaos in their
timely and readable *The Deconstruction of Christianity.* They are
uniquely gifted to decipher the terminology, simplify the philosophical
concepts, and give solid advice on how to respond to the trend. If
you have loved ones caught in the deconstruction web woven by
"exvangelical" YouTubers and TikTokers, let Childers and Barnett
guide you out of the confusing tangle.

> **GREGORY KOUKL,** president of Stand to Reason; author of *Street Smarts,*
> *Tactics,* and *The Story of Reality*

The greatest barrier to people even "hearing" what Christians say
today is their view of truth. Christianity is no longer treated as an
objective truth claim but only as an expression of personal emotion
and experience—*my* truth versus *your* truth. This is called the fact/
value split, and it is now permeating the church as well, where it is a
major factor in the movement to "deconstruct" historic Christianity.
This book will help you recover the conviction that biblical truth is
true to all of reality.

> **NANCY PEARCEY,** professor and scholar in residence at Houston Christian
> University, author of several books including *Total Truth* and *Finding Truth*

Alisa Childers and Tim Barnett have patiently combed through myriad books, articles, tweets, and YouTube videos to get to the issues at the heart of the "deconstruction of Christianity," which is one of the most significant challenges to Christianity in America today. They take deconstructionists' critiques head-on, seriously address their attacks on Christianity, and then provide strong arguments in favor of the faith given once for all to the saints (Jude 1:3).

DOUGLAS GROOTHUIS, PhD, professor of philosophy at Denver Seminary; author of *Christian Apologetics*, 2nd ed.

Well written and theologically sound, this book sheds much-needed light on the phenomenon called deconstruction. It is an excellent resource for the church in an age of misapprehension, confusion, and doubt regarding the truths of biblical Christianity. This is a must-read for church leaders and everyday Christians alike. I highly recommend it.

BECKET COOK, author of *A Change of Affection: A Gay Man's Incredible Story of Redemption* and host of *The Becket Cook Show* podcast

Every generation must defend the gospel anew. And like every generation, we must have a showdown with the wolves of our time. That's why Alisa Childers and Tim Barnett's book, *The Deconstruction of Christianity*, is a must-read. Childers and Barnett write with clarity, urgency, and courage. I love many things about this book, but one is that the authors speak plainly and clearly about the problem and the people causing it—there's no pandering on these pages. I thank God for Childers and Barnett, and pray that the Lord will use this book mightily. This book is the wake-up call that the true church needs.

ROSARIA BUTTERFIELD, author of *Five Lies of Our Anti-Christian Age*

This book not only helps us understand what deconstruction is or isn't, but more importantly it helps us understand how to be caring, loving, and thoughtful regarding people who are caught in the confusing cultural winds of our day.

DAN KIMBALL, author of *How (Not) to Read the Bible*, vice president and professor at Western Seminary

The past decade has seen a rise of deconversion stories with "exvangelicals" even creating communities for deconstruction. Yet behind every story is a devastated parent or loved one. How did this happen? What is deconstruction? Where can I find help? Look no further. In *The Deconstruction of Christianity*, Alisa Childers and Tim Barnett give an immensely important explanation of the how, what, and who of deconstruction. With clarity and compassion, they adeptly explain this tragic phenomenon that finds its genesis in a rejection of God's truth and a blind embrace of human experience. But there is hope. If your loved one has deconstructed, this is a must-read.

DR. CHRISTOPHER YUAN, speaker, author of *Holy Sexuality and the Gospel*, and producer of The Holy Sexuality Project video series for parents and their teens

As deconstructionism continues to be on the rise, more and more professing Christians are leaving the faith. This new book from my good friends Tim Barnett and Alisa Childers so eloquently explains everything you need to know about why people deconstruct their faith, and more importantly, how we can come alongside to help them build an even stronger faith. If you or someone you know is considering leaving Christianity, this book is a must-read. I trust it will be a valuable resource to aid the body of Christ for many years to come.

ALLEN PARR, author of *Misled: 7 Lies That Distort the Gospel (and How You Can Discern the Truth)* and founder of The BEAT YouTube channel

As a professor who works with hundreds of students a year at a Christian university, I have a front-row seat to the phenomenon of deconstruction. Some students are seeking honest answers to honest questions, wrestling through whether the faith of their upbringing can pass intellectual muster and offer them a more meaningful, loving, and just way to live. (Spoiler: It can!) But some find themselves drawn to the #exvangelical progressive Christianity so often pushed by online celebrities and social media algorithms. Alisa Childers and Tim Barnett have done us all a tremendous service. For its careful nuance, probing cultural analysis, biblical depth, and hope-filled defense of the historic faith, *The Deconstruction of Christianity* will be a top resource I recommend to anyone experiencing the trend (as old as Genesis 3) of lost faith.

> **THADDEUS WILLIAMS,** professor of theology at Biola University and author of *Don't Follow Your Heart: Boldly Breaking the 10 Commandments of Self-Worship*

In the guise of self-care and critical thinking, "deconstruction" is spreading like wildfire, burning whatever it touches and destroying the faith of many. This book's analysis of the issues, both logically and emotionally, will pour water on that fire. I can't overstate how important this book is for the great faith crisis of our time. Before you deconstruct, read this book.

> **MIKE WINGER,** teacher of BibleThinker online ministry

This book is so needed. In a conversation that is often full of broad brush statements and confusion, Alisa and Tim have accomplished what they set out to do—address deconstruction in a way that is reasonable, accurate, and filled with grace. I highly recommend this book.

> **JINGER DUGGAR VUOLO,** *New York Times* bestselling author of *Becoming Free Indeed: My Story of Disentangling Faith from Fear*

The Deconstruction of Christianity

THE
DECONSTRUCTION
OF
CHRISTIANITY

WHAT IT IS,
WHY IT'S DESTRUCTIVE,
AND HOW TO RESPOND

ALISA CHILDERS
AND TIM BARNETT

Visit Tyndale online at tyndale.com.

Tyndale and Tyndale's quill logo are registered trademarks of Tyndale House Ministries. *Tyndale Elevate* and the Tyndale Elevate logo are trademarks of Tyndale House Ministries. Tyndale Elevate is a nonfiction imprint of Tyndale House Publishers, Carol Stream, Illinois.

The Deconstruction of Christianity: What It Is, Why It's Destructive, and How to Respond

Cover illustration of an American church by Samuel Sloan (1815–1884), public domain.

Author photograph of Alisa Childers taken by Chrissy Katina of MagnifyU Photography, copyright © 2019. All rights reserved.

Author photograph of Tim Barnett taken by Ashley van der Walt, copyright © 2023. All rights reserved.

Cover designed by Dean H. Renninger

Published in association with the literary agency of William K. Jensen Literary Agency, 119 Bampton Court, Eugene, OR 97404.

The URLs in this book were verified prior to publication. The publisher is not responsible for content in the links, links that have expired, or websites that have changed ownership after that time.

The names of some of the individuals whose stories appear in this book have been changed to protect their privacy.

Library of Congress Cataloging-in-Publication Data

A catalog record for this book is available from the Library of Congress.

ISBN 978-4964-7497-1

Printed in the United States of America

29	28	27	26	25	24	23
7	6	5	4	3	2	1

For Dyllan and Ayden
That you might love the Lord and walk
with him all the days of your life
Mom (Alisa)

For Julianna, Jocelyn, and Alison
That you might love the Lord, delight in his
Word, and walk in the truth
Dad (Tim)

Contents

Foreword

APOSTASY IS NOTHING NEW. Ever since Paul mentioned in 2 Timothy 4:10 that his erstwhile colleague Demas had fallen in love with the things of this world and abandoned him, the church has been aware that there are those whose profession of Christianity, while often powerfully expressed in the moment, proves weak and transient in the long term. Every generation has its high-profile apostates. What is new is the cool postmodern terminology that has emerged in the English-speaking West for doing so: that of "deconstructing the faith."

On one level, the language of deconstruction in this context is something of a pose: Those who use the term and its cognates often have little grasp of its origins or its technical meaning. Thus, its use gives a novel, intellectual veneer of sophistication to something more prosaic: the age-old phenomenon of abandoning Christianity. The sophisticated linguistic theories associated with Jacques Derrida and his followers are not typically a direct inspiration for what is being described. Nor, one might add, is "deconstructing the faith" culturally akin to the Derrida project. Deconstruction (and its close relative post-structuralism) emerged as a force among French intellectuals in the wake of the Nazi occupation of France and the devastation of the Second World War. Its rejection of stable meaning was not something joyful and liberating; rather it spoke of a European despair. Only when this concept was transposed to America, where pre-9/11 the culture had a perennial optimism to it, was deconstruction welcomed as a positive, liberating force.

This loss of meaning points to one key affinity between postmodern American deconstruction and the current penchant for apostasy: Both see external authority as a problem of manipulative power structures and their demolition as liberating. Deconstruction in the technical sense might be seen to find inspiration in Nietzsche's comment that humans will never be free of God until they are free of grammar. In the same way, the contemporary "deconstructing the faith" movement thinks in less nuanced but substantially similar ways: We will never be free until we are free of God. Our current apostates present deconstructing the faith as a joyful discovery of meaning, not as a tragic and disorienting loss. Sadly, it really will prove to be the latter, no matter how cheerful the dime-a-dozen TikTok deconstructionists appear to their audiences. They do not feel the icy chill of the void into which they are plunging. Freedom, after the initial buzz has worn off, can indeed be a nightmare, with the responsibility of self-creation impossible and thus unbearable.

Rebellion against external authority is not an innovation in human behavior: From the Garden of Eden through Sinai to Calvary and beyond, human beings have sought to define themselves and their world on their own terms. But as noted, the language, or idiom, for this rebellion changes over time, which means that the church must keep two things in mind. First, she must not lose sight of the fact that the current problem with apostasy is not fundamentally different from the problem in the past. Demas rejected the faith for the same reason the TikTok apostate does: He loved the world more than he loved Christ.

Yet the idiom of apostasy does change, and thus it behooves those engaged in the important pastoral work to persuade those flirting with deconstruction of the error of their ways. And that means having a good sense of the specific logic and language of the times.

This is where Alisa and Tim's book is so helpful. Here the reader will find the current Christian deconstruction movement set against the broad background of postmodernism and explained both in terms of contemporary idiom and issues and basic biblical foundations. Dare one say it? Alisa and Tim help the reader to deconstruct the deconstructionists and thus to respond to them, both with arguments and with pastoral love and sensitivity. This is a timely book. I hope, ironically, that its time will pass—that the topic it deals with may be consigned to the dustbin of church history at some point. But for now, this deconstructing of the deconstructionists is a vital task.

Carl R. Trueman
Grove City College
Good Friday, 2023

PART I

#EXVANGELICAL

I (ALISA) WAS STANDING IN THE FOYER of a church where I had just spoken at a Christian worldview conference when I was approached by an elderly couple with downcast faces. Without wasting time on pleasantries, the man said, "Our son . . ." Surprised by his own tears, he stopped short. The gray-haired woman next to him laid her hand on his shoulder and continued. "Our son deconstructed. He isn't a Christian anymore. We don't know what to do."

"My wife and I did everything," the man said, shaking his head. "We brought him up as a Christian, raised him in church. We taught him to love God and his Word. We thought we'd done everything right. But several years ago he started claiming that the church is too exclusive. Then he complained that Christians are intolerant and unloving."

"Now he tells us we're toxic and won't let us see our grand-kids," his wife added. "What do we do? How can we get our son back and be invited into our grandkids' lives again?"

Sadly, this story represents countless similar scenarios in which parents, grandparents, pastors, spouses, and friends are faced with the tricky task of figuring out how to navigate the complex and sometimes volatile phenomenon that is sweeping up their loved ones.

I (Tim) sat across from Adam, a freshman in high school, at a local coffee shop. This was our first meeting, but I could tell right away that Adam was one of those kids who always needs to know why. He had been struggling with big questions about his faith, so his dad arranged for the two of us to have a conversation.

"I lost all my friends," Adam lamented. He recalled how his best friend of five years recently "came out" and wanted to know what he, as a Christian, thought about it. In a text message exchange, Adam carefully communicated his Christian convictions with truth and compassion. Sadly, Adam's friend took screenshots of their conversation and shared it with their high school friends. Soon he was being called "homophobic," and most of his friends from school wouldn't talk to him.

During our discussion, Adam mentioned that he'd discovered some TikTok videos that argue *from the Bible* that homosexual activity isn't a sin. With desperation, he told me, "If that's true, I might get my friends back." The pressure for Adam to capitulate to culture and adjust his beliefs was overwhelming. But we all feel it, don't we? Faithfulness to God comes at a cost. It's easier to submit to societal opinions than to stand on scriptural truth. Many Christians are feeling the pull to align their views with culture or their own personal preferences. For Adam, deconstructing the biblical view of sexuality wasn't just academic; it was personal. As he put it: "I might get my friends back."

These stories aren't unique. Perhaps you, like so many,

have someone in your life who is going through a process of deconstruction or who is being tempted to deconstruct their faith. Maybe you are experiencing heartbreaking loss and confusion, and are desperate for a lifeline. You are why we wrote this book.

It all started when I (Tim) was sitting on the back pew in an old chapel that more closely resembled a barn than a place of worship. I had been tasked with teaching a weeklong series on deconstruction for the morning Bible study. Through my research, I realized how much confusion there is about this topic and how much the church needs help addressing it. It also became clear that deconstruction is a transition away from historic Christianity and toward something else. For example, some who deconstruct their faith end up in so-called progressive Christianity. Given Alisa's work on this subject, I sent her a text message to see if she was going to write a much-needed book on deconstruction.

Meanwhile, I (Alisa) was beginning to think more deeply about the topic of deconstruction and noticed that not many Christian leaders were even talking about it. I had also noticed a couple of Tim's social media posts about deconstruction and thought, *He gets it!* I was so excited to see someone I trust tackle it head-on. Then one day, out of the blue, I received a text from Tim.

"Alisa, are you going to write a book on deconstruction?"

"Ugh. I'm trying to finish writing my second book and am drowning!" I replied.

"Want to write one together?" Tim asked, half-joking.

Immediately I knew this was destined to happen. "Let's talk," I typed. Those two words would lead to this moment.

If you're reading this book, you are probably not in deconstruction, but you may be trying to understand what's happening to someone you love. You might feel overwhelmed by the deconstruction stories dominating your newsfeed, the confusing and chaotic messages that often accompany the hashtags #deconstruction and #exvangelical, and the very real relational and emotional impact this phenomenon is having on your everyday life. If that's you, it's okay. Maybe it's time to press the pause button on social media. Put down your phone, close Twitter, and take a break from Facebook, Instagram, and TikTok. All of that will still be there when you return. Take a breath. Rest assured, we will walk you through what deconstruction is and how it works, and give you practical advice on how to relate with friends and loved ones going through it.

On the other hand, this concept might still be a bit abstract to you. You can see it happening, but it isn't touching your life in a concrete way. Maybe you simply want to understand why deconstruction seems to be so popular and learn more about what it is, where it originated, and how to respond.

If you are reading this book and *are* in deconstruction, we're really glad you've picked it up. While the book is primarily written to Christians who are experiencing deconstruction *from the outside*, we hope to present the topic in a way that is reasonable, accurate, and filled with grace for those experiencing it *from the inside*.

What you are about to read are the prayerful observations, thoughtful analyses, and honest conclusions of two people who have spent a significant amount of time collectively—as a team—living, studying, eating, sleeping, and breathing deconstruction.

We've listened to countless deconstruction stories. We've read books written by people who have deconstructed. We've jumped headlong into the deconstruction echo chambers on Twitter, TikTok, YouTube, and Instagram. We've met privately with proponents of deconstruction on Zoom. Our main objective in writing this book is to analyze the phenomenon of deconstruction and provide a biblical analysis and critique of its methods, trends, messages, and impact on the church.

This book is broken into three parts. In part 1, we identify deconstruction as it manifests in our homes, in our churches, and on social media. We define the word and give a thirty-thousand-foot view of how it has grown from a hashtag into a phenomenon, complete with conferences, coaches, and countless social media accounts. Then in part 2, we dig down into the details. We pull it all apart and analyze the many reasons *why* people are deconstructing, *how* they are deconstructing, and *what* they are deconstructing. We also consider *who* is going through it—the very real people undergoing deconstruction. We offer what we think is a better solution to the nagging doubts, difficult questions, and false ideas that haunt many Christians. Finally, in part 3, we focus on how we can best love and help those in our lives who might be in deconstruction. Please know that there is hope.

Let's dive in. What is deconstruction? Some might call it a movement. We think it's more like an explosion.

EXPLOSION

"It is time for us and your generation to declare war on this idolatrous deconstruction Christian movement!" declared Skillet front man John Cooper to the ecstatic applause of about fifteen thousand Christian youth at a popular music festival. Clips from Cooper's monologue were widely discussed on YouTube, Twitter, and TikTok and became the subject of several articles released by major Christian online platforms. *Relevant* magazine claimed Cooper was operating from "a fundamental misunderstanding of what 'deconstruction' is,"[1] while ChurchLeaders took a more neutral approach, allowing Cooper and some of his critics to clarify and further expound their opinions.[2] Soon, several others threw their proverbial hats in the online ring of the deconstruction conversation.[3] This flood of articles and social media commentary revealed a split between people who were defining deconstruction in two contradictory ways and seemed to be unaware of one another.

On the one hand, Cooper and the fifteen thousand or so youth at the Winter Jam festival were defining deconstruction as a move away from historic Christianity, which often results in deconversion and an almost religious zeal to deconvert others. The other group was defining deconstruction as a more straightforward process of "re-examining the faith you grew up with."[4] With those two definitions in mind, it's not difficult to see why Cooper's comments received such an explosive reception.

DECLARING WAR?

When speaking with the ChurchLeaders reporter, Cooper was careful to distinguish between people who ask questions about their faith and those who exit the faith altogether. He said he was calling out "formerly Christian leaders/influencers leaving the faith in a public way."[5] When Cooper declared "war" on deconstruction, he was speaking of *spiritual* warfare. Many Christians misunderstand spiritual warfare as referring only to power encounters with demonic spirits. Of course, there is some of that. But the fundamental nature of spiritual warfare is *not* power encounters; it's truth encounters.[6] It's a battle of *ideas*.

"We destroy arguments and every lofty opinion raised against the knowledge of God, and take every thought captive to obey Christ," writes the apostle Paul about the "weapons of our warfare" (2 Corinthians 10:4-5). The Bible also tells us that our enemy is not any group of people, but rather the "spiritual forces of evil in the heavenly places" (Ephesians 6:12). Jesus tells us about this enemy, called the devil, whom he describes as a murderer from the beginning, in whom there is no truth at all. Jesus says, "When he lies, he speaks out of his own character, for he is a liar and the father of lies" (John 8:44). In fact, he is the "deceiver of the whole world" (Revelation 12:9). Notice how the battlefield is in the realm of "opinions," "knowledge of God," "arguments," and "thoughts." As Christians, the primary weapon of our warfare is truth. If we want to "stand against the schemes of the devil," we must "put on the whole armor of God," which begins with "the belt of truth" (Ephesians 6:11, 14). We need to be vigilant to resist, oppose, and refute false

We need to be vigilant to resist, oppose, and refute false ideas while remaining loving and compassionate toward the people who are being taken "captive" by them (Colossians 2:8).

ideas while remaining loving and compassionate toward the people who are being taken "captive" by them (Colossians 2:8). Therefore, if deconstruction really is a movement that seeks to lead Christians away from truth and encourages them to deconvert from the faith, declaring spiritual war on it would be prudent, wise, and biblical.

However, if deconstruction simply means rethinking what you believe, engaging your doubts, or asking hard questions, declaring spiritual war on it would be unbiblical, fearful, and downright mean. After all, the Bible instructs us over and over again *not* to believe every spirit. We're told to "test the spirits to see whether they are from God, for many false prophets have gone out into the world" (1 John 4:1). John goes on to explain in verses 5 and 6 that Christians should evaluate the claims of spiritual teachers to determine whether they are speaking "from the world" or speaking truth from God. Specifically, we should consider whether or not these teachers listen to those who were sent by God. At the time when John was writing, this meant the apostles. Today, that means their words recorded in Scripture. In Philippians 1:9-10, Paul prayed that Christians would abound in love, "with knowledge and all discernment, so that you may approve what is excellent." In Acts 17:11, he also praises the Bereans for "examining" his words against the Scriptures to make sure he was telling the truth.

In addition, we are to be compassionate to those who ask questions because of a sincere desire to get at the truth. Jude assumes there will be doubters, instructing, "Have mercy on those who doubt" (Jude 1:22), and Jesus, rather than silencing doubters, is continually tender with them (more on this in chapter 5). Asking your hard questions, correcting your false beliefs, and facing your deepest doubts are all a natural part of maturing as a Christian.

So between these two definitions of deconstruction, which is correct? In order to bring clarity to the confusion, we need to answer the million-dollar question: What is deconstruction?

WHAT DOES IT MEAN?

Have you ever had a young kid ask you a question *and you had absolutely no idea what they were talking about*? A few years ago, while I (Tim) was celebrating my wife's birthday, my six-year-old daughter's face narrowed into a quizzical look as she asked, "Dad, what does a one-two smell like?"

Confused by her question, I said, "Julianna, one and two are numbers, and numbers don't have a smell." Logically speaking, she was making a category mistake. But try explaining that to a six-year-old.

Not at all impressed by my stellar critical thinking skills, and equally perplexed by my reply, she said, "No, Dad, what does a one-two smell like?"

Repeating the question didn't help. Now I was even *more* confused. I didn't know what else to say. Then my four-year-old, Jocelyn, observing our communication stalemate, said, "Dad, 'you look like a monkey and you smell like . . . one-two.' So, what does a 'one-two' smell like?"

When terms are not clearly understood, we can end up talking past one another. Multiple meanings create confusion, especially when it comes to a word as emotionally charged as *deconstruction*. This was on full display in the weeks following the John Cooper declaration and the subsequent op-eds, hot takes, and articles that put deconstruction front and center.

A decade ago, hardly anyone would have used the word *deconstruction* to describe their spiritual journey. Yet today, the word has made its way into our common vocabulary, along with words like *yeet*, *sus*, and *metaverse*. (If you don't know what those words mean, we'll pause for you to go ask a teenager.) In fact, our social media feeds are flooded with people detailing their faith deconstructions—people like Rhett McLaughlin and Link Neal (from *Good Mythical*

Morning YouTube channel), Joshua Harris (of *I Kissed Dating Goodbye*), Michael and Lisa Gungor (from Gungor), Jon Steingard (from Hawk Nelson), Kevin Max (from DC Talk), Phanatik (from The Cross Movement), and Derek Webb (from Caedmon's Call).

In the summer of 2019, the Christian world was shocked by news that Joshua Harris—the evangelical poster child for purity culture—had deconstructed his faith. A month later, it was Marty Sampson's turn. In a now deleted Instagram post, the former Hillsong worship leader informed his followers that he was "genuinely losing my faith."[7] Fast-forward six months to when *Good Mythical Morning* YouTuber Rhett McLaughlin detailed his "spiritual deconstruction" from Christian to "hopeful agnostic" in a video viewed more than 2.8 million times.[8] Next came Jon Steingard, the lead singer of the band Hawk Nelson. In a now deleted nine-image Instagram post, he wrote:

> After growing up in a Christian home, being a pastor's kid, playing and singing in a Christian band, and having the word "Christian" in front of most of the things in my life—I am now finding that I no longer believe in God. . . . I've been terrified to post this for a while—but it feels like it's time for me to be honest.[9]

DC Talk was a household name in Christian circles in the nineties. In fact, memorizing the lyrics to "Jesus Freak" was practically a spiritual sacrament. (Every church kid from that era knows exactly what was on the man's big fat belly that wiggled around like marmalade jelly.) That's why many were shocked when Kevin Max posted on Twitter, "Hello, my name is Kevin Max & I'm an #exvangelical."[10] Max followed up by explaining he's been "deconstructing for decades" and tweeting that he now follows "the Universal Christ."[11] This was confusing for Christians who had never heard of the Universal Christ, which is a belief in the "presence of the divine in literally 'every thing' and 'every one.'"[12]

It wasn't just famous musicians and artists announcing their exits from historic Christianity. Paul Maxwell, former theological content writer for Desiring God, an organization founded by John Piper, joined the fray. In an Instagram video, he said, "I think it's important to say that I'm just not a Christian anymore, and it feels really good. I'm really happy."[13]

The word being used to describe these experiences, and others like them, is *deconstruction*. Along with the higher profile deconstructions, there has been an explosion of TikTok, Instagram, and Twitter accounts dedicated to celebrating the mass exodus from a belief system that many have come to regard as toxic, oppressive, and abusive. Often, these memes, videos, and images are posted alongside the hashtags #deconstruction and #exvangelical. For example, at the time of this writing, a quick search on Instagram reveals the #deconstruction tag being used on 340,000 posts. On TikTok, videos using the deconstruction hashtag have accumulated 714 million views.[14]

To call something a movement would imply a group of people *moving* together, united around common principles and sharing the same goal. Deconstruction is a bit like a movement in the way people find community, share stories, and tend to reject the same set of beliefs they now deem harmful. But because deconstruction can lead to so many different destinations, with some people landing in agnosticism, some in progressive Christianity, some in secular humanism, and some in a more self-styled spirituality, it's more like an explosion, blasting out in all different directions. There's also been an explosion in *how* the word is used.[15] If you ask ten different people to define *deconstruction*, you might get eleven different definitions. That's because there is no agreed-upon, authoritative, univocal understanding of what it means. When someone says, "I'm deconstructing my faith," they could mean anything from asking questions, experiencing doubts, and correcting beliefs to rejecting Scripture, following cultural norms, or leaving Christianity altogether. But if deconstruction means everything, it means nothing.

Take, for example, the case of Joshua Harris. Many Christian teenagers were given a copy of his bestselling book, *I Kissed Dating Goodbye*, which practically became canon in the evangelical culture of the late 1990s and early 2000s. Nearly two decades later, a week after announcing his divorce, Harris posted a picture of himself pensively staring out over a serene lake, surrounded by beautiful ice-capped mountains, with a caption that read,

> The information that was left out of our announcement is that I have undergone a massive shift in regard to my faith in Jesus. The popular phrase for this is "deconstruction," the biblical phrase is "falling away." By all the measurements that I have for defining a Christian, I am not a Christian.[16]

When Harris made his big announcement, virtually no one questioned his definition of deconstruction as being synonymous with "falling away." At the time, that seemed to be the general understanding of what someone meant when they said they had "deconstructed." But for many today, deconstruction doesn't always involve walking away from faith but instead may entail a redefinition of that faith.

In his book *After Doubt*, A. J. Swoboda defines faith deconstruction as "the process of dismantling one's accepted beliefs."[17] Swoboda sees this as a "journey of questioning, critiquing, and reevaluating previous faith commitments."[18] This is a much broader definition that includes not only people abandoning their faith but also, say, an evangelical Christian who is questioning a secondary doctrine like young-earth creationism or doubting a denominational distinctive like dispensationalism while remaining committed to the faith. So one person could use the word to describe their decision to leave Christianity but another could use it to mean their choice to reject young-earth creationism while remaining evangelical. Can you see why so many are confused by the word?

There has been an effort by Christians to solve this ambiguity problem. Since the word *deconstruction* covers such a large landscape, some have proposed a distinction between "good deconstruction" and "bad deconstruction." For example, pastor and *New York Times* bestselling author John Mark Comer said this:

> The first thing that must be said about deconstruction is that there is a good type of deconstruction. . . . This

is the type of deconstruction where Jesus, and others, used Scripture to critique the world's corruption of the church. But then there's another type of deconstruction, that of Western millennials, who use the world to critique Scripture's authority over the church.[19]

Similarly, Grammy Award–winning rapper and producer Lecrae described two types of deconstruction happening in the church. In a Twitter thread, he wrote, "One type of deconstruction actually involves using scriptures to deconstruct unhealthy ideas and practices."[20] He calls this "healthy" deconstruction. Conversely, he continues, "Many millennials are using culture to challenge scripture. This often leads to culture taking precedence over scripture & sadly people begin to deconstruct themselves out of the faith. We begin to question the Bible because it doesn't line up w/ culture."[21] Lecrae calls this type of deconstruction "unhealthy"[22] and "dangerous."[23]

Both Comer and Lecrae recognize that all "deconstruction" is *not* the same. Furthermore, they communicate the value of asking questions, rejecting legalism, standing against abuse, reforming beliefs, and engaging doubts. They express compassion for the hurt and struggles people are going through, and both propose a way forward that communicates an emphasis on God and his Word. Consequently, they provide an important distinction between two different approaches to examining faith—one biblical; the other unbiblical.

While we agree with all of that, we want to make a

suggestion. When we started our investigation of deconstruction, we also thought adding adjectives to the word (like *healthy* versus *unhealthy* or *good* versus *bad*) would help solve the confusion. But now we actually think it makes things worse.

BAPTIZING WORDS

Although we certainly understand why some Christian thought leaders and influencers are using the word to encourage discernment, reformation, and healthy questioning, there are a number of reasons why the word *deconstruction* should not be baptized, redeemed, or Christianized to mean something healthy or positive. First, what pastors call "good deconstruction" (i.e., using the Scriptures to challenge the ideas you hold) doesn't match the common use of the word in the culture, which usually calls for the rejection of Scripture as a standard. In fact, the further we got into our research, the clearer it became that we wouldn't find many people in the deconstruction explosion who still believed in Scripture as their absolute authority. It seemed the only people who were using the word that way were Christian pastors and apologists who were trying to keep people in the faith.

For the majority of people from the broader culture in the deconstruction movement, the Bible is seen as a tool of oppression to be rejected, not a standard of truth to be affirmed. In fact, most major deconstruction platforms bristle at the idea that anything other than one's personal conscience should guide an individual toward breaking free from oppressive systems (perceived or actual) and toxic theology, which is defined as any doctrine or practice that someone deems harmful.

Ironically, many in the deconstruction community agree with us on this point. In the deconstruction online community, if you use the Bible to "deconstruct," or if you remain an evangelical Christian during or after deconstruction, then you never *really* deconstructed. For example, Andrew Kerbs runs the Instagram platform @deconstruct_everything with over 24,000 followers. In response to someone who wrote, "Do not deconstruct without the Bible in hand, or apart from the local church," he replied, "So . . . don't actually deconstruct is what I'm hearing you say."[24] Another popular deconstructionist posted a meme conveying a similar sentiment. At the top a hypothetical evangelical pastor is quoted as saying, "I don't have a problem with deconstruction, you see I too have deconstructed." Underneath that statement is a picture of a Chihuahua cutting his eyes in skepticism and disapproval. The caption below reads, "I'll eat my hat if the next thing they say isn't some variation of 'you just have to do it biblically.'"[25]

When Christians co-opt the word, redefining it, the deconstruction community thinks we're being deceptive. David Hayward, a former pastor, warned his followers of evangelicals who use the word *deconstruction* with a particular agenda. He said, "Some people use the word *deconstruction* to lure you back into the fold. Don't go for it."[26] Even worse, many deconstructionists attribute bad motives to Christian leaders using the word. In an article titled "The Age of Deconstruction and Future of the Church," Kurtis Vanderpool warns, "There will be a long line of evangelical leaders attempting to co-opt and redirect deconstruction for their own purposes. It is a desperate attempt to hold on to their people, hold on to their influence, hold on to their way of life without having to be held accountable for what their way of life has produced."[27]

Here's the point: Many in the deconstruction spaces don't think an experience can be rightly called deconstruction if the one claiming to have deconstructed remains a historical Christian or holds to biblical authority. And frankly, we agree.

Second, when people redefine words, the first casualty is clarity, and communication is compromised. This is why some people are confused about whether or not Mormons are Christians. After all, Mormons espouse belief in God, Jesus, and the gospel. But there's a problem. What they mean by God, Jesus, and the gospel is radically different from what Christians mean. As many have said, they have the same vocabulary but are using a different dictionary. For example, the Mormon god is "an exalted man"[28] with "a body of flesh and bones as tangible as man's."[29] For Mormons, Jesus is the created spirit brother of Lucifer. Furthermore, the Mormon gospel is the good news that if we obey God's commandments well enough, "we can become like our Heavenly Father" and "live in the highest degree of the celestial kingdom of heaven."[30] This includes leading our own worlds populated by our own spirit children.[31] So it turns out, when Christians and Mormons talk about God, Jesus, or the gospel, they are talking about completely different things. Notice that when a Mormon says, "I believe in Jesus," or "I'm trusting in God," it's not clear which Jesus, or which God, they're talking about. Communication is compromised. Likewise, when

Christians co-opt and redefine the word *deconstruction* to mean something completely different from what the culture means, confusion abounds.

Third, while we understand the temptation to baptize the word, it can come across as fairly awkward. If you attended youth group in the nineties, you might have heard a youth pastor say, "Don't get high on weed; get high on the Most High," or "You don't need a boyfriend because Jesus is your boyfriend." These were such cringeworthy statements because some youth pastors were trying to baptize words. In an attempt to be relevant and meet students where they were, they radically redefined terms, and their ability to connect with students actually decreased rather than increased, along with their credibility. Let's not make the same mistake today.

Philosophical baggage

Another concern has to do with the word's philosophical baggage. The word *deconstruction* can be traced back to the twentieth-century French philosopher Jacques Derrida, known by many as the father of deconstruction. For Derrida, deconstruction meant "dismantling our excessive loyalty to any idea and learning to see the aspects of the truth that might lie buried in its opposite."[32] Ultimately, Derrida didn't believe that words could be pinned down to singular meanings. In their book *Cynical Theories*, James Lindsay and Helen Pluckrose write, "For Derrida, the speaker's meaning has no more authority than the hearer's interpretation and thus intention cannot outweigh impact."[33] Derrida applied deconstruction to both literary texts and political institutions. Today, it's being applied to all areas of life, including religious belief. Many people deconstructing their faith have no idea who Derrida is, yet his postmodern philosophy lives on in their deconstruction testimonies. In other words, they may not have heard his name, but they are using his playbook. We'll discuss this further in chapter 8.

Deconstruction's postmodern roots lead us to avoid using the term in any sort of positive sense. This might seem like nitpicking over semantics, but it's vital to make some important distinctions. Maybe an illustration will help. If you live in America, you've probably seen T-shirts, hats, and signs with the words Black Lives Matter or Make America Great Again. You probably also know that each of these slogans represents a set of beliefs. That's why some wouldn't be caught dead wearing a BLM T-shirt (even though they affirm that black lives do, indeed, matter), while others would rather stick their hand in a blender than wear a MAGA hat (even though they want America to be great). These acronyms are loaded with political and ideological baggage. They aren't just simple, straightforward statements. Behind each mantra is a movement.

In a similar way, the word *deconstruction* has philosophical baggage. And when Christians wear the deconstruction label, they need to understand what's behind it. Whether people realize it or not, faith deconstruction is a form of postmodern deconstruction. And here's the irony: If we attempt to completely detach current deconstruction from the ideas of Derrida (the father of deconstruction) and define it subjectively, we are literally deconstructing the word *deconstruction* à la Derrida. And if the meaning of that word signifies any number of different things, at best we will be equivocating.

At worst, we will have bought into the assumptions of post-modernism hook, line, and sinker.

A question of authority

As Christians, we want to use accurate language to describe our understanding of how to live as followers of Jesus, and when we use the word *deconstruction* according to its common usage today, we find that the concept it describes is not present in the Bible. When advising us on how to evaluate our beliefs, Scripture talks about using discernment (Hebrews 5:14), seeking understanding (Proverbs 2:2-5), abounding in knowledge and approving what is excellent (Philippians 1:9-10), and holding fast to what is good (1 Thessalonians 5:21). Nowhere in Scripture do we find approval for the practice of deconstruction.

Jesus never says, "Therefore go and make disciples of all nations, baptizing them in the name of the Father and of the Son and of the Holy Spirit, and teaching them to deconstruct everything I have commanded you." Instead, Jesus commissions his followers to make more disciples and to "obey everything I have commanded you" (see Matthew 28:16-20, NIV). There is no Great Decommission.

The practice of deconstruction is fundamentally at odds with Christianity. Here's why. First, deconstruction has little to do with trying to achieve correct theology. Take, for example, Melissa Stewart, a former Christian, now an agnostic/atheist with a TikTok following of over 200,000. She describes how lonely and isolated she felt during her own deconstruction. Discovering the #exvangelical hashtag, she says, opened up a whole new world of voices who related with what she was going through. Her TikTok platform now gives her the opportunity to create that type of space for others. In an interview on the *Exvangelical* podcast, she commented on the deconstruction/exvangelical online space:

> My biggest experiences with it were people talking about what they went through—talking about their stories—and it was very personal and focused on the human beings who have come out of this rather than on whether or not a certain kind of theology is right or wrong.[34]

She gets it. Deconstruction is *not* about getting your theology right. It's *not* about trying to make your views match reality. It's about tearing down doctrines that are morally wrong *to you* to make them match your own internal conscience, moral compass, true authentic self, or whatever else it's being called these days. Yet the goal for *all* Christians should be to align our beliefs with the Word of God, despite our own personal feelings or beliefs on the topic.

Second, there is no end goal, or destination, to the deconstruction process. There is just a never-ending skepticism of your view. As David Hayward said, "There isn't a right way to deconstruct, nor is there a right destination. You do you."[35]

Derek Webb, former lead singer of Caedmon's Call, wrote, "The cycle of de & reconstruction is existentially exhausting. What I've found helpful is to simply stop constructing. 'Belief' is just too heavy a term. Other than maybe cause & effect, I'm done 'believing.' Hypothesizing in real-time + permanent uncertainty = a start."[36]

Third, with deconstruction, there is no external authority to tell you what your view should look like. *You* are the ultimate authority. As one deconstructionist wrote, "I am not looking to adhere to any type of guidebook, any type of 'how to,' or any person telling me I must do it a certain way. I'm done being told what I must do to be doing things the *right* way."[37] Notice the rejection of any external authority, including the Bible. In her book *Faithfully Different*, our friend Natasha Crain writes, "Deconstruction doesn't usually imply a deconversion to atheism, but it's certainly a deconversion of its own kind—from a worldview rooted in the authority of the Bible to a worldview rooted in the authority of the self."[38]

MY KINGDOM FOR A DEFINITION!

As Natasha succinctly articulated, at the heart of the deconstruction explosion is a rejection of biblical authority. Deconstruction emphasizes personal autonomy—the authority of the *self*. So here's the big reveal. After months of research, practically living in the deconstruction and exvangelical online spaces, and eating/drinking #deconstruction, we have seen deconstruction characterized in different ways. However, there is one dominant expression that can be summed up in one sentence. When we use the word *deconstruction*, here's what we mean:

> Faith deconstruction is a postmodern process of rethinking your faith without regarding Scripture as a standard.

We could say a lot more about it, and we will. In fact, we will spend a great deal of time in this book defending this definition and demonstrating it to be true. We want to be clear what we are analyzing and critiquing, and what we aren't. We understand that there are people questioning, doubting, and critically examining their Christian beliefs according to what they find in Scripture (a healthy process!) and that they might be calling that deconstruction. But

At the heart of the deconstruction explosion is a rejection of biblical authority. Deconstruction emphasizes personal autonomy—the authority of the self.

we hope to demonstrate that, as Christians, we *already* have language for that. Our research has shown that deconstruction goes beyond just rethinking and asking questions—it's a specific process or methodology. It's *how* someone goes about rethinking their faith that makes the difference.

Now for a few more definitions. Much of this book will engage with the movement of deconstruction and the thought leaders who write the books, lead the seminars, organize the conferences, and run the social media platforms. We will call these thought leaders deconstructionists. When we use the word *deconstructionist*, we are talking specifically about the most influential voices online who are actively attempting to dismantle historic Christianity, discredit the church, and promote an atmosphere of faith deconstruction. However, when we write about deconstructionists, we are *not* talking about the Christian high school student who has become confused by a YouTube video he watched about supposed Bible contradictions. We are *not* talking about a woman who is just realizing she has been spiritually abused and is trying to find her way out. We are *not* talking about your sons, daughters, coworkers, friends, and loved ones who are critically examining their beliefs and are wading in the confusion of doubt. These situations would require a different response. We give some practical advice on this in chapter 12.

As we'll see in the next chapter, deconstruction isn't concerned with rethinking just any beliefs. Its primary concern is leaving behind what's characterized as "evangelical" beliefs. Many deconstructionists, in fact, are proud to call themselves exvangelicals.

EXVANGELICAL

"A god that requires belief in it in order to avoid eternal punishment while also not providing evidence of its existence is not a loving god." #exvangelical[1]

"I'm not going to derive my cosmology from four thousand-year-old legends of a jealous, bloodthirsty demigod." #exvangelical[2]

"If abortion is terminating a living thing you created that's still in formation stages, doesn't that mean god aborted an entire planet with the 'great flood'?" #exchristian #exvangelical[3]

"In abusive relationships, one person convinces another person that they are worthless and no one else could ever love them. That's why people stay. This is also how the church operates." #exvangelical[4]

These quotes grieve the heart of every Christian who values the authority of the Bible. Not only do they misrepresent God and genuine Christianity, but they also express an almost religious zeal to deconvert others with a confidence that would make the most fire-and-brimstone preacher jealous. *Exvangelical* doesn't simply mean "no longer evangelical." The exvangelical hashtag is like an iceberg, a piece of ice that has broken off a glacier, with 90 percent of its mass concealed below the waterline. With #exvangelical, there is the tiny bit you see on top—the TikTok videos, the Instagram posts, the graphic quotes, and the Internet memes. However, hidden under the surface is a giant mountain-like structure of beliefs and experiences that supports and sustains every hashtag proudly posted on social media. Most often, the deconstruction and exvangelical hashtags are placed together. This isn't a coincidence. An explosion blasts out in all different directions *from a singular starting place.* That point is the church; more specifically, the evangelical church. The one thing virtually all deconstruction stories have in common is what they say they are leaving behind.

LEAVING EVANGELICALISM?

Blake Chastain grew up in an evangelical church and began to deconstruct during college. Although he attends a mainline church, he articulates that he is, to some degree, agnostic.[5] In 2016 he birthed the hashtag #exvangelical, which has since grown into a movement with multiple millions of views on TikTok and over 100,000 impressions on Twitter every day.[6] He also started the *Exvangelical* podcast, which now functions as a type of community where others who have left their evangelical upbringings can process their experiences together. But #exvangelical isn't just about an individual leaving an evangelical church. It has to do with a particular understanding of what evangelical actually means. As we'll see, for many in the #exvangelical community, *evangelical* is perceived to be synonymous with misogyny, racism, homophobia, and the political support of Donald Trump.

For there to be an exvangelical, there must be an *evangelical*. But this is where things get murky. In his book *The Real Scandal of the Evangelical Mind*, Carl Trueman writes, "For there to be a scandal of the evangelical mind, there must be not just a mind, but also a readily identifiable thing called an 'evangelical' and a movement called 'evangelicalism'—and the existence of such is increasingly in doubt."[7] So, what is an evangelical? When we look back in history, we discover the word *evangelical* has always lacked definitional precision. Historian David W. Bebbington is famous for characterizing the evangelical movement according to its four main emphases. According to Bebbington, evangelicals were historically focused on the Bible as the source for essential truth, the cross as the atoning sacrifice of Christ, personal conversion as necessary for salvation, and activism primarily expressed as preaching the gospel.[8] However, this description is fairly broad, and doesn't provide specific doctrinal criteria such as a statement of faith to determine its boundaries. It's no wonder, then, that a 2022 study by Ligonier Ministries and LifeWay Research revealed that 43 percent of US *evangelicals* believe "Jesus was a great teacher, but he was not God," 56 percent of these *evangelicals* believe "God accepts the worship of all religions, including Christianity, Judaism, and Islam," and 38 percent believe "religious belief is a matter of personal opinion; it is not about objective truth."[9] These are the responses of evangelicals, not exvangelicals. But how can someone identify as an evangelical *and* deny the deity of Christ? It's because the word *evangelical* today has morphed to mean almost anything.

"When asked if I am an evangelical," Trueman writes, "I generally respond with a question: What exactly do you mean by that term? In a world in which everyone from Joel Osteen to Brian McLaren to John MacArthur may be called an evangelical, I want to know into what pigeonhole my answer will place me."[10] In many cases, exvangelicals use *evangelical* as a catchall term to "pigeonhole" people into a particular position. With the political overtones, scandals, and general negative attitudes surrounding the movement, the word *evangelical* has become a dirty word in many people's minds.

In the deconstruction movement, essential Christian truths like the doctrine of final judgment, substitutionary atonement, and biblical authority are often rightly associated with evangelicalism, but also lumped together with white supremacy, Christian nationalism, and Western civilization in general. This is one

The exvangelical hashtag can tell us only that someone left; it does not tell us what they left.

reason the mantra "decolonize your theology" has become so popular in deconstruction circles. Of course, it should go without saying that white supremacy is evil and that conflating the gospel with one's national identity is wrong. This book is not meant to be a defense of evangelicalism. It would be beyond the scope of this book to dive too deeply into those complex issues. But for our purposes, it must be understood that #exvangelical carries a lot of baggage because the word *evangelical* carries a lot of baggage. Because of this, the exvangelical hashtag can tell us only *that* someone left; it does not tell us *what* they left.

WHAT ARE THEY LEAVING?

There are plenty of self-identified evangelicals who believe and behave in abhorrent ways. Whether it's a televangelist seeking millions of dollars for a private jet or a high-profile pastor caught in another sex scandal, there's no shortage of examples. If exvangelicals were simply leaving because of those types of behaviors, we'd be right there with them. But they're leaving more than that. They're not merely renouncing bad beliefs and behaviors; they're rejecting sound doctrine.

Blake Chastain penned a blog post in which he fleshed out what it means to use the exvangelical hashtag.[11] He referred to it as a "working definition," acknowledging that it's a bit fluid and has yet to be concretized in its usage. Nevertheless, Chastain characterized what exvangelicals are leaving behind (his definition of evangelicalism) under five basic points:[12]

1. A literal reading of the Bible
2. A belief that women are to be submissive to men

3. A belief in the sanctity of heterosexuality/
   heteronormativity and a rejection of homosexuality
   as sinful
4. The assumption that the American way of life is best
5. Identification and partnership with political and
   social conservatism

So according to Chastain, this is what the exvangelicals are rejecting. Given the lack of clarity on the word *evangelical*, let's leave aside the question of whether or not this list accurately reflects the evangelical movement as a whole. Instead, we'll evaluate each point to see if it describes a bad belief that ought to be rejected or sound Christian doctrine that should be preserved.

Literalism?

Should we read the Bible literally? Well, it depends on what you mean by literal. Of course, Christians have historically believed that the entire Bible, from Genesis to Revelation, is the inspired and authoritative Word of God. This means that it communicates objective truth that isn't meant to be interpreted subjectively. But reading it literally doesn't mean *taking everything in it* literally. The Bible employs figures of speech like metaphor, simile, euphemism, hyperbole, and personification. It is made up of sixty-six books that were written in different time periods by different authors, who were communicating through different genres. Some books of the Bible are

Reading the Bible literally means believing that the Bible communicates literal truth, but not always in a literal way.

history (like many books in the Old Testament such as Joshua, Judges, and Ruth), and others contain law codes (like Deuteronomy and Leviticus). Some are made up of poetry (like Psalms and Song of Solomon) while others communicate general principles of wisdom (Ecclesiastes and Proverbs). Some are instructive (like Paul's epistles), and some are books of prophecy (like Isaiah, Jeremiah, and Ezekiel).

According to the *Merriam-Webster* dictionary, the word *literal* does not always mean exact equivalence. It's also defined as: "adhering to fact or to the ordinary construction or primary meaning of a term or expression; free from exaggeration or embellishment; characterized by a concern mainly with facts."[13] In other words, reading literally means believing that the Bible communicates literal truth, but not always in a literal way.

However, in the deconstruction movement, rejecting a "literal reading" of the Bible often means rejecting the idea that the text has a literal, objective meaning the Christian needs to discover and accept. Biblical interpretation becomes subjective, or the Bible is rejected altogether.

Patriarchy?

Second, should women be submissive to men? Part of God's design for marriage is communicated quite clearly throughout Scripture as being a union of one man with one woman who become one flesh for one lifetime. Jesus himself affirmed this in Matthew 19 when the Pharisees asked him a question about divorce. He replied by appealing to the definition of marriage in the Genesis creation narrative, stating: "Have you not read that he who created them from the beginning made them male and female, and said, 'Therefore a man shall leave his father and his mother and hold fast to his wife, and the two shall become one flesh'? So they are no longer two but one flesh. What therefore God has joined together, let not man separate" (verses 4-6). Both men and women are made in God's image (Genesis 1:27; James 3:9), but there are all sorts of differences between them, and they come together in marriage to become one flesh (Genesis 2:24).

Paul lays out household codes in Ephesians 5 that begin by telling spouses to submit to one another "out of reverence for Christ" (verse 21). Women are to submit to their husbands, and husbands are to love their wives as Christ loves the church. There is much spirited debate within Christianity about the role of women in ministry and leadership. For example, even though I (Alisa) am a complementarian (I believe that men and women are equal in value but different in roles), I grew up in the evangelical Foursquare denomination, in which there is no office a woman can't hold, including senior pastor of a congregation. Growing up, I didn't even know that many churches didn't ordain women pastors. I just thought it was some obscure Baptist thing! It simply isn't true that Christianity teaches that women have to submit to all men. In fact, nowhere in the Bible is this taught. The Bible teaches that wives should submit to their husbands, but it doesn't require every woman to submit to every man.

As we'll learn more about in chapter 8, in the deconstruction movement, complementarianism is "inherent misogyny"[14] and used synonymously with the word *patriarchy*, which is rejected as oppressive to women. This assumes that submission is inherently oppressive. However, Jesus himself submitted to the Father when he walked the earth (Mark 14:36; John 5:30; 1 Corinthians 11:3; Philippians 2:5-8).

Homophobia?

Third, is the idea that heterosexuality is sacrosanct a bad belief we should jettison, or is it sound doctrine? Simply put, the Bible teaches that God made two different sexes—men and women—that were designed to come together into one flesh (see previous section). The act of sex was designed to be between one man and one woman in the context of marriage. Anything outside of that is described in Scripture as "sexual immorality." And it's not just a few so-called "clobber" passages that teach this. It's the narrative of Scripture from cover to cover. In her *Mama Bear Apologetics Guide to Sexuality*, Hillary Morgan Ferrer describes the biblical understanding of sexual intercourse: "Sex is a married couple repeating their marital vows in bodily form."[15] In other words, sex is something designed by God to fully unite two human beings into one flesh. It's deeply valuable, holy, and incredibly powerful. Because of this, God has placed boundaries of protection around it. This isn't a uniquely evangelical belief. The Eastern Orthodox and Roman Catholic Churches hold to this sexual ethic as well. For the historic Christian (not just the evangelical), this is a nonnegotiable.

Yet in the deconstruction movement, the biblical language surrounding gender and sexuality is condemned as harmful. As Chastain puts it, "'Exvangelical' is also a repudiation of evangelicalism. It affirms what evangelicalism condemns. We embrace moral and religious autonomy. We embrace the LGBTQ community fully."[16]

Nationalism?

Fourth, does Christianity teach that the American way of life is the best? Obviously there was no America when the Bible was written. However, the Declaration of Independence was built upon the idea that God exists, that we are all created equal by him, and that he has granted us certain fundamental rights that the government must respect. This does not make America a "Christian nation" in any rigid sense, but it does allow people from all walks of life, religions, and philosophical systems to practice their beliefs with freedom. We think that's a good thing. Many Americans—evangelicals, Muslims, New Agers, and people from all walks of life—think so too. Does this mean that American exceptionalism (the idea that America is unique in its history, values, and political system and is therefore destined to play a distinct and positive role in the world) is a core tenet of Christianity? Certainly not. If America were to disappear, God's redemptive plan would continue. (We all know God's redemptive plan for the world is Canada. Can I [Tim] get an eh-men? Get it?)

Christians all over the world love their home countries and feel a sense of loyalty to their cultures and fellow citizens. There's nothing wrong with that, as long as the Christian's primary loyalty is to Christ and his Kingdom. Here in America, there is much discussion about "Christian nationalism." Like deconstruction, *nationalism* is one of those terms that means various things to different people. It's been defined as everything from "devotion and loyalty to one's own country"[17] to the claim that white Christian men have "the freedom to seize property, to make money, and to dominate others" to the merging of "Christian and American identities."[18] The implication is "to be a good American, one must be Christian."[19] We don't have the time or space to analyze these definitions here, and we acknowledge that there have certainly been people who claim to be Christians who have done and said false, heretical, and even dangerous things in the name of Christ. We also acknowledge that the accusation of Christian nationalism is often lobbed at evangelicals simply because they voted for a certain candidate or hold political opinions that are classically conservative. Ultimately, Christianity doesn't teach that "the American way of life" is best. But to the extent that America does reflect Christian values or allows freedom of religion, Christians can certainly celebrate this.

Conservatism?

Finally, should political and social conservatism be assumed to have God's blessing? For Christians, politics will flow downstream from theology. In other words, how we vote and engage politically will be informed by what we believe about God and what he says in his Word. A person's feelings about a political view don't determine whether or not Christianity is true. However, many Christians land under a classic definition of conservatism because of their theological beliefs about the nature of man. One central aspect of conservatism is the goal of limiting the role of the government. Limited government reflects the biblical teaching that humans are inherently sinful. In other words, power must be separated because too much power in the hands of one person or governmental body can have devastating consequences.

Political and social (as opposed to classical) liberalism approaches the question from a different understanding of human nature, assuming that the problem with society is not the sinfulness of humanity but an unfair system. The belief that human nature is malleable, that we can re-create institutions (such as marriage) at will, and that human value is not intrinsic and doesn't necessarily begin at conception means that liberalism also often lines up with issues that pose a threat to the nuclear family and the lives of unborn children.

This makes it especially repugnant to Bible-believing Christians. Dr. Douglas Groothuis, a conservative philosopher and professor at Denver Seminary (who is not affiliated with any particular political party), put it this way: "A conservative seeks to ameliorate ills as much as possible and is quick to critique ill-fated and unrealistic attempts to fundamentally change human nature. Conservatives, given their constrained view, are eagle-eyed to spot the unintended consequences of political overreach (or statism)."[20]

Simply put, it's fair to say that many evangelicals are political and social conservatives. There are reasons for this that would go beyond what we will be able to cover in this book, but due to the biblically informed pro-life and pro-family ethic and because they prefer to serve the poor by supporting private charities rather than by increasing the power of the state, many Christians (not just evangelicals) will not vote for liberal candidates. This doesn't mean that if you vote for a Democrat, you can't be a Christian. It simply means there are reasons so many Christians vote conservative, including some that have to do with biblical doctrines such as the nature of man.

While we may disagree with Chastain on his characterization of these points of evangelicalism at times, we do agree that these are some of the main issues that seem to inform deconstruction stories and have caused many to rethink their core values and religious beliefs. This case study demonstrates that many deconstructionists are not just rejecting bad beliefs. In many cases, they're rejecting sound Christian doctrine.

DECONSTRUCTION AS REVIVAL?

There are, no doubt, aspects of evangelical culture that need to be reformed. There are plenty of fair criticisms against Christians that could be addressed. Some think that this change needs to come through deconstruction. Kurtis Vanderpool is a certified life coach who offers "deconstruction coaching" as an option on his website. In an article for *Relevant* magazine, Vanderpool wrote, "I believe deconstruction is from God. I believe deconstruction is the revival evangelicals have been praying for for centuries."[21] Vanderpool sees deconstruction as a reawakening—a move forward for evangelicals. But as we will see in the next chapter, deconstruction isn't moving toward God; it's moving away from God. It's not a revival. It's a rerun.

RERUN

BACK IN THE NINETIES, American families would gather around their twenty-three-inch color televisions for the much-anticipated prime-time programming block on ABC called TGIF. "It's Friday night!" the theme song began, as our favorite sitcom celebrities would take turns hosting the weekly event, introducing that evening's shows and giving little teasers about what the audience was about to watch. Back then, there were no on-demand DVRs or streaming platforms like Netflix or Hulu. If you wanted to watch something on any given night, you had about three or four choices on network television. You couldn't rewind live TV, so if you weren't ready to watch at precisely the program's start time, you might miss something. There was also the possibility you would never see it again. In that case, you could only hope that this particular episode would be aired as a rerun. When a network needed to fill a time slot—such as when the regular season ended—they might run an older episode.

In many ways, deconstruction is like a rerun. We've seen it play out in the pages of Scripture. While *deconstruction* is a new word being applied to faith, it's actually an old idea. Indeed, it goes all the way back to the Garden of Eden.

THE ORIGIN OF DECONSTRUCTION

We are all familiar with the story of the Fall. Many of us grew up in Sunday school hearing about how Adam and Eve disobeyed God by eating the forbidden fruit, introducing human sin and death into the world. But the fall of mankind didn't begin when the pair took their first bite. That is, it didn't begin with a disobedient deed. Rather, it began with a *deconstructed idea*.

When the serpent approached Eve with the tantalizing notion that God was holding out on her, he started by questioning what God had actually said. In Genesis 3:1, he asked, "Did God actually say, 'You shall not eat of any tree in the garden'?" Deconstructed beliefs nearly always begin with questions. It's *not* that questions are bad. Questions can be good. Jesus himself asked over three hundred of them in the Gospels alone.[1] But not all questions are *honest* questions. When it comes to faith, some questions seek answers, and some questions seek exits. There are questions that seek after truth, but other questions seek to avoid truth. (More on this in chapter 11.) In Genesis 3, Satan sought to deceive Eve by questioning God's word. Incidentally, his game plan hasn't changed. In our time he is asking the same question in different contexts. For example, "Did God really say marriage is between one man and one woman for one lifetime?" "Did God really say murder (and therefore abortion) is wrong?" "Did God really say people will go to hell for their sin?" "Did God really say Jesus is the only way?" "Did God really say there are only two genders?" "Did God really say . . . ?" So, first, Satan questions what God has said.

Second, Satan moves from *questioning* God's word to *denying* it. He claims that what God said is untrue by declaring, "You will not surely die" (Genesis 3:4). Satan doesn't seek to refute God's existence. No, his crafty scheme is even more insidious. He undermines what God has said *so he can replace truth with a lie* (Romans 1:25). Well, what's the lie? This leads to the next point.

When it comes to faith, some questions seek answers, and some questions seek exits.

Third, Satan *deconstructs* who God is. In this short dialogue, we see Satan twist the meaning of God's words so he can deconstruct God's character. Think about the implications of his argument:

> The serpent said to the woman, "You will not surely die. For God knows that when you eat of [the fruit] your eyes will be opened, and you will be like God, knowing good and evil." So when the woman saw that the tree was good for food, and that it was a delight to the eyes, and that the tree was to be desired to make one wise, she took of its fruit and

ate, and she also gave some to her husband who was
with her, and he ate.

GENESIS 3:4-6

First, Satan deconstructs the idea that God is loving. After
all, how could a loving God withhold something that appears
to be pleasing to the eyes? Surely a loving God wouldn't for-
bid something they desired. (Does that sound familiar?) The
implication is, God is *not* loving. Satan persuades Adam and
Eve to believe the lie that God must not care about them; he
must like keeping things from them; he must be cruel. Of
course, none of this is true. We know God *is* love. "Anyone
who does not love does not know God, because God is love"
(1 John 4:8). But Satan succeeds in deconstructing their
belief in God's love and goodness.

Second, Satan deconstructs the idea that God is truthful. Satan—the father of lies—convinces them to believe
God deceived them about the consequences of disobeying
his command. God said they would die (Genesis 2:17).
Satan says, "You will *not* surely die" (Genesis 3:4, emphasis added). The implication is, God wasn't telling them the
truth. Therefore, he can't be trusted. Of course, Satan is the
one who cannot be trusted. John 8:44 tells us that Satan is
the "father of lies" and that there is no truth in him at all.
God, on the other hand, cannot lie. "God is not man, that he
should lie, or a son of man, that he should change his mind"
(Numbers 23:19).

Finally, Satan deconstructs the idea that God is sufficient. Adam and Eve begin to believe they are responsible
for taking care of themselves. They think they need to be

their own gods. This implies that God is *not* enough for them. It's only *after* Adam and Eve have deconstructed who God is—not loving, not truthful, not enough—that they eat the fruit.

Deconstruction is as old as humanity itself. It began with Satan—the father of faith deconstruction—and continues today. As Carl Trueman observes, "In time immemorial, people have lost their faith. . . . It's interesting because now it's used with this pseudo-intellectual language of 'deconstruction' in order to describe it. It's old thinking packaged in trendy postmodern language."[2] Like Adam and Eve, when we ignore or reject God's Word, we cut ourselves off from the primary source of truth about what God is like.[3] As a result, we open ourselves up to deconstructing beliefs about God. In particular, we begin taking our cues about God not from his Word, but from other sources, like cultural norms and personal preferences. This isn't speculation. It has played out many times throughout history.

Following cultural norms

In the days of the prophet Jeremiah, the Israelites engaged in all kinds of wicked behavior. But none was more egregious than sacrificing their children to Baal. Speaking through the prophet, God said,

> Hear the word of the Lord, you kings of Judah and people of Jerusalem. This is what the Lord Almighty, the God of Israel, says: Listen! I am going to bring a disaster on this place that will make the ears of everyone who hears of it tingle. For they have

forsaken me and *made this a place of foreign gods*; they have burned incense in it to gods that neither they nor their ancestors nor the kings of Judah ever knew, and they have filled this place with the blood of the innocent. They have built the high places of Baal to burn their children in the fire as offerings to Baal—*something I did not command or mention, nor did it enter my mind.*

JEREMIAH 19:3-5, NIV, EMPHASIS ADDED

Notice that God was angry and ready to bring fierce judgment against his people, and he told us why. The Israelites were sacrificing their children as burnt offerings. Where did this idea come from? God certainly didn't command it. In fact, the text says the idea didn't even enter his mind. So then where did the idea originate? Thankfully, we're not left guessing. In the surrounding pagan culture, child sacrifice was a normal part of religious worship. Tragically, rather than looking to the Word of God, the Israelites let the cultural beliefs, values, and practices of the pagans around them inform what they believed about God. The sad irony is that God's Word contains a stern warning against this very thing.

When the LORD your God cuts off before you the nations whom you go in to dispossess, and you dispossess them and dwell in their land, *take care that you be not ensnared to follow them*, after they have been destroyed before you, *and that you do not inquire about their gods*, saying, "How did these nations serve their gods?—that I also may do the

same." *You shall not worship the LORD your God in that way, for every abominable thing that the LORD hates they have done for their gods, for they even burn their sons and their daughters in the fire to their gods.*
DEUTERONOMY 12:29-31, EMPHASIS ADDED

As we learn from the Israelites, you can't determine what God is like by looking at the culture. The Israelites surveyed the surrounding nations and concluded that God must *like*—and, possibly, demand—child sacrifice. After all, that's what the other nations did for gods like Baal and Molech.

So what does this ancient story have to do with modern deconstruction? We are all prone to imagine a god that is more like our culture (or ourselves) than who God truly is. If we're not careful, this can distort our view of him. For example, in the last twenty years, Western culture has become much more affirming of homosexuality and transgender ideology than ever before. In fact, it's not merely affirmed; *it's celebrated*. Consequently, some have argued that a loving God could not be less inclusive or accepting than our culture. God is love, after all. This, of course, requires an updated definition of the word *love*.

Biblically speaking, the definition of love begins with the nature and character of God. It's one of his attributes. God, through the apostle Paul, spells out what this looks like in the life of a Christian in 1 Corinthians 13:1-13. He explains what love is and what it isn't. Love is patient and kind. It doesn't envy or boast. It isn't irritable or resentful. Then things get interesting. The passage goes on to explain that love "does not rejoice at wrongdoing, but rejoices with the truth" (verse 6). According to the Word of God, it's not loving to affirm or celebrate something that is sinful, harmful, or untrue. This is the opposite of our culture's definition of love, which is more along the lines of accepting, affirming, and celebrating whatever someone deems as "their truth." When Christians adopt this unbiblical definition of love, it's not because they have been informed by Scripture or have interpreted it more accurately. Instead, it's because they are following a cultural shift. Sadly, as the culture becomes more LGBTQ-affirming, many churches go right along with it.

Gender and sexuality aren't the only issues where the cultural view is influencing the church. As we continue to be surrounded by affluence in the West, it is unthinkable for some that God wouldn't want us all to be happy, healthy, and wealthy. Prosperity becomes the measuring rod of God's goodness toward us, and happiness becomes the meaning of life. Success is measured by an impressive career or high income, and greater honor may be bestowed on those who have "made it" by the world's standards. When the church is influenced by culture in this way, those who are sick or poor can be chastised for not having enough faith or for not giving enough money and resources to the church. This mentality would have been unthinkable in most times and places throughout church history, when persecution, hardship, and struggle were the norm. Just imagine approaching a Christian who was driven from his home and business in Mosul by ISIS and saying, "Hey, you really need to believe God for a new Bentley!" That would be not only ridiculous, but also an idea foreign to Scripture.

As technology advances, the world shrinks. Because of

the internet and social media, we have access to more people from more cultures than ever before—many of us now know sincere Muslims, Hindus, Buddhists, and people of other religious traditions. This creates a wonderful opportunity to get to know people outside of our immediate cultural context and to share the gospel far and wide. But living in a pluralistic society (different religions coexisting in the same space) means we are being exposed to more opinions, ideas, religious philosophies, and values than ever before. This can influence Christians to adopt a type of religious pluralism (the belief that all religions are equally valid). Sincerity, not truth, becomes the new criterion for salvation.

If we're honest, the influence of cultural norms on our understanding of Christianity cannot be overstated. All of us—despite our political and denominational backgrounds—need to ask ourselves an honest question: *Where do my beliefs look more like the world than God's Word?*

The tragedy of the Israelites sacrificing their sons and daughters goes beyond their evil actions. Israel should have known better. They should have known that the Lord *hates* child sacrifice. But how would they know that? They didn't have to read God's mind or get some personal, private message from him. They should have known it *because it was written in their Law.* Moses wrote, "You shall not worship the LORD your God in that way, for every abominable thing that the LORD hates they have done for their gods, for they even burn their sons and their daughters in the fire to their gods" (Deuteronomy 12:31). The problem is, these Israelites didn't know their Scriptures. They had false ideas about God because they ignored, or possibly rejected, the primary source they had about God—*his Word*. Sadly, most Christians don't know their Scriptures either.

Losing knowledge of (and love for) God

Statistics show that biblical literacy is at an all-time low. In fact, as we mentioned in the previous chapter, recent data shows that about half of American evangelicals believe God learns and adapts to different circumstances and accepts worship from all religions. More than half of the same group think that most people are good by nature. Nearly 40 percent of American evangelicals have bought into the idea that religious belief is not a matter of objective truth, but merely a matter of personal opinion. Over 40 percent don't even believe Jesus is God![4]

Like the Israelites, *we* should know better. The Bible teaches that God does not change (Malachi 3:6; James 1:17), that Jesus is the only way to God (John 14:6), and that humans are born with a sin nature (Psalm 51:5; Romans 5:12). Scripture tells us that Jesus is the truth (John 14:6), and that he is the same yesterday, today, and forever (Hebrews 13:8). As we'll discuss further in chapter 6, the Bible teaches that Jesus is God (John 1:1). It's evident that many Christians have adapted their beliefs about God to accommodate popular beliefs in culture rather than to match what God said about himself. Think about how fashionable these ideas are in the media. Nearly every cultural message we binge on Netflix is telling us that we are perfect just as we are and that we should live our truth. It is really tragic that Christians can quote *The Office* but can't quote the Covenants,[5] or that they know more about Marvel's Iron Man than they do about the Bible's God-man.

The only way to guard against false ideas about God is to fill our minds with true ideas about him. But thinking rightly about God doesn't come naturally. Scripture says we were all, by nature, enemies of God (Romans 5:10), "children of wrath" (Ephesians 2:3), who did "not accept the things of the Spirit of God" (1 Corinthians 2:14) before we were saved by grace. So our natural inclination is to think wrongly about God. That is why we must look to Scripture—God's Word—for guidance and authority on what he is like. *We need to go to his Word because only God can tell us what God is like.* And he has. However, many of us are too distracted to listen.

We need to go to God's Word because only God can tell us what God is like.

The prophet Hosea said,

Hear the word of the LORD, O children of Israel,
    for the LORD has a controversy with the inhabitants
        of the land.
There is no faithfulness or steadfast love,
    and no knowledge of God in the land. . . .
My people are destroyed for lack of knowledge;
    because you have rejected knowledge,
    I reject you from being a priest to me.
And since *you have forgotten the law of your God*,
    I also will forget your children.

HOSEA 4:1, 6, EMPHASIS ADDED

Why was there no knowledge of God? Because the Israelites had forgotten the law of God. They had neglected his special revelation to them. It's interesting that Hosea mentions they have *no love for God* in the same breath that he mentions they have *no knowledge of God*. That's not a co-incidence. There is a direct link between "knowledge of" and "love for." Here's an analogy that might be helpful.

Let's imagine you said, "Tim, tell me about your wife."

And I (Tim) replied, "My wife has blonde hair, two eyes, teeth, and a nose."

You might respond by saying, "No, tell me what she's *like*."

Now imagine if my original response was the best I could offer. What would you conclude about my relationship with my wife? You would probably think I didn't know her very well. From that encounter, would you conclude that I actually *love* my wife? Probably not. You would also likely think I was a fairly dim brute with the sensitivity and emotional IQ of a block of wood.

Next, imagine that when you asked what my wife is like, I responded with, "Stacey is one of the hardest-working women I know. When she's not busy consulting for a chemical manufacturing company, she's paying bills, folding laundry, packing lunches, pumping iron, bandaging scrapes, cook-ing dinner, and reading stories. She's one of those 'morning people' who wake up with a smile and a seemingly endless supply of energy. (Yeah, one of *those* people.) She's a chemist by training, who loves to experiment with new culinary crea-tions. In her downtime, she enjoys cuddling into her favorite blanket with a book in one hand and a peppermint tea in the other. Stacey's kind and generous, faithful and trustworthy, smart and funny. But what I appreciate most is how she consistently puts the needs of others before her own. Her life and love are a portrait of Christ's life and love."

You might be a bit more convinced that I actually love Stacey when I am able to describe specific, personal details I have observed about her. The love I have for my wife is connected to the knowledge I have of her. It's my love for her that drives my desire to know more about her, and the more I know about her, the more I love her. In the same way, love for God is always tied to knowledge of God.

Jesus said this: "Whoever has my commandments and keeps them, he it is who loves me. And he who loves me will be loved by my Father, and I will love him and manifest myself to him" (John 14:21). There are two verbs applied to God's commandments in this verse: *has* and *keeps*. The first word is *echō*, which means "have," "hold," or "possess."[6] The second word is *tēreō*, which means "keep," "guard," or "observe."[7] If we truly love God, we will both *have* and *keep* his commands. Being aware of his commands helps us know the God who gives these commands. And God's commands are not independent of who he is; they flow from his nature.

If you want to know God, read his Word. The Bible is primarily a story about God. He is the main character. Over and over, the Bible says, "God loves"; "God says"; "God does." Every time we read about God, we get to know what he is like. We get to know his desires, his personality, his character. There is nothing greater than knowing our good God. Sadly, this is often in conflict with what culture says is good. That's why it's so important for Christians to stay connected to God through his Word, which is truth.

Prioritizing personal preferences

"All that the LORD has spoken we will do, and we will be obedient." These are the words Israel spoke in response to Moses reading aloud the Book of the Covenant (God's law) in Exodus 24:7. Then Moses threw the blood of sacrificed oxen onto the people to signify that they were now bound by a blood oath to keep their word. This blood was also a symbol of God vowing to keep his word to lead them into the Promised Land. This would have been a deeply impactful event, with the blood droplets remaining on their skin for days—and on their clothing indefinitely—as a reminder of this solemn agreement.[8] Not long after, Moses was called to spend forty days on the mountain of God, where he would receive the Ten Commandments, written on stone by the finger of God himself. From the vantage point of the Israelites below, this would have been a powerful and magnificent sight, with the glory of God wrapping around the mountain like a cloud and blazing like a devouring fire at its pinnacle.

Forty days started to feel like an unreasonable amount of time for the impatient Israelites, who had all but presumed Moses dead by this point. They asked Moses' brother, Aaron, to make a god who could go before them (Exodus 32:1). Without hesitation—really, it's quite shocking how quickly Aaron cooperated—Aaron instructed them to bring their wives' and children's gold earrings, which he promptly fashioned into an image of a golden calf. He must have done a great job because the people were so impressed, they declared, "These are your gods, O Israel, who brought you up out of the land of Egypt!" (verse 4). Now, one would think that the idea of God's people turning so quickly to idols would be enough to make Aaron grieve (or at least wince?). But no, Aaron's response was to go ahead and build an altar for the thing. Then the Israelites had a big party, and let's just say God's wrath was kindled. Moses prayed for them, and God's anger relented, but then Moses came down the mountain only to have his own anger burn hot. He broke the tablets Charlton Heston–style and ground the golden calf to powder, scattering it on the water and making the Israelites drink it.

There's a lot to unpack here. When Moses went to receive the law from God, the people grew impatient and created their own god—the golden calf. They wanted a god who would meet them on their terms, not his. They deconstructed their view of God (and literally deconstructed all their gold) and reconstructed a god of their own making. But this was not a god who had any power or ability to love them and care for them. It was not a god who could challenge them, correct them, or (conveniently) punish them. It was impotent. It was simply a hunk of melted gold they could look at, and they could project on it their own emotions, desires, and opinions. If only they had resisted the urge to deconstruct the idea that God would keep his word, the horrific bloodshed that followed this event would have been avoided. (Read through the end of chapter 32 for more, but be prepared. It ain't pretty.)

The Israelites had the law of God. They had vowed to believe it and obey it. But when God didn't just snap to and give them what they wanted, they abandoned him and sought whatever else they thought would meet that need.

Their decision was not based on what was objectively good and true. It was based on their personal preference.

It wasn't just in Bible times that people turned to personal preference to construct their ideas about reality. Thomas Jefferson famously took a razor to the New Testament and carefully cut out the history of Jesus' life and his moral teachings. Then he glued parts of them together, leaving out most references to the supernatural, such as miracle stories and the Resurrection. Jefferson believed that the teachings of Jesus provided "the most sublime and benevolent code of morals which has ever been offered to man."[9] However, if you remove the deity of Jesus, his miracles, and his resurrection from the narrative, you may have a "sublime" Jesus who taught great ethics but not a *divine* Jesus who can save you.

Most people today are not taking scissors and glue to their physical Bibles, but they are altering and revising the parts of Scripture they don't like. Whereas Jefferson liked the moral teachings of Jesus, many today would see those teachings as backwards, archaic, and outdated. Maybe you've heard statements like, "Oh, that was just Paul's view of sexuality." *Snip!* "That's just what Moses thought God wanted." *Snip!* "I could never believe in a God who . . ." *Snip!* Today, we live in a culture where human beings are defined by their individual inner feelings and desires.[10] We are encouraged to live in a way that lines up with those feelings and desires, which become our ultimate authority. Anything that challenges that notion is considered to be oppressive, especially Bible verses that contradict your own personal expression.

The apostle

Being in love with the world

The apostle Paul dealt with his share of people who claimed to follow God before turning away. Consider Demas. Many Christians today may not even know who that is. Unlike Adam and Eve, Demas doesn't come up in any of the classic Sunday school stories. He didn't write any books of the Bible. There's no Bible cartoon depicting his story or children's board book illustrating his contribution to Christian history. But he was a significant player in the early church. Paul tells us Demas was a "fellow worker" (Philemon 1:24). He also gets a shout-out in Paul's letter to the church in Colossae: "Luke the beloved physician greets you, as does Demas" (Colossians 4:14). The inclusion of this special greeting indicates people knew who Demas was. It's not hard, then, to imagine that Demas was a well-known Christian in the first century.

But something happened. In Paul's last letter, we find out that Demas walked away. Paul writes, "For Demas, in love with this present world, has deserted me" (2 Timothy 4:10). Paul was imprisoned in Rome, facing a death sentence. And in this time of need, Demas deserted him. But Demas didn't just abandon his friend; he may have abandoned his faith. We don't know for sure, but it appears Demas was an apostate. An important clue is the phrase "in love with this present world." In other words, he was reluctant to share in Paul's sufferings; he put his own self-guided sense of comfort and satisfaction before Christ's call to deny himself and pick up his cross (see Matthew 16:24). Demas traded eternal hope for earthly treasure.

Just a few verses earlier, Paul describes how "the time of [his] departure has come" (2 Timothy 4:6). He writes, "I have fought the good fight, I have finished the race, I have kept the faith. Henceforth there is laid up for me the crown of righteousness, which the Lord, the righteous judge, will award to me on that day, and not only to me but also to all who have loved his appearing" (verses 7-8). Notice how Paul contrasts those who keep the faith because they love Jesus (verse 8) with those, like Demas, who leave the faith because they love the present world (verse 10). One loves the appearing of his eternal Savior, and the other loves the temptations of the present world. Sometimes, the Bible uses the word *world* to signify the entire universe (John 13:1; Hebrews 1:2), and sometimes it simply refers to the people who inhabit the earth (John 3:16; 1 John 4:9). However, most often—as in the passage referring to Demas—it means something more like the sinful inclinations that rule the culture (Matthew 18:7; John 15:19; Romans 12:2; 1 Corinthians 2:12; 1 John 2:15; 4:5).

Focusing on this world is a common sentiment in deconstruction stories. Take, for example, one of the most famous and influential examples, the deconstruction of Rhett McLaughlin. McLaughlin and his YouTube cohost, Link Neal, posted their deconstruction stories on their wildly popular channel, *Good Mythical Morning*. Like Demas, Rhett explained that his focus has shifted from an eternal perspective to an earthly one: "It's not so much what happens after you die, but what happens while you're alive," he said.[11] He also articulated, "If I don't *have* to believe [Christianity], then why would I?" His cohost, Link, put it this way in his own deconstruction video: "Why was I working so hard to make Christianity work for me if it wasn't even true?"[12] It's not difficult to see that both Rhett and Link came to a place in their spiritual journey where they no longer found Christianity beautiful. The world gave them a much more palatable option.

Deconstruction is nothing new. People have been abandoning the standard of God's Word and engaging in a process of rethinking—and often abandoning—their faith since the beginning. That's why the biblical record contains so many warnings about leaving or redefining the faith. Consider Paul's first letter to Timothy. In it, he describes those who "have wandered away" (1:6 and 6:10), who "made shipwreck of their faith" (1:19), who "will depart from the faith" (4:1), who "denied the faith" (5:8), who "abandoned their former faith" (5:12), who "strayed after Satan" (5:15), and who "swerved from the faith" (6:21). If you're keeping track, that's eight references in one short letter. Since the time of Christ, people have been "falling away" from the faith.

The announcement of Demas's desertion may have rocked some of the early Christians. After all, this guy was traveling with the apostle Paul. We wonder how his family and close friends took the news. We wonder if it caused other Christians to question and leave their own faith. We wonder what Demas would have posted if he'd had Instagram or TikTok. We wonder if Demas went through a process that looks a whole lot like what we see manifesting today as deconstruction. Of course, the Bible doesn't explicitly use that word. But the same motivation existed thousands of years before postmodern philosophers coined the term. Though the deconstruction explosion may have looked different then, the impact it caused was likely the same. That's because, after any explosion, there's fallout. In the next chapter, we're going to explore the fallout of deconstruction.

4

FALLOUT

"THERE'S NOTHING MORE WE CAN DO," the oncologist told my wife's family as they stood around my father-in-law's hospital bed. This devastating news caught everyone by surprise.

I (Tim) was stuck at Chicago's O'Hare Airport on my way home from a speaking event when I got the call I'll never forget. "Tim, my dad is dying," my wife said as she sobbed into the phone.

I was speechless, unable to process the news. "Wait, what? I don't understand. There must be some mistake. Weren't they going to talk about next steps? This doesn't make any sense," I replied, shocked and confused.

Just a few months earlier, my father-in-law was experiencing terrible pain from what doctors thought was a benign cyst growing near the base of his spine. After further tests, however, they discovered it wasn't a cyst. It was cancer—an extremely aggressive malignant tumor. Now, given its size and location, there was nothing they could do to save him.

One month later, he was gone.

Nothing prepares you for the news that someone you dearly love is dying. Words like *heartbroken* and *helpless*, *shocked* and *sad*, *devastated* and *disoriented* fall short of expressing how you feel. It's as if a piece of you is dying too. Many people haven't experienced the shock of finding out that they're losing a loved one. But they have experienced the shock of finding out a loved one is deconstructing. This may, at first, seem like a strange connection to draw.[1] After all, there's hardly anything more devastating than a loved one dying. However, many who have gone through deconstruction liken it to a "kind of death." For example, in his free downloadable "Deconstruction Guide," David Hayward, also known as the Naked Pastor, writes,

> For many, [deconstruction] is a traumatic experience . . . *a kind of death*. As a result, deconstruction may be accompanied by grief over the loss of faith, certainty, and the fellowship that often accompanies them.[2]

Deconstruction is a death of sorts. Those who deconstruct experience a death of their beliefs, their community, their confidence, their relationships, and, quite possibly, their faith. It's not difficult to see why it's so painful. Christianity isn't something one experiences in isolation. First Corinthians

12:12-31 explains that we are all members of the body of Christ. Just as a physical body is made up of arms, legs, eyes, ears, fingers, and toes, the church body is made up of many parts. And each Christian is an integral and important part of the whole. If an appendage gets cut off, it hurts. There is pain, grief, and loss, and time is needed to process and recover.

Derek Webb, former lead singer of the Christian band Caedmon's Call, announced he had walked away from his faith and produced a solo album he described as a "deeply personal tale of two divorces."[3] The songs are his reflections on his divorce from his wife and his divorce from God. His pain is palpable and well-articulated. Responding to the Calvinist understanding of salvation Webb had formerly believed, he writes that there are only two options: Either God isn't real, or Webb himself simply wasn't chosen. He goes on to say he may never find out which is true. "Either way, my heart is broken," he writes in the haunting lyrics.[4]

A terrible feeling comes over you when you finally face those doubts you've been stuffing down for years. Especially when you've dedicated your entire life to loving and serving God. Especially when your whole identity is wrapped up in him. Especially when your heart deeply loves a being who you've come to believe may have just been a figment of your imagination. That terrible feeling turns into a sick thud at the very bottom of your stomach when you finally become intellectually persuaded that God doesn't exist. It's disorienting. It's destabilizing. It's terrifying. It's as if darkness becomes a physical property that wraps itself around your entire psyche like a python slowly coiling itself around its unsuspecting prey.

Many in the deconstruction community have expressed the anguish of walking through it. As I walked through my own faith crisis, I (Alisa) also experienced this torment.[5]

But deconstruction doesn't affect *only* the one going through it. It also impacts those who love the person going through it. When deconstruction leads to a rejection of faith, that can feel like a death both to the one deconstructing and to their loved ones. Like physical death, deconstruction can leave loved ones shocked, confused, and grieving. We've heard this sentiment time and time again from parents with grown children who have announced their deconstruction. This is the pain of parents who did their best to train up their children in the way they should go (Proverbs 22:6) but now face the devastating pain that their kids have deconstructed their faith. In some cases, this decision has led to distanced or strained relation-

When deconstruction leads to a rejection of faith, that can feel like a death both to the one deconstructing and to their loved ones.

ships between them. This is the grief experienced by pastors who, despite their best efforts to disciple their flock and lead them in biblical truth, have watched their congregants walk away. This is the heartache of wives and husbands who have stood by helplessly as their spouses deconstructed, and who now have to navigate the complicated and heartrending reality of being married to someone who may think their worldview is toxic or abusive. Progressive Christian author Sarah Bessey says, "I think there is always a sense of grief that comes along with deconstruction."[6] While some claim to feel a sense of freedom and happiness in their deconstruction, others are confused and grieving. But many of you reading this book are mourning a loss as well.

A BURIAL AND A BATTLE

There are two responses, broadly speaking, to this issue. In many ways, we feel like we are writing with both tears in our eyes and a sword in our hand. At times, having a loved one in deconstruction is like going to a burial. Tears flow, and words fail. In these moments, we "weep with those who weep" (Romans 12:15), "comfort those who are in any affliction" (2 Corinthians 1:4), and "bear one another's burdens" (Galatians 6:2).

At other times, however, responding to deconstruction is like going into battle. The same Scriptures that command us to "have mercy on those who doubt" (Jude 1:22) also tell us to "hold firm to the trustworthy word as taught" and "rebuke those who contradict it" (Titus 1:9). The Bible is clear about God's attitude toward those who draw others into sin and unbelief. From the lips of Jesus himself come the words "Temptations to sin are sure to come, but woe to the one through whom they come! It would be better for him if a millstone were hung around his neck and he were cast into the sea than that he should cause one of these little ones to sin" (Luke 17:1-2).

On multiple occasions, the biblical authors caution us about possible threats to our spiritual well-being. As we mentioned in chapter 1, we are at war, not with people, but with falsehoods about God and his Word. Even so, we must be willing to confront those who contradict the truth revealed in

Scripture. In his parting words to the leaders of the Ephesian church, Paul sternly warned of a danger within the church. He told them to "be alert" because there were individuals who, "speaking twisted things," would "draw away the disciples after them." He called them "fierce wolves" (Acts 20:29-31). Interestingly, Paul didn't invent this term. He got it from Jesus. Speaking to the crowds in his famous Sermon on the Mount, Jesus said, "Beware of false prophets, who come to you in sheep's clothing but inwardly are ravenous wolves" (Matthew 7:15). Just as there were wolves in the first century (see also 2 Peter 2:1-3), there are wolves today. And their goal is the same: to draw people after them, away from "the faith that was once for all delivered to the saints" (Jude 1:3) and toward their own views. Those who lead others astray may (and probably do) truly believe their views are better than the beliefs of those they hope to draw away after them. But regardless of motives, the result is the same: Their false views—no matter how sincerely believed—will ultimately destroy those who follow them, as surely as sheep are devoured by wolves.

Second Timothy chapters 3 and 4 are a tremendous help to those of us trying to understand what is going on with the deconstruction explosion. Take a moment and slowly and carefully read through 2 Timothy 3:1-7:

> But understand this, that in the last days there will
> come times of difficulty. For people will be lovers
> of self, lovers of money, proud, arrogant, abusive,
> disobedient to their parents, ungrateful, unholy,
> heartless, unappeasable, slanderous, without

self-control, brutal, not loving good, treacherous, reckless, swollen with conceit, lovers of pleasure rather than lovers of God, having the appearance of godliness, but denying its power. Avoid such people. For among them are those who creep into households and capture weak women, burdened with sins and led astray by various passions, always learning and never able to arrive at a knowledge of the truth.

Those are profound yet stinging words that predict so much of what we see manifesting today. Paul goes on to explain that these are people who are opposed to the truth (2 Timothy 3:8). In chapter 4:3-4, he makes another prediction: "The time is coming when people will not endure sound teaching, but having itching ears they will accumulate for themselves teachers to suit their own passions, and will turn away from listening to the truth and wander off into myths." First Timothy 4:1 tells us, "The Spirit expressly says that in later times, some will depart from the faith by devoting themselves to deceitful spirits and teachings of demons." So the deconstruction phenomenon should not take us by surprise. We should expect that as time goes on, we will witness people becoming deceived and leaving the faith. Verse 16 gives us good practical steps to stay on the right track through the chaos: "Keep a close watch on yourself and on the teaching. Persist in this, for by so doing you will save both yourself and your hearers."

Romans 16:17 also exhorts Christians to watch out for people who create division and place obstacles in front of good and right beliefs. We are actually instructed to *avoid* them. In Hebrews 2:1 we learn that we must pay close attention to the good teaching we've been given so we don't "drift away from it." Overall, the Bible describes a great battle over truth. In that battle, we are to be consistent, vigilant, and careful in making sure that what we believe lines up with reality. Bad and untruthful ideas are harmful to people, so we should make every effort to speak truth into those lies with hearts filled with compassion and love. As Paul instructs in 2 Timothy 2:24-25, we should gently correct bad ideas so that people who hold them can come to repentance as they learn what is true.

When we "destroy arguments and every lofty opinion raised against the knowledge of God, and take every thought captive to obey Christ," as we are commanded in 2 Corinthians 10:5, we are not attempting to destroy *people*. Rather, we want to destroy the ideas that would seek to enslave people to false understandings of God—to help them, instead, to "continue in what [they] have learned and have become convinced of," the things taught by inspired Scripture (2 Timothy 3:14, NIV).

NOT-SO-SECRET AGENDA

One of the main concerns with the deconstruction explosion is the obvious agenda to deconvert evangelicals. There are countless platforms dedicated to providing a place to welcome Christians into the process of deconstruction. These are promoted as "safe spaces," but in many cases, they are carefully orchestrated to foster an environment of doubt and unbelief. In her book review of *Gaslighted by God*, self-described faith deconstruction coach Angela J. Herrington begins by explaining that she is constantly on the lookout for resources to help people through their faith deconstruction, particularly those "that aren't pushy or have hidden agendas to convert you to a specific belief system. Well, good news! I found another one!"[7] She then says the book will help you discover "that your faith is largely built upon bad translations, human error, and manipulative false doctrines designed to protect the church's power."[8] Well, she's right about one thing. The agenda certainly isn't hidden!

Deconstruction platforms are promoted as "safe spaces," but in many cases they are carefully orchestrated to foster an environment of doubt and unbelief.

Another example of the not-so-secret agenda comes from 2015 when a Nashville church made headlines after its pastor announced one Sunday morning that it would become fully inclusive of LGBTQ+ identities and relationships. This came as a shock to many members of the congregation, who sat in silence, though others stood and applauded. Within three weeks, the church's giving was cut almost in half, and attendance dwindled significantly.[9] Although this declaration came on the heels of a three-year public discussion on the topic, the pastor had been sowing the seeds of deconstruction privately for many years. In a Facebook video on the church's journey to LGBTQ+ affirmation, the pastor reflected on his approach. He explained that at its start, there were three groups of people in the church—those who were deconstructed, those who were in deconstruction, and those who had no idea what deconstruction was but thought they were in a Bible-believing evangelical church. Of that third group, he said, "I still had a really strong desire to convert. . . . I was very evangelical."[10] Then he went on to explain his secret agenda:

> I knew they didn't know who I was. And I knew
> that group didn't know what I was doing. But I was
> okay with that, and I justified that because I thought
> it was in their best interest for them to stay in that
> blind space as long as they were in the pipeline of
> being converted by me to a more progressive way of
> thinking. Before I got them over to progressivism,
> I just wanted to get them into the throes of
> deconstruction.[11]

Although not every deconstructionist is this open or this intentional, much of the exvangelical/deconstruction social media presence is focused on making converts, which is indeed very similar to the evangelical world that serves as the punch line of its jokes and the punching bag upon which all manner of its fury is unleashed. One popular deconstructionist said, "I'm not here to tell people where they should end up—I'm just here to hang out with them on the journey."[12] Of course, scrolling through his Instagram account tells a different story. From the meme that displays a man with a look of hopeful confusion as he thinks, *When you realize you haven't even thought about God for weeks and your life has only gotten better*[13] to the caption, "Poor Satan, there's only so much evil he can do. . . . He's no match for Evangelicalism,"[14] there's no end to the aggressive and deeply cynical view of evangelical Christianity presented in post after post.

Nevertheless, we want to be honest about the fact that we *are* here to tell people where they should end up. We don't just want to "hang out" with you on the journey; we want to hang out with you in eternity. If Christianity is true, the stakes are life and death. The destination of deconstruction matters. That's why we seek to persuade everyone to trust in the true Jesus as their Lord and Savior. Jesus says, "Whoever believes in him is not condemned, but whoever does not believe is condemned already, because he has not believed in the name of the only Son of God" (John 3:18). So there it is: Tim and Alisa's not-so-secret agenda. We want to identify our motivation here so you know we aren't writing this book merely with weapons drawn. We are writing it with broken hearts as we watch people walk away from eternal life.

PART 2

#DECONSTRUCTION

As we've said, deconstruction isn't one-size-fits-all. Every deconstruction story is unique because every person is unique. There are, however, some elements common to all deconstruction stories. Every act of deconstruction contains three basic components: (1) a *process* of deconstruction, (2) a *belief* being deconstructed, and (3) a *person* deconstructing. In other words, every act of deconstruction has a *how*, a *what*, and a *who*. First, there is the process of deconstruction. This concerns how someone deconstructs their faith. Second, in our context, there is a person's faith being deconstructed. But what does that mean? In other words, is it true Christianity being deconstructed, or is it something else? Third, there's a person deconstructing. Without a person, there's no deconstruction. This may sound trivial, but it's often overlooked in this discussion. In trying to understand deconstruction, we need to ask, *Who* is deconstructing? What (if anything) do we know about them?

So if we're going to understand the act of deconstruction, we need to examine these three questions. But before we do, we need to ask another one: Why are people deconstructing in the first place? What causes deconstruction? There's a reason people deconstruct. Most people don't make a conscious choice to enter into deconstruction. It's often triggered by a crisis that initiates the process. It's typically not something people choose. In many cases, it happens *to* them.

5

CRISIS

IF DECONSTRUCTION IS THE EXPLOSION, then *crisis* is the burning fuse that detonates it. Virtually every deconstruction story speaks of a trigger event (or several) that sets the whole thing off, leading to disillusionment with Christianity or the church. But the crisis event alone isn't enough to send someone into deconstruction. Two different people can grow up in the same house with the same parents, same church, and same youth pastors. They can even experience very similar crisis events, yet one can end up in deconstruction and the other may emerge with their faith even stronger than before. So although a crisis of faith and deconstruction are often conflated, they are actually distinct. After all, a crisis doesn't necessarily cause deconstruction. It simply makes someone a good *candidate* for deconstruction.

If a faith crisis doesn't always lead to faith deconstruction, what could be some of the other factors? While it's not possible to quantify all of them, it's clear that one's faith *foundation* is important. Consider what Jesus has to say about the foundation of our faith in the parable about a sower who sows seeds on four different types of soil. Some seeds fall along a path, others in rocky soil, still others among thorns, and some in good soil. Jesus' parables are sometimes hard to understand. Fortunately, in this case, Jesus interprets the parable for us. He says the sower represents someone who is "sowing the word," and the soils represent the four types of people who hear the Word.

Jesus describes the stony soil this way: "Other seed fell on rocky ground, where it did not have much soil, and immediately it sprang up, since it had no depth of soil. And when the sun rose, it was scorched, and since it had no root, it withered away" (Mark 4:5-6). When he interprets the meaning of the seeds that fell on the rocky soil, he says, "These are the ones sown on rocky ground: the ones who, when they hear the word, immediately receive it with joy. And they have no root in themselves, but endure for a while; then, when tribulation or persecution arises on account of the word, immediately they fall away" (Mark 4:16-17). So according to Jesus, there will be some who receive the Word and flourish temporarily, then "fall away." And Jesus tells us why: They don't have deep roots. Shallow faith can last for a season. But when confronted by a crisis of faith, there's no foundation to hold it up.

FOUNDATION + CRISIS

I (Alisa) was living in Chatsworth, California, when the now-famous Northridge earthquake rocked Southern California on January 17, 1994, at 4:30 a.m. I had just graduated from high school and was asleep in bed at my parents' house when it felt like someone lifted our house off the ground, slammed it back to the earth, and then began to jostle it back and forth like a kid shaking up a snow globe. Despite all my years of school earthquake drills, my fight-or-flight response kicked in, and apparently *flight* was what my body chose. I jumped out of bed in a flash and ran so fast, I seemed to float on air through the kitchen and into the entryway, where my mom and sisters were already gathered. By the time the shaking stopped, my mom's fine china lay shattered all over the kitchen floor, along with everything else that had previously sat undisturbed in a drawer or cabinet. Despite the shock and momentary terror of the event, our house was left standing with nothing but some minor damage to the chimney. Many of our neighbors weren't so fortunate.

We piled into the car and set out to assess the damage to the neighboring communities with an ominous sense of somber reflection. As the sun came up over our valley, we observed entire rows of homes demolished, with only one or two left standing on a particular street. We drove by the Northridge Mall, the ever-constant hangout of my childhood and teen years, which now lay in rubble. The giant sign designating the iconic Bullock's department store had slid off what was left of the building and was now lying on the ground alongside bent steel beams, collapsed drywall, and broken concrete.

Since then, I've learned there is quite a bit that goes into securing a building to withstand an earthquake. When buildings are erected in earthquake zones today, they aren't necessarily constructed with the intention of avoiding all damage, but they are built with the goal of *saving lives*.[1] This means it's vital not only to give the building a solid base, but also to reinforce the walls with a type of bracing that is distributed evenly to help absorb the force of the earthquake and take pressure off the rest of the structure. Then the ceilings are braced likewise. In order to earthquake-proof a house, the builders must be intentional about everything from the base level to the roof. That way, if an earthquake ever hits, there will be some unavoidable damage, but the structure will remain intact to protect the people inside.

In this way, the entire infrastructure is like our faith foundation. The earthquake is like the crisis or trigger that tests the soundness of that foundation. The combination of the foundation and the crisis will influence what happens next. As with a building, each person's faith foundation is constructed from an almost endless list of unique variables. And as with an earthquake, the crisis can vary between types of movement (earthquakes can quake up and down or side to side), its magnitude (which relates to the size of the fault line), and so on. These variables together will impact how much damage is done. This is why each deconstruction is unique. Each person's spiritual foundation, from base to roof, is different. That foundation intersects with

Not every candidate for deconstruction ends up deconstructing their faith.

different types of crises, with several sometimes appearing at once.

When theological crises of all sorts meet various types of inadequate foundations/faith structures, one can become vulnerable to deconstruction. Let's take a look at several types of crises that can turn people into candidates for deconstruction. As we'll see, not every candidate ends up deconstructing their faith.

Suffering

"If you take my son, we're done!" Drew screamed as he sobbed into the steering wheel of his car in the hospital parking lot. Drew had just come from the neonatal intensive care unit, where his son, Linden, lay in his mother's arms. Linden had been born prematurely and unable to breathe on his own. After further testing, doctors discovered he had multiple holes in his heart and some brain bleeding. Linden later required a feeding tube for his daily nutrition.

Throughout this process, Linden saw a dozen specialists, but Drew and his wife, Jane, were still left with more questions than answers. Doctors chalked up Linden's developmental delay to a "failure to thrive," but there was no clear diagnosis. So finally, in a moment of desperation, Drew asked the doctors to level with him: "We're tired of all the question marks. What does Linden's future look like?" The doctors said they didn't have those answers. Drew and Jane didn't know if Linden would ever be capable of living on his own. They didn't know if they would bury their son. They just didn't know. This news brought Drew to the brink. Sitting in his car, feeling frustrated, tired, hurt, and confused, trying to process every parent's worst nightmare, he was left feeling abandoned by God and wondered if he should walk away.

It might surprise you to learn that Drew isn't some luke-warm Christian. He isn't Christian in name only. Drew is a young pastor of a thriving church plant in San Antonio, Texas, and a talented Christian illusionist. But Drew encountered a profound moment of doubt when his son's life was at stake. In an interview, he said, "Doubt drives you in one of two directions. It either pushes you to run away from God, or it pushes you to run toward God." That day, in the car, Drew said it felt like God "was bear-hugging me as I pounded on his chest."[2]

We'd love to tell you that Linden has been completely healed, but that hasn't happened. There's no big red bow on this story. Linden continues to develop slowly, and Drew and Jane celebrate each new milestone. But they are still in it—living in the midst of suffering. They have experienced unanswered prayer, unexpected suffering, and unwanted hardship—all of which could lead someone to doubt the goodness of God and even his existence. This crisis made Drew a good candidate for deconstruction. One deconstruction resource describes suffering as one of the pillars that cause people's faith to crumble, pointing out that this is the number one reason many people begin to deconstruct.[3]

But it doesn't have to be. Drew and Jane have firsthand experience with suffering and the doubts that result from it. But rather than leading them to deconstruct their faith, this experience has allowed them to experience the love of God like never before. Drew ended the interview by saying, "Over the last year, here's what I've learned: No matter what happens to my son, God is still good. If there's a miracle and he heals him, he's good. And if he doesn't, he's still good."

Doubt

When reading about Drew challenging God regarding his son, you might be thinking, *But pastors aren't supposed to talk like that, are they?* One of the beautiful realities we find in Scripture is that we have permission to be real with God—even when that means expressing our frustrations, our worries, and our doubts.

Just read Psalm 13. David finds himself surrounded by his enemies, and he begins to wonder where God is or why he is allowing this to happen. In deep despair, David writes, "How long, O LORD? Will you forget me forever? How long will you hide your face from me?" (verse 1). But there is something telling about David's prayer. As he honestly questions God and pours out his heart, David draws closer to God. Before he receives his answer, he ends with praise: "I will sing to the LORD, because he has dealt bountifully with me" (verse 6). It's no surprise that both the Old and New Testaments refer to David as a man after God's own heart (1 Samuel 13:14; Acts 13:22).

Or take Habakkuk, an Old Testament prophet who was overwhelmed by the rebellion and violence of his own people. He cried out to God, "O LORD, how long shall I cry for help, and you will not hear? Or cry to you, 'Violence!' and you will not save?" (Habakkuk 1:2). Interestingly, God didn't smite Habakkuk or punish him for asking questions. *God answered* (see verses 5-11). The answer launched Habakkuk into a whole new round of doubts and questions, as God promised to punish Judah's sin by allowing them to be taken captive by Babylon. Yet God didn't scold Habakkuk for questioning him.

When a storm threatened to capsize their boat, Jesus' disciples couldn't believe he was sleeping through this treacherous experience. They woke him and asked, "Teacher, do you not care that we are perishing?" (Mark 4:38). Think about that question. The disciples accused Jesus of not caring enough. One might think the natural response would be for Jesus to rebuke them for doubting his provision and protection. Instead, he rebuked the wind and the sea. After all was calm, he asked them why they were so afraid and had no faith. He pointed out their lack of faith, but he didn't shut down their questions or scold them for asking them. In fact, it's clear that when they expressed their doubt, he performed a miracle to give them evidence to help bolster their faith. By calming the storm, Jesus proved his dominion over the natural elements, providing his disciples ample reason to trust him.

There are many more examples throughout Scripture of God's people pouring out their hearts to him, asking the tough questions, expressing doubt over his goodness and sovereignty, and even despairing of life. Every doubter eventually comes to a crossroads where they must decide whether to continue to move toward God or to move away from him. David was honest with God. Habakkuk questioned God. Jesus' disciples accused him of not caring about them. In every case above, the doubters brought their questions to God, and God responded with tenderness. Jesus can handle our doubts. There is evidence of God's existence

Jesus can handle our doubts.

and the truthfulness of Christianity all around us. We can fall back on this evidence when it feels as if God is silent. We can trust him even when there are situations that seem overwhelming or when we have been harmed by those who claim to be representatives of Christ.

Jinger Duggar Vuolo, the sixth child of Jim Bob and Michelle Duggar, approached her doubts in this way. America watched Jinger and her siblings grow up on the popular TLC reality series *19 Kids and Counting*. The family were devout followers of now-disgraced minister Bill Gothard. who founded the Institute in Basic Life Principles (IBLP). The IBLP is an ultraconservative organization that teaches women to shun birth control; to avoid wearing pants, shorts, tank tops, or any other clothing deemed by the organization to be immodest; and to be totally subservient to their husbands. Popular culture was generally to be avoided while the authoritative role of Gothard himself was emphasized. Jinger described these teachings as "cult-like," and told *People* magazine, "The fear kept me crippled with anxiety. I was terrified of the outside world."[4] Although Gothard never married or had children, his teachings on family, modesty, and women in particular are extreme and unbiblical, even being described by Jinger as "superstition."[5] Gothard was accused of sexual misconduct by over thirty women in 2014 and resigned from IBLP, though his profile and resources are still featured on the website.

Jinger began to doubt what she had been taught all her life, but she did not deconstruct. In her memoir, *Becoming Free Indeed: My Story of Disentangling Faith from Fear*, she noted that the Christianity she grew up with was a mix of truth and false teaching tangled together: "Instead of deconstruction, my faith journey is one of disentanglement. . . . I've spent eight years unthreading my faith: separating truth from error."[6] Jinger rejected the urge to turn to herself as the authority for truth or to reject Christianity altogether. Because Jesus can handle our doubt.

Politics

We would be remiss if we failed to mention the impact the 2016 election had on the deconstruction explosion. One of the dominant expressions of #exvangelical and #deconstruction on Twitter, Instagram, and TikTok can be summarized with this tweet: "80% of evangelicals supporting Donald Trump was the last straw for me. I walked out of church and never went back. #exvangelical #ExChristian"[7] On another popular deconstruction-themed Instagram page, @eve_wasframed wrote: "I was raised as an evangelical, charismatic Christian (think Jesus Camp upbringing) and believed that way for 25 years. Everything started to unravel for me in 2016 when Evangelicals [sic] outright worship of Trump gave me the motivation to question the faith I had held so dearly."[8] The impact that evangelical support of Donald Trump played in producing faith crises cannot be overstated. Charges of Christian nationalism, hypocrisy, moral decay, and white supremacy are peppered throughout the myriad deconstruction stories populating social media platforms. While it's not possible to assess all of these claims, there was some genuine hurt and confusion over the political atmosphere within the church. The accusations continue to be debated, and meanwhile, hardline political disagreements still affect the faith of many people.

Purity culture

Many Christians remember the church's emphasis on abstinence during the 1990s and early 2000s, with many Christian teenagers pledging to remain virgins until marriage. In many cases, these vows were formalized at "purity balls," official ceremonies/dances in which teen girls received purity rings from their fathers as a symbol of their vow. With ministries like True Love Waits bursting on the scene in 1993 and Joshua Harris's *I Kissed Dating Goodbye* being published in 1997, virtually every youth group in America was talking about sex . . . or more accurately, talking about *not* having sex. Many Christian teens wanted to know the clear and specific boundaries (how far is too far?), so the emphasis shifted from simply abstinence to overall purity. As Christian parents sought to teach their teens that sex was intended to be enjoyed only within the confines of biblical marriage, they also wanted to help their kids understand that purity was a much broader category, including everything from one's thought life (pornography and lust) to the physical acts that lead up to and include sexual intercourse.

As author Amy Davidson notes, "In the original curriculum, truth and grace were fairly balanced, but by the time this message reached youth groups, things often went sideways." Davidson continues, "Students who weren't virgins were compared to chewed gum, half-eaten lollipops, flowers without petals, or used pieces of tape. There were even youth activities to emphasize these points."[9]

There were definitely missteps in purity culture, and in some cases, downright abuse. Linda Kay Klein, a self-described deconstruction and purity culture recovery coach, says her nightmares, shame, and PTSD-like symptoms were the result of purity culture, and she credits it as being the catalyst of her own deconstruction. The sex education she received in her youth group included teaching girls they must remain sexless in mind and body,[10] which led her to break up with her high school boyfriend for fear of being named a Jezebel.[11] Klein also recalls that her youth pastor was convicted of trying to seduce a twelve-year-old girl. Although she mistakenly applies what she experienced in her youth group to *all* evangelical churches, she represents a great many in the deconstruction explosion who have experienced a crisis related to purity culture.

The Bible

In his article, "Deconstructing and Losing Faith by Reading the Bible," Christian author Dan Kimball notes that there are an increasing number of videos on TikTok and YouTube with stories of how reading the Bible led many into deconstruction.[12] A common sentiment among these stories is that the Bible is archaic, contradictory, and even immoral. On one popular deconstruction Instagram page, the author asked his audience to describe in one sentence how "messed up" different passages of Scripture are. One example he gave was Judges 11, in which Jephthah made a vow that if God gave the opposing army into his hand, he would take the first thing that came out the front door of his house and present it as a burnt offering. The deconstructionist wrote, "God makes passionately, faithful man murder his own child because of a technicality in the wording of his prayer. (Judges 11)"[13]

When telling their deconstruction stories, many people reveal a deep sense of disillusionment with the darker and more violent stories told in the Bible, which they were not really exposed to while growing up in church. However, as in the case above, often these stories are plucked out of their contexts and interpreted in the least charitable and most simplistic ways possible. For example, the story of Jephthah in the Old Testament is a historical narrative in which a man took a vow that God never sanctioned or approved of. In fact, as we discussed earlier, the Old Testament actually condemns child sacrifice (Leviticus 18:21; Deuteronomy 12:31; 18:10) and includes examples of when God's wrath was stirred against those who committed it (2 Kings 21:6).

So there is more going on in Judges 11 than is represented by the deconstructionist. God did not "make" Jephthah murder his own child but rather instituted a law in which that was forbidden. Jephthah did this on his own . . . *if that's even what happened.* The Hebrew word used for "burnt offering" is *olah*, which can also mean "ascent" or "a going up." (The same word is used this way in Ezekiel 40:26.)[14] It's important to note that when translating the Bible from Hebrew to English, context plays a significant role in determining the meaning of a word. So, many scholars think that in a context where a daughter's *virginity* is emphasized, Jephthah must have meant he was dedicating his daughter into permanent service to God (perhaps at the Tabernacle), not burning her as a sacrifice. When Jephthah's daughter realized what her father had done, she went into the mountains to weep for her virginity.

Interpreting difficult passages like this in light of the whole of Scripture, and with a careful consideration of context and nuance, doesn't fit the "God is evil" narrative. Sadly, passages like this one are often used as proof texts to demonstrate that the Bible is morally flawed and to portray a God who promotes oppression, murder, and/or genocide.

Morality/toxic theology

In the deconstruction movement, certain doctrines and ethics taught within Christianity, such as God's design for marriage, gender, and sexuality, are rejected as "toxic," corrupt, or morally repugnant. In June 2021, a deconstructionist asked this question on Twitter: "What was the first doctrine or belief change that began your deconstruction?"[15] As hundreds of replies rolled in, she tweeted, "For me it was the rapture, so my eschatology was the first little world that got rocked." Those who replied pointed to their churches' teachings on multiple topics, including interracial dating, complementarianism, hell, prayer, and biblical inerrancy. A frequent theme among respondents was their rejection of the doctrine of original sin: "Original sin and the toxic abuse it leads to."

A pro-deconstruction progressive Christian parenting blogger discussed the phrase "Jesus died for you/your sins." She wrote, "While I realize that statement won't psychologically damage every kid, if it damages ONE, it's not worth using. Period."[16] Notice that "statement" is what Paul calls "the gospel"—the good news: "Now I would remind you, brothers, of the gospel I preached to you . . . that Christ died for our sins" (1 Corinthians 15:1, 3). That statement can cause discomfort because it acknowledges our sinfulness, but that does not change the reality: The gospel saves.

Often people who deconstruct their faith claim to be taking the moral high ground. For instance, many no longer believe that homosexuality is sinful. A Twitter user responded this way: "My thought process in 8th grade: 'actually Lady Gaga is awakening me and gay people aren't bad. If God made them that way, then that means he loves them so everyone else should as well.'"[17] Of course, God does love all people regardless of our sin struggles. In fact, it is because of Jesus' love for the world that he gave his life to offer the free gift of salvation to everyone who believes in him (John 3:16).

One deconstruction resource on Instagram sees complementarianism (the belief that men and women have equal value but different roles) as morally problematic as well, asserting that it fosters environments that are "much more likely to harbor abuse," "discriminate against women," and lead to a "miserable life."[18]

Then she pointed out certain stories in which real abuse was handled poorly by churches, where the women were told to reconcile with their abusive husbands under threat of excommunication. This was also tied up with a lack of inclusivity for the LGBTQ+ community, racial minorities, and those who are neurodivergent.[19] We are well aware that some churches have made mistakes and even engaged in abusive behaviors in the way they have taught and implemented certain doctrines. But often, deconstructionists believe that it's the doctrines themselves that are the problem.

Abuse

One anonymous survivor shared her story of sexual and spiritual abuse through the online platform Buzzfeed. She wrote, "My dad sexually abused me [when I was 9] and used religion to keep me quiet. He said things like, 'If God forgave me, then you're supposed to forgive me too.' 'What WE did was a sin.' 'You tempted me.' My church REALLY pushed purity culture, and I was terrified of revealing how 'damaged' I was. I resigned myself to having a life without marriage and a family because I was impure."[20] Stories like this one are horrific examples of the abuse some have endured at the hands of those who claim the name of Christ. Our hearts are rightly grieved when reading them, and it's not difficult to imagine why many who have experienced something like this end up walking away from the faith. Christian parents should never abuse their children but should bring them up in the training and instruction of the Lord (Ephesians 6:4). God's Word refers to children as a "heritage from the LORD" (Psalm 127:3) and tells us how tenderly and lovingly Jesus treated them (Matthew 18:1-6).

Scripture is clear that we are to be tenderhearted and kind to one another (Ephesians 4:32), to love one another with a brotherly affection, outdoing one another in showing honor (Romans 12:10), and to look not only to our own interests, but also to the interests of others (Philippians 2:4). Jesus himself said to do to others what you would want them to do to you (Matthew 7:12). Clearly abuse and mistreatment have no place among Christians or the church.

Sexual abuse damages people and dishonors God. It contradicts his design for sex, which is clearly articulated in

Scripture. As a reflection of Christ's love for the church, sexual activity belongs only within a committed marriage relationship between one man and one woman (1 Corinthians 6:18; Ephesians 5:3; 1 Thessalonians 4:3-5; and Hebrews 13:4, to name a few, but there are many more!). These passages not only instruct individuals about God's design for sex, but they also serve to protect those who might otherwise become the unwilling victims of someone else's sexual appetite.

If everyone followed God's perfect ideal for how we are to interact with one another, there would be no abuse. It's fallen people, not Christianity, who are abusive. Jesus came to set captives free. He said, "The Spirit of the Lord is upon me, because he has anointed me to proclaim good news to the poor. He has sent me to proclaim liberty to the captives and recovering of sight to the blind, to set at liberty those who are oppressed, to proclaim the year of the Lord's favor" (Luke 4:18-19). And for those who have been abused, oppressed, and taken advantage of, Solomon, one of the psalmists, expresses the heart of God toward them: "He delivers the needy when he calls, the poor and him who has no helper. He has pity on the weak and the needy, and saves the lives of the needy. From oppression and violence he redeems their life, and precious is their blood in his sight" (Psalm 72:12-14). God also instructs us, his followers, to tenderly care for those who've been mistreated. For instance, the apostle Paul tells us to "bear one another's burdens, and so fulfill the law of Christ" (Galatians 6:2).

These beautiful truths speak against the idea that Christianity is abusive, so what is behind the broad accusations of abuse against the faith as a whole? Many deconstructionists seem to take a subjective approach in determining what qualifies as abusive, toxic, and legalistic, leading to trauma. There certainly are valid examples of abuse in the church, such as sexual assault and abuses of power. But many deconstructionists go further, saying that some historic orthodox teachings of Christianity—such as penal substitutionary atonement (Jesus paying the penalty for our sins on the cross), the doctrine of hell, and complementarianism—are abusive by nature. Therefore, many in the deconstruction online space claim to have been abused simply because they were taught these ideas. For example, one deconstructionist posted a graphic meme on Instagram that claims Christianity *itself* is abusive, even when practiced in a healthy church environment. The caption next to the meme states:

> The religion itself, from many people's perspective, is abusive and harmful. I didn't leave the faith because of the church or the people. I left the church because of the church. Then I continued to faithfully have a "relationship with Jesus" for many years. Eventually, it became clear to me that the very faith itself was what I couldn't make peace with.[21]

One popular deconstructionist put it this way: "Penal substitutionary atonement theory (PSA) is psychological abuse always!"[22]

DECONSTRUCTION ISN'T INEVITABLE

Greg grew up in a violent inner-city home, where his entire family was eventually reached and discipled by a hyperfundamentalist and very legalistic church. In a candid tweet, he revealed, "The wounds inflicted were real and it has taken decades to recover."[23] But as we mentioned earlier, *not every candidate for deconstruction ends up in deconstruction.* Greg could easily have blamed God for the very real failings of the people who claimed to represent him. He could have conflated the abuse and violence of his childhood with the more difficult doctrines of God's justice, wrath, and judgment. He could have let roots of bitterness against the legalistic Christians in his life grow into weeds of cynicism and unbelief. *But that's not what happened.* In fact, today Greg runs a national ministry that equips youth leaders everywhere to "see the Gospel advanced and disciples made among today's youth."[24] In a Twitter thread explaining the trauma of his past, he wrote:

> I never thought once about becoming a "progressive
> Christian" or abandoning my Christian faith because
> of trauma. Jesus has been my anchor in the storm.
> He alone has been my firm foundation. The intense
> violence I witnessed growing up, the pain of being
> abandoned by my biological father, the shock of
> almost dying four times before the age of eleven, the
> anxiety of being raised in a high crime rate area by
> a single shame-fueled mom, the guilt of constantly
> failing to measure up to the impossible standards of
> a super legalistic church . . . all of this is NOTHING
> compared to the overwhelming love of Christ. Don't
> buy the lie that abandoning the historic Christian
> faith is your only option if you've been hurt by life or

by the church. It's not. My life is proof of that. Jesus loves you. Christianity is true. And, yes, life is hard. But pain and trauma are not excuses to leave the faith. They are reasons to cling that much more to Christ. They are reasons to run to Jesus every day. As Spurgeon said "I have learned to kiss the wave that throws me against the Rock of Ages." May the waves that are battering you, not sink your faith, but bring you closer to Jesus.[25]

We hope Greg's story encourages you. His life is a testimony of what can happen when someone fully surrenders their life to Christ and bears the beautiful fruit of love, grace, forgiveness, and true spiritual freedom.

While the triggers described in this chapter might be valid reasons to become confused about what Christianity is and cause someone to wrestle with the nature of God along with the truthfulness of certain teachings and doctrines, none of them is a good reason to leave the historic faith or redefine it according to one's subjective preferences. But for us to be able to know which beliefs and practices to hold on to and which ones to reject, we must root our understanding of Christianity in the authority of the Scriptures, not in the authority of the self.

UPPER STORY

AFTER COVID-19 HIT, a flood of contemporary Christian music (CCM) artists announced their deconstructions within a few months of each other. With concerts halted, many artists found themselves at home with no touring opportunities for the first time in their careers. No doubt this provided ample time to rethink the beliefs they'd been singing about and making a living by. Many took to social media—one of the only ways to connect socially during that isolating time—to express their change of belief. In July of that year, I (Alisa) invited Skillet front man John Cooper and his wife, Korey, who is the band's guitarist and producer, along with singer/ songwriter Jeremy Camp and his wife, Adrienne, singer and former front woman of the Benjamin Gate, to discuss deconstruction within the CCM industry. Before this special live

YouTube event, I released a trailer to generate interest and help promote the discussion.

The trailer opens with quick flashes of headlines describing the deconstruction stories of several Christian celebrities over the somber piano-driven opening to the Skillet song "Anchor."

"What's going on in Christianity?" asks John Cooper. "Why are so many people falling away from their faith?"

After more quick cuts and quotes from these deconstructionists, the voice of Jeremy Camp is heard: "One day I'm going to see Jesus face-to-face. Even when I cannot see, I still believe."

Then I come on-screen and say, "Most of them [deconstruction stories] being from CCM music, it just felt like gut punch after gut punch after gut punch. Be good, be kind, do all this good stuff. They're borrowing that from the Christian worldview."[1]

The trailer generated quite a buzz and was viewed over 150,000 times across all platforms. It caught the attention of deconstructionist Janice Lagata, who created a parody video of the trailer with other deconstructionists, Jo Luehmann and Julia, who goes under the Instagram moniker That Loud Deconstructing One.

"What's going on with dietary preferences? Why are so many people walking away from meat?" asks Janice plaintively.

Julia adds, "One day I'm gonna taste the perfect steak. Even though COVID stole my sense of taste, I still believe."

Jo Luehmann observes, "Most of them even being from meat-eating families, it just felt like gut punch after gut punch after gut punch." She continues, "Use heat. Use spice.

Use all this good stuff. They are borrowing that from meat recipes."[2]

Obviously, they were using humor to try to make the point that our religious beliefs are just personal preferences. As a result, it would be silly to fret over the religious views of our friends in the same way it would be weird to worry too much about whether they choose to get their protein from chicken or peas. In this view, religious preference is no different from dietary preference. Walking away from Christianity is like walking away from chicken.

The comedic comparison between religious beliefs and food choices highlights a fundamental flaw underlying the deconstruction movement. In fact, it's central to what's wrong with deconstruction. Francis Schaeffer, the brilliant philosopher and theologian who was prophetic in understanding the times, saw all this coming back in the 1970s. "Schaeffer wrote that the problem with communicating Christianity to a new generation was centered on a new view of truth that detached it from objective and knowable reality," writes philosopher Douglas Groothuis.[3] This "new view of truth" seems to be at the heart of the deconstruction movement.

WHAT MAKES SOMETHING TRUE?

To better understand what Schaeffer is referring to, let's look at two different ways the word *truth* is typically used. When I (Tim) teach about truth to audiences, I begin with a simple statement: "My computer is on the podium."[4] Then I ask, "Is that statement true?" At this point, some are probably wondering if this is a trick question. After all, everyone can clearly see my sixteen-inch MacBook Pro sitting right there. Once we agree the statement is true, I have a second question: "What *makes* the statement true?" The thing that makes the statement "My computer is on the podium" a true statement is—drumroll please—my computer sitting on the podium. If my computer were sitting not on the podium but on the floor, the statement would be false. This may sound simple, but it has important implications.

This commonsense notion is technically referred to as the correspondence theory of truth. It's a fancy phrase that simply means a statement is true if it corresponds with (or matches up with) reality. Douglas Groothuis, professor of philosophy at Denver Seminary, put it this way in his massive tome *Christian Apologetics*: "A belief or statement is true only if it matches with, reflects or corresponds to the reality it refers to. . . . In other words, for a statement to be true, there must be a *truth-maker* that determines its truth."[5]

Notice a couple of things. First, the truth of the statement is independent of anyone's beliefs and desires. Someone may not *believe* my computer is on the podium, but that doesn't change reality. Furthermore, someone may not *like* that my MacBook is on the podium (maybe they're anti–Apple products). In any case, the person's belief and preferences are irrelevant to the truth of the statement. This is called objective truth. Describing objective truth, apologist Greg Koukl says, "If the 'truth maker,' the condition that makes a statement true, is something about the *object* itself—something outside us, so to speak, unrelated to our own thoughts, desires, feelings, or beliefs—then the truth is an *objective* truth."[6] So objective truth is what corresponds to the world "out there."

There's another way the word *truth* is used. This "truth" isn't determined by the object; it's determined by the subject. In this view, truth is relative to what a person believes. It's called subjective truth or relativism and is the belief that what is true or false depends completely on the individual, the "subject." The individual's beliefs, tastes, or preferences are the "truth maker." Something can be "true" for one person, but the exact same thing may be "false" for someone else. So, for example, you might hear someone say, "Christianity is *true for you*, but it's not *true for me*."

Although many people think this way, relativism is actually self-defeating when the truth of a statement proves itself false. For example, "There are no English sentences longer than three words" is a self-defeating statement since it is an English sentence longer than three words. Now take the relativists' claim, "All truth is relative." We hear some version of this assertion all the time. But if we apply the claim to itself, it refutes itself. In other words, "All truth is relative" is a self-defeating declaration since it's an example of an objective truth claim, the kind of truth the claim denies. If the claim is objectively true, then it is objectively false.

Now that we've laid out the difference between objective truth and subjective "truth," it's time for a test. (Don't worry; you'll do great.) Listed below are five statements. We want you to identify what *kind* of truth claim is being made: objective (fact) or subjective (preference).

1. The average gravitational pull of the Earth is 9.8 meters per second squared.
2. *She-Hulk* was the worst TV show of all time.

3. Coke tastes better than Pepsi.
4. The Empire State Building is located in New York City.
5. ZoeGirl is the best CCM band ever.

If you read the statements above and concluded that numbers 1 and 4 are objective facts, and numbers 2, 3, and 5 are subjective preferences, congratulations. You passed the test! (And if you believe number 5 is correct, you obviously rock.)

Okay, here's a bonus question:

6. Christianity is true.

Is this merely a subjective claim, or is it an objective claim? Notice this is a religious claim. And many people believe religion is just a matter of subjective preference rather than objective fact. Before we give you the answer, we need to talk about Schaeffer's two-story building.

TWO-STORY BUILDING

In her book *Total Truth*, author Nancy Pearcey builds upon the insight of Schaeffer and describes a "two-tiered truth."[7] Pearcey writes,

> As Schaeffer explains, the concept of truth itself has been divided—a process he illustrates with the imagery of a two-story building: In the lower story are science and reason, which are considered public truth, binding on everyone. Over against it is an

upper story of noncognitive experience, which is
the locus of personal meaning. This is the realm of
private truth, where we hear people say, "That may
be true for you but it's not true for me."[8]

According to Schaeffer and Pearcey, our culture divides
truth into two realms.[9] In the lower story are things like math,
science, logic, and facts. "All dogs are mammals," "insulin
controls type 1 diabetes," and "2 + 2 = 4" are all lower-story
truths. Schaeffer called this "true truth."[10] In the upper story
are likes and preferences, such as your favorite kind of cheese
or which row you like to sit in at the movie theater. In this
house, facts go downstairs, and preferences go upstairs. Now
back to our question: Does religion belong in the lower story
or the upper story? In other words, is religion a matter of
fact about reality, or is it a matter of private, personal belief?
Pearcey says contemporary culture has relegated religion (as
well as morality) to the upper story, "which takes it out of the
realm of true and false altogether."[11]

Christianity is "true truth"

When we say, "Christianity is true," there's a common confusion that occurs. Our contemporary culture thinks we're
claiming, "Christianity is true *for me*." They assume we're
making a subjective claim, not an objective one. That's
because religious beliefs have been pushed into the upper
story. Like choosing ice cream, many people assume that religious beliefs are based on your tastes or what works for you.

But we're not merely claiming that Christianity is our
personal preference. We're claiming that Christianity is true

to reality—it fits the way the world really is. It's objectively true. As Pearcey says, it offers "a unified, integrated truth that stands in complete contrast to the two-level concept of truth in the secular world."[12]

Christianity is *not* simply about finding a way of life that works for us or fits our personal tastes. In fact, sometimes Christianity will not *feel* like it's working for us. Former atheist J. Warner Wallace put it this way:

> I'm not a Christian because it "works" for me. I had a life prior to Christianity that seemed to be working just fine, and my life as a Christian hasn't always been easy.
>
> I'm a Christian because it is true. I'm a Christian because I want to live in a way that reflects the truth. I'm a Christian because my high regard for the truth leaves me no alternative.[13]

While standing before Pilate at his trial, Jesus said, "For this purpose I was born and for this purpose I have come into the world—to bear witness to the truth. Everyone who is of the truth listens to my voice" (John 18:37). Jesus didn't come bearing witness to *a* truth, or *his* truth. He came as a witness to *the* truth. Following Jesus means following the truth. He is the Truth, after all (John 14:6). But following Jesus comes at a cost. Jesus says, "Anyone who would come after me, let him deny himself and take up his cross and follow me" (Matthew 16:24). Since the cross is an instrument of death, the implication of Jesus' words is that all those who come after him must be willing to lose their lives for the sake of the truth. Jesus also says, "Whoever loses his life for my sake will find it" (Matthew 10:39). Of course, that doesn't prove Christianity is true. However, it does show that Christianity, from the beginning, was founded on a belief in objective truth.

Moreover, Jesus also made claims about himself that went beyond mere opinion. In John 8:48-59, some Judeans accused Jesus of being demon-possessed. After a bit of tense conversation, they asked him outright, "Who do you think you are?" (verse 53, NIV). Jesus replied, "Very truly I tell you, . . . before Abraham was born, I am!" (NIV). This is an incredibly significant statement because of what happened earlier in Jewish history. If we go back to the account of God speaking to Moses from a burning bush, we find that when Moses asked God's name, God responded with, "Say this to the people of Israel: 'I AM has sent me to you'" (Exodus 3:14). So when Jesus said, "I am," he was identifying himself not only as some kind of vague deity, but as the true God of the Old Testament. The Jews understood this to be blasphemy, and they picked up rocks to stone Jesus.

Throughout his life, Jesus demonstrated his deity. He forgave sins (Matthew 9:1-8), which caused the religious leaders to accuse him of blasphemy because forgiving sins is something only God can do. He accepted worship on multiple occasions (Matthew 2:11; 14:33; 21:9; 28:9; John 20:28). The claim of Jesus' deity is important because if it's not true, then Jesus was just "living his truth." That would actually make him a liar or a lunatic for claiming to be God, as C. S. Lewis famously pointed out.[14] However, if his assertion is true, then it's true to reality.

This is one of the reasons the resurrection of Jesus is such a bedrock teaching. The Resurrection is a fact about reality—an objective truth—that isn't just true for those who believe it. Jesus was either raised from the dead, as a historical event in reality, or he wasn't. If he wasn't, then Christianity is false. If he was, then Christianity is true for everyone, whether they believe it or not. Because of that, it has eternal consequences for everyone. This is why the apostle Paul is so adamant in 1 Corinthians 15:14 that "if Christ has not been raised, then our preaching is in vain and your faith is in vain." Paul is letting us know that the value of Christianity depends on it being objectively true, so if someone were to dig up the body of Jesus or prove the Resurrection was a hoax or a fraud, it would demonstrate that the entire belief system of Christianity is objectively false and worthless. That's a bold claim! This is why religion cannot be placed in the upper story, in the realm of preference. If Christianity is true, it makes exclusive claims about itself. Jesus claimed, "I am the way, the truth, and the life. No one comes to the Father except through me" (John 14:6). He predicted his own death and resurrection (John 2:19; 10:18), and then he proved his claims true by raising himself from the dead.

Christianity is not merely subjective truth; it is true truth. It is truth that explains reality.

Christians should reject the idea that religious and moral truth belong in the upper story. In fact, they are just as objective as scientific truth. Christianity is not merely subjective truth; it is true truth, as Schaeffer points out. It is truth that explains reality.

The primal heresy

The idea that we determine our own truth—subjective truth—is "the heartbeat of our age."[15] But it actually goes back to the beginning, as we pointed out earlier. In fact, Greg Koukl calls this "the primal heresy."[16] Giving an interpretative paraphrase of Genesis 3:1-6, Koukl writes:

"Has God said?" the Deceiver challenged. "He's lying. He's holding out on you. He is not good. What do *you* want? What does *your* heart tell you?"

"The fruit seems good to eat. It delights my eyes. It will make me wise. I want it."

"Then take it. Be free of him. Truth is not out there. Truth is within. Make your own rules. Follow your own heart. Be true to your own *self*." . . .

At the Fall, an alternative "truth" prevailed, the truth within, "my truth." The revolt in the Garden was a rejection of the *external* source of truth in exchange for an *internal* authority. Self-rule replaced God's rule. Mankind embraced itself.[17]

So deconstruction began in Eden, when Satan walked Adam and Eve into the "upper story." This primal heresy permeates the deconstruction explosion. For a movement that prides itself on being tolerant, nonjudgmental, and open-minded, there emerges a dogmatic orthodoxy. The word *orthodoxy* is defined as "a belief or a way of thinking that is accepted as true or correct."[18] The word *heresy* means "a belief or opinion that does not agree with the official belief or opinion of a particular religion."[19] Among many deconstructionists, certain beliefs are practically considered heretical, even though deconstruction is not an official religion.

For example, it's taboo to tell someone what they *should* believe about religious truth. This is why making judgments about someone's deconstruction has become unacceptable. For example, on a popular deconstruction Facebook page, a graphic meme explains what it looks like to "hold space for someone else." The quotation reads: "It means that we are willing to walk alongside another person in whatever journey they're on without judging them, making them feel inadequate, trying to fix them, or trying to impact the outcome."[20] That same Facebook page posted a graphic meme stating, "If whatever communities we find ourselves in, we refuse the notion of 'I'm right and you're wrong,' and we come with a posture of humility and healing is our end goal, it changes everything."[21] Notice that the same platform that exists to encourage people to change their current, traditional beliefs is touting the importance of not judging someone else's belief journey. But why encourage a journey at all unless you think the starting point ought to be abandoned? Doesn't that require judging that traditional Christian beliefs are, in fact, wrong?

Regardless of any contradiction between their stated goals and what they do in actual practice, the deconstruction movement claims to be about being nonjudgmental and tolerant, and Schaeffer's two-realm theory of truth helps us understand the thought process behind this. Most of the deconstructionists advocate an upper-story deconstruction grounded in private, personal preferences rather than a lower-story experience grounded in public, objective facts. This also explains why many modern "deconstruction coaches" refuse to tell people where they should land in their deconstruction. After all, if deconstruction belongs in the upper story, then each destination is a matter of personal preference and equally valid. Of course, they're quick to say where one *shouldn't* land—evangelical Christianity.

In a video titled *Our Journey of Faith Deconstruction*, Jo Luehmann and her husband share their stories. She says,

> This is the thing with deconstruction that I really think it's important to understand. Everyone lands wherever they land. There is no right place to land with deconstruction. Some people land away from faith. Some people land in a different type of faith. Some people become agnostic. Some people become a different type of Christian. Some people become atheists. And all of those routes in deconstruction are valid and to be respected.[22]

The reason "there is no right place to land" is that, for Luehmann, deconstruction is in the upper story, where objective right and wrong do not exist. Luehmann isn't alone. Psychology professor and deconstruction coach Katie Blake notes that she "isn't trying to get people back to their Christian faith."[23] In the article titled "Deconstructing? There's a Coach for That," Blake says, "Generally, I don't use the term 'reconstruction' in my work. . . . I find that term can imply what is an OK outcome and what is not an OK outcome in someone else's faith journey. That is not for me to decide." Tipping her hat to practices like mindfulness, yoga, social psychology, and the Enneagram,[24] she articulates that belief-building should be "self-determined," which she describes as a "rare work of art."[25]

Why won't Blake offer "outcomes" or tell you what to believe? It's because she's thinking of deconstruction as an upper-story process. As philosopher and Baylor University professor Francis Beckwith points out, if religious beliefs belong in the realm of personal preference, then they are "incapable of being judged or assessed by third parties."[26]

Crystal Cheatham is another deconstruction coach. She is an LGBTQ rights activist and founder of Our Bible App, a progressive Christian community claiming "to *uplift* you, *affirm* your goodness, and *dig into the hard stuff*—**without the baggage** of toxic theology."[27] Included in the list of "toxic theology" is the idea that religious truth is objective. She says, "One of the toxic traits of evangelicalism is the belief that there is only one right way to do it, and we can't swing back into the rut of saying that one way is how you do it correctly." Cheatham says, "People find all sorts of paths and we encourage it."[28] Our Bible App's stated mission says, "Through highlighting devotionals that are pro-LGBTQ+, pro-feminism, and encouraging of interfaith inclusivity— we hope to provide a tool that is needed to create healthy spiritual habits."[29] From that, it seems that all paths are valid, except the historically Christian path.

On his web page, deconstruction coach Kurtis Vanderpool writes, "Deconstruction is a deeply personal and emotional experience and no one else can tell you where it should lead or how you should do it. Find your own way forward that leads to peace, acceptance, and purpose with a companion and guide through deconstruction coaching."[30] Notice— again—the contradiction. Why would you need a "guide" if no one else can tell you where to go?

Once again, we see upper-story thinking rear its relativistic head. One way to expose it is to replace the word *deconstruction* with something from the lower story, and see if it still works. For example, let's replace the word *deconstruction* with the words *heart attack*, then read the sentence again: "A *heart attack* is a deeply personal and emotional experience and no one else can tell you where it should lead or how you should do it." You see the problem.

HEART ATTACK

My (Tim's) dad had a heart attack on May 3, 2019, which nobody saw coming. My dad has been 165 pounds since he was in high school. He exercises daily and eats healthy. However, after feeling intense chest pain in the middle of the night that wouldn't go away, he headed to the hospital. After getting the results from some blood work, doctors rushed him into the operating room for an emergency life-saving surgery. According to the heart specialist, my dad had two blockages. The most concerning blockage was in the left anterior descending (LAD) artery, which supplies blood to the largest part of the heart. It was 99 percent blocked. This is known as the widow-maker heart attack because of its deadly track record. Most patients require immediate surgery to survive.

Heart attacks are lower-story events. Since they are

objective facts about reality, the way doctors react isn't merely a matter of preference. A heart attack calls for a specific medical response. This is because the heart has a purpose or goal. The purpose of the heart is to pump blood throughout the body. With the heart's objective purpose in mind, highly skilled medical professionals were able to save my dad's life. But what if my dad's doctors had relativized the heart's purpose? What would you think if they told my dad, "No one should tell you where your heart attack should lead or how you should respond to it. Follow your heart [sorry . . . couldn't resist]. Find your own way forward. All routes are equally valid. We're not here to tell you what to do." In this hypothetical scenario, my dad would be dead. That's because the doctors would have been treating a lower-story problem with an upper-story solution.

Contrast what my dad's doctors actually did with the approach taken in a video titled "No goal!!!!!!" by "Naked Pastor" David Hayward. He says, "When you're deconstructing, it's wise not to set a goal or envision an outcome. Totally wipe the slate clean. Enjoy the here and the now."[31] He also recommends not reconstructing: "Don't reconstruct . . . because you're only going to reconstruct into another theology that you'll have to eventually deconstruct later."[32]

Here's the question: Why does the goal matter when a doctor responds to a heart attack, but the goal *doesn't matter* when a person responds to a faith crisis? The answer is fundamental to understanding deconstruction. Deconstruction treats your religious beliefs as if they are nothing more than personal preferences in the upper story.

UPPER-STORY AUTHORITY

How we view religious truth also impacts how we view religious authority. Once again, think about what makes something true. If religious truth is merely an "upper-story" truth, then the "truth maker" is *you*. Who's in charge of upper-story truth? You are. You are the final authority of what is true and meaningful. You are "the man upstairs," so to speak. Ideas have consequences. Pearcey comments on where we find ourselves today: "Religion is not considered an objective truth to which we *submit*, but only a matter of personal taste which we *choose*."[33] The deconstruction movement isn't about *submitting* to the truth. Instead, it's about people *choosing* their own truth. As Angela Herrington, quoted on the Deconstructing Mamas Facebook page, expresses it: "We're taught to value the voice of authority over our own and that's really upside-down and backwards."[34]

This is clearly illustrated in a Facebook post from Chris Kratzer, a pastor and author of *Stupid Sh— Heard in Church*. He writes about counseling a woman through her faith deconstruction. At one point he realized that the apostle Paul's writings about penal substitution were very distressing to her. Eventually she asked him what he thought about some specific verses in Paul's letters.

I told her, "he's wrong."

She replied, "I'm allowed to do that? It's ok to say he's wrong?" I could hear, over the phone, the shackles break free from around her heart and the monstrous god hiding under her bed was revealed as a fraud created by men. She started breathing for the first time.

Folks, this is what's wrong with much of Christianity. All authority is given to a book and then given to church people who claim its authority for themselves. If you can't say Paul is wrong, it's going to be harder to say that they are wrong. That's the design.

The most dangerous thing in all of Christianity is a person who reads the Bible in front of them who has not learned to read the mind of Christ within them, and see it as our ultimate Light.[35]

Kratzer's post illuminates an important thrust within the deconstruction movement. Notice who's in charge of what's true. It's *not* the apostle Paul, who was inspired by God, whose words are referred to as Scripture. It's the "mind of Christ" within the individual that trumps Scripture. On another post, Kratzer put it like this: "I think there is something beautifully transformative in our spiritual journey when we begin to spend less time studying the Bible and far more time writing our own."[36]

Here's the problem with that way of thinking, and it's really quite simple. Write this down, stitch it on a pillow, or tattoo it on your forehead: *The mind of Christ will never disagree with the words of Christ.* According to 2 Timothy 3:16, "All Scripture is breathed out by God and profitable for teaching, for reproof, for correction, and for training in righteousness." This means that every word in the Bible is inspired by God and thus reflects the mind of Christ. But lest anyone think we are engaging in circular reasoning by saying the Bible is God's Word because the Bible says so, let's look at what Jesus says about Scripture. He affirms the Old Testament Scriptures over and over again saying things like, "God commanded" (Matthew 15:4), and referring to them as "the word of God" (Mark 7:13) and "the commandment of God" (Mark 7:8). He even appeals to the authority of the Scriptures to fight temptation in the wilderness. It would be beyond the scope of this book to launch into an in-depth defense of biblical authority, but we recommend studying up on it for yourself. *Christ and the Bible* by John Wenham is a good place to start.[37] The main point here is that if we don't let the words of Christ inform what we believe about the mind of Christ, we will effectively be sending Christ upstairs and putting him in the realm of "my truth." The end result will probably be a Christ that reflects *our* minds rather than *his*.

> The mind of Christ will never disagree with the words of Christ.

Deconstruction is a flawed process. It assigns religious belief to the upper story, treating truth as a matter of personal preference, and makes the individual the ultimate authority. So if we don't want Christians to deconstruct, what *do* we want Christians to do? That's the question we turn to next.

REFORMATION

When I (Alisa) was a kid, I wasn't allowed to watch scary movies. Not that I would have wanted to. I once spent an entire two hours and thirty-four minutes facedown on a pillow, pretending to be asleep, when some friends decided to watch the movie *Aliens* at a sleepover. It was at one of those all-night parties that I came to learn about the story of "Bloody Mary." As legend goes, if you stand in front of a mirror and say the name Bloody Mary over and over, she will appear and climb out of the mirror and scare you . . . or kill you . . . or show you your future husband or something. Who knows. I sure as death never tried it. Needless to say, I had exactly zero interest in trying to summon a bloody ghost who would definitely haunt my nightmares for the foreseeable future. In fact, for years I avoided looking into the bathroom mirror at night.

The words *Bloody Mary* conjure up feelings of fear and trepidation. Many kids refuse to even say the words, worried about what might result. Similarly, some deconstructionists misconstrue any critique of deconstruction as being motivated by fear. They think conservative Christians, terrified of losing power, have turned deconstruction into a bogeyman in an attempt to shut down sincere questions. "The only thing more detrimental to a church than people leaving are people staying and questioning leadership. Hence the smear and fear campaign they are currently running on the word [deconstruction]. They're legitimately scared," one deconstructionist tweeted.[1]

Are Tim and Alisa scared of people "staying and questioning leadership"? Nope. In fact, we are constantly *encouraging* Christians to question Christianity and its leaders. We're not afraid of questions. We welcome them. Leaders who can't be questioned and lack accountability make churches ripe for spiritual abuse. Socrates famously said, "The unexamined life is not worth living."[2] We would add, the unexamined faith is not worth believing. An examined faith is a *healthy* faith. That's why it's important that we examine and reexamine our beliefs. Every Christian should know *what* they believe and *why* they believe it. And this means being open to asking hard questions. (More on this in chapter 11).

Every Christian should know what they believe and why they believe it. And this means being open to asking hard questions.

So then, why are we concerned about Christians using the word *deconstruction*? It's *not* because we are on a "smear and fear campaign" against the deconstruction bogeyman. Neither of us is going to collapse into the fetal position at the sound of this four-syllable *d*-word. It's because we care about clarity. As we've seen, deconstruction isn't just about questioning beliefs; it's about rejecting Scripture as the source of *objective* truth and authority.

We'd like to propose a better way to reexamine your faith.

REFORMATION, NOT DECONSTRUCTION

There's a significant difference between *de-* words and *re-* words. The English prefix *de-* means "do the opposite of" or "remove from." When applied to verbs, it almost always reverses the verb's action. *De*hydrate, *de*activate, and *de*stabilize, for example, all mean the opposite of the original verb. When you dehydrate a tomato in the hot sun for your homemade pasta sauce, you're causing it to do the opposite of hydrate. Likewise, at the most basic level, *de*construct means "do the opposite of construct." The emphasis is on tearing down, not building up.

Re- words, on the other hand, work a bit differently. The prefix *re-* denotes "moving back to the original." So when you *re*cover, *re*store, or *re*build something, you are bringing it back to its original purpose and definition. Both *de-* words and *re-* words are directional, but *re-* words signify moving back to something. When you recover from the flu, you return to a normal state of health. When Jesus healed a man with a withered hand, he told the man to stretch out his hand, and "his hand was *restored*" (Mark 3:1-6, emphasis added).

It's a lot easier to deconstruct something than to restore something. My (Tim's) dad encouraged my younger brother and me to take auto shop in high school. He thought this would provide practical skills we could use throughout our lives. (He's probably right, but I still go to him when my SUV makes a strange noise.) While my friends were playing in the band, singing in the choir, and practicing for the next musical, I was changing brake pads, replacing spark plugs, and figuring out how to remove grease from under my fingernails. The high school I attended had two auto shops devoted to training future mechanics. Teachers would bring their vehicles to us for oil changes, brake jobs, and anything else they thought we could handle. Of course, this was all done under teacher supervision. It was a good arrangement. We got hands-on experience, and they saved a few bucks.

One class assignment involved disassembling and reassembling an engine. (Don't worry, this was a model motor, not one from a teacher's car.) Taking apart an engine is surprisingly simple. For the most part, you don't need many instructions. You just need a good ratchet and a socket set. Rebuilding an engine, on the other hand, is a different matter. If you want a working engine, you need to make sure *everything* goes where it's supposed to. (I may have finished with a few parts left over on my first attempt.) Reassembly requires knowing where things go and how things fit together. It involves forethought, knowledge, and skill.

There are certainly many areas where the church has lost its way. Like an old car, there are parts that are broken, missing, or added that don't belong. But the solution isn't to send the whole thing to the scrapyard. There's a better way.

SEMPER REFORMANDA

One popular claim from deconstructionists is that deconstruction "has long been seen as a healthy expression of Christian faithfulness."[3] As proof, we're told to just "ask Martin Luther."[4] Martin Luther is famous for challenging the church on what he saw as serious abuses and initiating the Protestant Reformation. Many deconstructionists compare what they're doing with what Luther did: *reforming.* For example, Derek Webb, former lead singer of the Christian band Caedmon's Call, tweeted, "'Deconstructing' is part of 'reforming.' I'd like to think your church deacons would be comforted knowing that we're following the reformation's cry of 'semper reformanda' (always reforming), calling out teachings and practices that the church should repent of and leave behind."[5] But is *that* what's actually happening? Are deconstructionists just doing what the Reformers did?

"Always reforming" (Latin: *semper reformanda*) is an expression many Christians are familiar with, though few know where it comes from. Theologian Michael Horton traces the phrase back to a devotional book written by Jodocus van Lodenstein, a Dutch Reformer, in 1674.[6] The whole Latin phrase is *ecclesia reformata, semper reformanda secundum verbi Dei*, which means "the church is Reformed and always being reformed according to the Word of God." The last part of the sentence is significant. The church isn't always reforming to keep up with contemporary culture, or to get rid of old, dusty orthodoxy. Rather, it's always being reformed *according to Scripture.* That's what the Protestant Reformation was all about. Although the process wasn't always tidy in its execution, the goal was to remove aspects of Christianity that had deviated from divine revelation. There would have been no Reformation without Scripture. The Reformers, like Luther and Calvin, weren't responsible for reforming the Church. *The Word of God reformed the Church.*[7] The purpose of the Reformers was to recover the original, not tear everything down and create something new. Pastor Kevin DeYoung says, "The motto of the Reformation was not 'Forward!' but 'Backward!'—as in, 'Back to the sources!'"[8] But that ultimate "source" of truth is God's Word, not something else. DeYoung concludes, "*Semper reformanda* is not about constant fluctuations, but about firm foundations. It is about radical adherence to the Holy Scriptures, no matter the cost to ourselves, our traditions, or our own fallible sense of cultural relevance. . . . The only Reformation worth promoting and praying for is the one that gets us deeper into our Bibles, not farther away."[9]

Now, is deconstructionist Derek Webb encouraging people to be constantly reforming in light of Scripture? No. Webb has walked away from Christianity, including Scripture, and even quipped on a podcast, "Either it's all chaos—or there is a god who is both all-loving and all-powerful, and he's just a f— a—. It's kinda gotta be one of the two."[10] But what he describes as deconstruction isn't reforming according to God's Word; it's *rejecting* God's Word. That's *not* what Luther did. And that's *not* what early Christians did. For example, the Bereans were commended because they "were more noble than those in Thessalonica; they received the word with all eagerness, examining the Scriptures daily to see if these things were so" (Acts 17:11). The Bereans only "received" Paul's message after seeing if it lined up with Scripture.

When Christians find themselves struggling with questions about their faith, a better practice is *reformation*, not deconstruction. Remember, we defined deconstruction as a process of rethinking your faith *without requiring Scripture as a standard.* By contrast, reformation is the process of correcting mistaken beliefs *to make them align with Scripture.* The key distinction is the role God's Word plays in the process.

A TALE OF TWO PAINTINGS

To better understand the distinction between reformation and deconstruction, consider stories about two different paintings. Both paintings are of Jesus, and both are now famous—but for different reasons.

Salvator Mundi

The first painting is called *Salvator Mundi*, which is Latin for "Savior of the World." It depicts Jesus wearing a Renaissance-era robe while holding a transparent orb in his left hand and giving a blessing with his right. Art experts long believed this was a copy of a lost original by Leonardo da Vinci, who is widely regarded as one of the greatest artists who ever lived. Painting in the late fifteenth and early sixteenth century, he is best known for the *Mona Lisa* and *The Last Supper.* Fewer than twenty of his paintings are known to still be in existence.

Though the exact history of *Salvator Mundi* is fuzzy, it was sold at auction in the late 1950s for under $100. By the time it was sold to some art dealers at a Louisiana auction in 2005, the painting was in pretty rough shape. That's because *Salvator Mundi* was painted on a wood panel, and natural expansion and contraction caused severe damage to the painting. Also, it received some crude touch-ups and overpainting along the way. It desperately needed extensive restoration.

That's where respected art restorer Dianne Dwyer Modestini comes in. Armed with solvents, cotton, varnish, and a few other tools, she began the slow, meticulous process of restoration.[11] After removing layers of caked-on varnish and overpainting, Modestini discovered something odd about *Salvator Mundi*. Jesus had *two* right thumbs. Art experts call this a *pentimento*, which means "repentance" or "second thought." In this case, the artist drew one thumb, but reconsidered the position and painted over it with another thumb. Because significant revisions like this one are most often made by the artist and not a copyist, this discovery suggested to many in the art world that *Salvator Mundi* wasn't a daVinci copy. It was a daVinci original.[12]

News of a "lost Leonardo" made headlines.[13] People lined up for hours at museums in New York and London to catch a glimpse of it. Some in the art world were calling this the "male *Mona Lisa*." In 2017, *Salvator Mundi* went to auction in New York. After an exciting bidding war, the painting sold for $450,000,000, setting a record for the most expensive painting ever sold. The painting continues to be shrouded in mystery. In 2021, curators at the Prado Museum in Madrid downgraded the painting from "by Leonardo" to "attributed works, workshop or authorised and supervised by Leonardo."[14] Unfortunately, no one has seen the painting since it was last sold. Some speculate it might be on the Saudi Arabian crown prince's $400 million superyacht.[15] (Where else would one keep a $450 million painting but on their superyacht?)

Ecce Homo

Our second story begins in a small town of a few thousand people, located in northeastern Spain. On the wall of a small Roman Catholic church is a fresco depicting Jesus before his crucifixion, staring off to the side while wearing a crown of thorns. The artist, Elías García Martínez, painted the fresco in the 1930s. The name of the piece, *Ecce Homo*, comes from John 19:5, the account of how Jesus was paraded by Pilate before the murderous mob after being flogged, mocked, and forced to wear a crown of thorns and a purple robe. Hoping he'd done enough to satisfy the crowd, Pilate declared, "Behold the man!"—"*Ecce homo*," in Latin.

Enter Cecilia Giménez, an eighty-year-old amateur art restorer. Upset over how the painting had deteriorated, Giménez took it upon herself to restore it. (She swears she had the permission of the priest.)[16] This is where the story takes a twist. In her attempt to restore the painting, she butchered it. The "restored" painting looked nothing like the original. When a picture of it was posted on the internet, it became a viral sensation. If you have never seen it, we encourage you to look it up online. It is guaranteed to make you laugh and brighten your day.

Things didn't turn out the way this elderly artist expected. She didn't have the skills required to restore the sacred portrait. Instead, she made an unholy mess. Rather than what you might expect from an accomplished artist, *Ecce Homo* looks more like Picasso got drunk and painted a proboscis monkey with his left hand. Since news broke about the botched restoration, thousands of tourists have flocked to the small town to see the art abomination for themselves. Visitors are happy to spend their money on mugs, T-shirts, and other *Ecce Homo* souvenirs, all featuring the deformed face. But the painting is valuable only as a faddish joke. And that kind of value is shallow and fleeting.

Now think about how these two paintings relate to reforming and deconstructing. Both paintings needed work, but different approaches to restoration led to very different outcomes. *Salvator Mundi* is an example of a reformation approach, with the goal being to restore the work to its original glory. In this case, a skilled expert facilitated the restoration, revealing something valuable underneath—what many believe to be an authentic da Vinci. The overpainting and deterioration had concealed the painting's true identity. That stuff needed to be stripped away so the painting could be restored to its original state. So an internationally renowned, skilled expert with impressive credentials, ample experience, and a long history of impeccable restorations was brought in. After six years of carefully restoring the *Salvator Mundi* with vigilant patience and attention to detail, she had to hand it back over. She even describes "suffering separation anxiety and depression over losing the painting, and with it her connection to the enigmatic painter who was its author."[17] The value of *Salvator Mundi* went beyond mere dollars, and the weight of its significance remains a topic of discussion among da Vinci scholars and art aficionados to this day.

Ecce Homo is an example of a deconstruction approach. When an amateur painter took matters into her own hands, the result was a haphazard and embarrassing rendition that bore no resemblance to the original. As a result, the process didn't restore the original; it ruined it. When it comes to rethinking faith, *the process matters*. There's a life-or-death difference between recovering the original and distorting the original. But because deconstructionists don't see the value of biblical Christianity, they prefer to "improve" it according to their own personal beliefs and preferences rather than to recover the original, which they feel is harmful or oppressive. Many leave their community of believers and deconstruct in online spaces, a move that is, in many ways, like handing their faith over to an amateur art restorer. This often leads to an *Ecce Homo* outcome—a distortion of authentic Christianity or a rejection of it altogether.

One person wrote, "#EvangelicalismIsUnreformable because any way you slice it, the primary belief is that child sacrifice saved the world." She adds, "There are no comebacks for this one."[18] If you feel annoyed by this, there's a good reason. A post like this demonstrates a lack of understanding of Christianity—or worse, an intentional misrepresentation of it. And it's not the only one. It's representative of many such distorted descriptions of Christian doctrines displayed on social media by deconstructionists. Be on the lookout for this common fallacy in the deconstruction movement.[19] If someone claims to be deconstructing Christianity but mischaracterizes it like this, they may be deconstructing something, but it's not Christianity.

BUT WHY IS THE BIBLE THE STANDARD?

If someone doesn't believe Scripture is true and authoritative, obviously they can't be expected to reform their views in light of the Bible. After all, biblical reformation can only be done by Christians who are questioning or doubting *but still believe God's Word is their ultimate authority*. So what about those who reject God's Word? Where reformation is not an option, we turn to apologetics. The word "apologetics" comes from the Greek *apologia*, which means defense.[20] It is a discipline that seeks to give good reasons to believe that the claims of Christianity are true, including the assertion that the Bible is the authoritative Word of God. Francis Schaeffer referred to apologetics as *pre-evangelism*.[21] This is the idea that God uses well-reasoned answers and arguments as a springboard to the gospel of Jesus Christ. In his book *Mere Apologetics*, Oxford theologian Alister McGrath says, "Apologetics lays the ground for this invitation; evangelism extends it."[22] But apologetics isn't merely pre-evangelism to the culture. It's also *post-evangelism* to the church. After all, the challenges to faith don't evaporate once you become a Christian. In many ways, they intensify. This is where apologetics can serve to strengthen the faith of believers. For example, when I (Alisa)

> *Biblical reformation can only be done by Christians who are questioning or doubting but still believe God's Word is their ultimate authority.*

was in a major faith crisis over ten years ago, God used apologetics to help rebuild my faith. I was a believer, but I needed to know that what I believed was true.

So far, we've approached this topic from the perspective that the Bible is God's Word. We are Christians, and that's the Christian view. But we don't have to simply assume it or believe it "because the Bible says so." We believe the Bible is the Word of God because we have good evidence to come to that conclusion. Entire books have been written that give robust arguments for the veracity, inspiration, and authority of the Bible. This is not one of those books. Having said that, we'd like to give you a very brief sketch of one of those arguments. In a sentence, we believe the Bible is God's Word because of Jesus. The reasoning goes something like this: Jesus taught that he is God. God approved Jesus' teaching by raising him from the dead. The logical conclusion is that Jesus actually *is* God. Since Jesus is God, we should believe what he taught about the Scriptures. Jesus proclaimed that the Old Testament is divinely inspired, and he predicted the inspiration of the New Testament.

The first thing to notice about this argument is that it rests on three key premises: that Jesus claimed that he is God, that God proved Jesus' message true by resurrecting him, and that Jesus affirmed that the Old Testament is divinely inspired and predicted the inspiration of the New Testament.[23] Logically speaking, if those premises are true, the conclusions that follow—that Jesus is God and the Bible is divinely inspired—must also be true. Of course, for the conclusions to be true, there would need to be good reasons to support the three premises that don't depend on simply asserting the Bible is true. Each premise would need to be defended using criteria that can help determine the truthfulness of the historical claim (referred to as "criteria of authenticity").[24] Rather than rehearse all the arguments here, we want to simply sketch out how one could make the case.

Let's begin with the first of the three premises: Jesus claimed to be God. While many different lines of evidence could be cited, one compelling piece of evidence comes from Jesus referring to himself as "the Son of Man." This title is recorded in each of the Gospels, which fits a criteria of authenticity scholars call multiple attestation. This means that we have more than one source to support a particular claim. But this self-designation of Jesus also rarely shows up outside the Gospels, which fits a criteria called dissimilarity that scholars use to identify authentic sayings of Jesus.[25] The "Son of Man" designation is a reference to a divine figure in the vision recorded in Daniel 7:13-14, where Daniel describes "one like a son of man" coming on the "clouds of heaven," who is presented before "the Ancient of Days," given "an everlasting dominion," and worshiped by "all peoples, nations, and languages." This reference would have been recognized by those at Jesus' trial, when the high priest asked, "Are you the Christ, the Son of the Blessed?" and Jesus responded, "I am, and you will see the Son of Man seated at the right hand of Power, and coming with the clouds of heaven" (Mark 14:61-62). With this statement, Jesus was claiming to be God himself! The high priest knew exactly what Jesus was saying and charged him with committing "blasphemy" (Mark 14:64).

A second line of evidence that Jesus claimed to be divine

comes from the early Christian belief that Jesus is God. Philosopher William Lane Craig states, "Within twenty years of the crucifixion a full-blown Christology proclaiming Jesus as God incarnate existed. How does one explain this worship by monotheistic Jews of one of their countrymen whom they had accompanied during his lifetime, apart from the claims of Jesus himself?"[26]

So we have reason to believe the first premise of our argument for the inspiration of Scripture is true: Jesus claimed to be God. Now let's move on to the second premise: God authenticated Jesus' claims by raising him from the dead. For Christians, Jesus' bodily resurrection is fundamental. Though Christians disagree on some secondary issues, the apostle Paul taught that this is a matter of "first importance" (1 Corinthians 15:3-4). After all, he said, "If Christ has not been raised, your faith is futile and you are still in your sins" (1 Corinthians 15:17). While Christian apologists take different approaches when arguing for the resurrection,[27] one type of argument builds a case on three facts: the empty tomb, the experiences numerous people had with what they considered to be the risen Jesus, and the disciples' unexpected belief that Jesus had risen from the dead.[28] Regardless of the apologetic approach, the conclusion is the same: The resurrection of Jesus is the best explanation of the historical evidence. And it isn't just a historical event. It's theologically significant. As Craig points out, "It is the divine vindication of Jesus' radical personal claims."[29]

There are really good reasons to believe that Jesus claimed to be God and that God proved Jesus' claim by raising him from the dead. If those propositions are true, then it follows necessarily that Jesus *is* God. We should reiterate that, for the Christian, this shouldn't be controversial. These are the foundational beliefs necessary for salvation. Paul says, "If you confess with your mouth that Jesus is Lord and believe in your heart that God raised him from the dead, you will be saved" (Romans 10:9).

With the first two premises establishing that Jesus is God, we can move on to the third premise of our argument for inspiration: Jesus taught that the Old Testament is divinely inspired, and he promised the inspiration of the New Testament. If Jesus is God, we can trust what he says, including what he says about Scripture. So what did he have to say? When responding to Satan's temptations in the wilderness, Jesus began each Old Testament quotation with "It is written" (*gegraptai* in Greek).[30] Theologian John Wenham says this implies Scripture is the "permanent, unchangeable witness of the Eternal God, committed to writing for our instruction."[31] Furthermore, Jesus constantly used Scripture to settle arguments and answer questions. For example, he cited Genesis 2:24 when asked about divorce (Matthew 19:3-6). This is because Jesus knew the Old Testament had divine authority.

Moreover, Jesus explicitly named God as the author of Old Testament passages. For example, Jesus tells the Pharisees they reject "the commandment of God" so they can establish their tradition. Then he immediately quotes Moses' words in Exodus: "For Moses said, 'Honor your father and your mother'; and, 'Whoever reviles father or mother must surely die'" (Mark 7:9-10). Don't miss what Jesus does here! He attributes two Old Testament verses to *both* God *and* Moses.

For Jesus, what Moses said is also what God commanded. That's why he ends the discussion by condemning the Pharisees for "making void the word of God" (Mark 7:13) by their tradition. Jesus calls these two verses from Exodus "the word of God."

Many will accept that Jesus taught the Old Testament is divinely inspired, but where did Jesus teach that the New Testament will be divinely inspired? Well, he didn't do so *directly*. After all, there was no New Testament while Jesus walked the earth. Having said that, Jesus promised the apostles all that was necessary to facilitate the writing of the New Testament.

First, Jesus promised that his apostles would be taught by the Holy Spirit. During what is known as the Upper Room Discourse just before his crucifixion, Jesus said, "The Helper, the Holy Spirit, whom the Father will send in my name, he will teach you all things and bring to your remembrance all that I have said to you" (John 14:26). So the apostles were promised the Holy Spirit, who would teach them and help them remember everything that had taken place.

Furthermore, we're told this teaching would have divine authority. Jesus said the Holy Spirit "will guide you into all the truth, for he will not speak on his own authority, but whatever he hears he will speak, and he will declare to you the things that are to come" (John 16:13). So according to Jesus, the apostles would receive divine revelation—authoritative truth from God. Commenting on the scope of this promise, New Testament scholar Craig Blomberg writes, "While Jesus' promise encompasses more than simply inspiring his disciples to write further Scripture, it surely includes what

John understood himself to be doing in producing [his] Gospel."[32] And it wasn't just John. Paul puts all the apostles on par with the prophets. He tells the Ephesians the "household of God" is "built on the foundation of the apostles and prophets, Christ Jesus himself being the cornerstone" (Ephesians 2:19-20). Likewise, Peter reminds his readers of "the predictions of the holy prophets and the commandment of the Lord and Savior through your apostles" (2 Peter 3:2). Again, there seems to be an equivalency of authority between prophets and apostles. That's why Peter, almost as an aside, places Paul's writing with "the rest of the Scriptures" (2 Peter 3:16, NKJV).

So Jesus put the pieces in place with the New Testament. But did he really expect the apostles to write the New Testament? During the Last Supper, Jesus passed the cup, saying, "This cup is the new covenant in my blood, which is poured out for you" (Luke 22:20, NIV). This is called the new covenant because there was already an old covenant. But just as the old covenant was accompanied by authoritative writings—the Old Testament—it was reasonable to expect the new covenant to have authoritative writings—the New Testament. Commenting on 2 Corinthians 3:14, in which Paul writes, "When they read the old covenant, that same veil remains unlifted," Bible scholar Michael J. Kruger notes that "covenants are written documents."[33] Philosophy professor Steven Cowan concludes,

> The fact that [Jesus] appointed the apostles as his
> authoritative spokesmen, the fact that he promised
> them the supernatural guidance of the Holy Spirit

both to recall his earthly teaching and deliver to
them further divine revelation, and the fact that they
and Jesus would naturally have expected the writing
of new covenant documents, provide sufficient
reason to believe that Jesus promised the inspiration
of the [New Testament].[34]

Therefore, since Jesus is God and taught that Scripture is inspired, it follows that the Old and New Testaments are divinely inspired.

If you've never read an apologetic argument like this, we hope this one got you thinking or even strengthened your trust in Scripture. Remember, it's okay to ask questions about biblical inspiration and authority. But questioning biblical authority is not the same as deconstructing it.

MARTIN LUTHER THE DECONSTRUCTIONIST?

As we've seen, some people are using Martin Luther—the great Reformation theologian—as an example of deconstruction. The implication seems to be that deconstructionists have a theological heavyweight in their corner. But did Luther *really* deconstruct? Luther believed God revealed himself through his Word. For Luther, Scripture was his ultimate authority. As a result, he conformed his beliefs and behavior to the Bible. Is that what deconstructionists are doing today? Are they using God's revealed Word to get back to the faith once for all delivered to the saints? To suggest that this is all that people are doing—"deconstructing like Luther"—is to misunderstand what's really going on. Or worse, it deceives people into thinking they are merely doing what Luther did.

By all means, do what Luther did. But please know that what Luther did isn't what the vast majority of people posting #deconstruction are doing. Luther formed and reformed—examined and reexamined—his beliefs *in light of Scripture*. In his journey, he had a guide (Scripture) and a goal (sound doctrine). True, Luther questioned the church's traditions, abuses, and theology. Yes, it was messy, and he wasn't perfect in his search for truth. But his goal was not to deconstruct the fundamental truths of Christianity. Today many people, like Luther, are questioning, reexamining, and changing their views. But *how* many of them are doing it is fundamentally different. As we will see in the next chapter, some are rethinking their beliefs in light of sociology, personal experience, and personal preferences. Scripture isn't their starting point or ultimate authority. For some of them, it's just one more thing to be deconstructed.

TOXIC

FROM THE PERSPECTIVE OF DECONSTRUCTIONISTS, there is no false theology to be corrected. There is only "toxic" theology to be deconstructed. *Toxic theology* is a catchall term being used to describe any doctrine one deems harmful. Here's an example. In a TikTok post[1] viewed close to 900,000 times (at the time of this writing), a deconstructionist explains what an abusive relationship looks like. She says, "The abuser will break down the victim's self-worth and self-esteem and make them feel broken and worthless without them so they'll be dependent on the abuser." The video then flashes to her playing the part of a Christian responding with "Oh yeah, that's really horrible that people do that." Playing the part of deconstructionist, she says, "Right? So then when a church teaches you that you're born broken and a sinner and worthy of eternal punishment, it's . . ." Back to the Christian: "True. We're all sinners unworthy of what Jesus did for us." Deconstructionist: "I'm gonna start from the beginning. You let me know where I lost you."

Short videos like this have persuasive rhetorical power because they appeal to emotions, present a compelling false comparison, and keep it short enough to prevent anyone from analyzing it too deeply and thoughtfully. Unfortunately, many people can't spot the missteps. Is the church's teaching of original sin—that we're born with a sin nature—equivalent to an abuser trying to control their victim? Is telling people they're sinners a type of "toxic theology"?

Think of it this way. Imagine a scenario in which someone recognizes that a particular person is "broken" and then proceeds to beat on that individual's chest forcefully, causing deep bruising. Is this just their toxic way of trying to control the other person or beat them into submission? If that's the case, many would call that abuse. We would too—*unless* the person pounding on the other one's chest is trained in CPR and the chest they're pounding on lodges a heart that has stopped beating. That changes the narrative, doesn't it? In that case, the "broken" person will die without intervention, and the person performing chest compressions is actually saving their life. However, if someone were to tell a perfectly healthy person they were "broken" and then proceeded to pound on their chest cavity, an observer wouldn't call the hospital first, but rather, the police. To refer to original sin as "toxic" makes sense only if it's *not* true. If it *is* true, the gospel is the cure.

Further, this comparison between the church and

abusers would apply only if original sin *actually did* teach that humans are worthless. It doesn't. In fact, it's quite the opposite. Christianity teaches that every human has been made in the image and likeness of God, and this gives every person inherent dignity, value, and worth (Genesis 5:1-2). We are not worthless. We are image bearers. But that image is distorted by sin. Romans 5:12 tells us, "Sin came into the world through one man, and death through sin, and so death spread to all men because all sinned." Original sin teaches that we all have inherited a sin nature from Adam, and that sin nature bends us toward sin. However, there's a cure for our sin problem, and it's Christ's sacrificial death on the cross. Therefore, helping someone understand their need for the cure is both a healthy and loving thing to do *because it's true*. And if it's true, it would be unloving to tell someone otherwise.

But rather than focusing on whether or not the doctrine of original sin is true, there's an assumption slipped into this video. It's so subtle it would be easy to miss. It's the assumed *motive* the church has for teaching original sin. When characterizing the abuser, it's pointed out that the *reason* for telling someone they are broken is so that the person can be *controlled*. This is often true in abusive relationships. However, this motive is then projected onto the church, and voilà! You have a beautiful teaching sullied by interpreting it through the lens of abuser vs. abused.

It's not surprising that this video turns away from questions of truth and toward questions of motivation and power because on many of these social media platforms, people aren't all that concerned with what is objectively true. And when objective truth is denied or swept aside, all you are left with is *power*. As Greg Koukl writes, "Remember, relativism is the ultimate negation of truth, and when truth dies, power is all that remains."[2] Think about it. Picture a gawky middle schooler placing his backpack on the curb while waiting for the school bus. Then a tall, muscular high schooler walks over and says, "Hey, that's my backpack!" Who decides between them? Who or what is the truth maker in this scenario? If there is no objective truth they can appeal to, then it all comes down to who is bigger and stronger. In other words, if truth is not decided by what corresponds with reality, then might makes right—and the high schooler just got himself a new backpack. After all, he's just living *his* truth.

Of course, most people don't live as if stealing someone's personal property is in the upper story of Schaeffer's two-story house. But most people today do live as if religious truth were in the upper story—in a place without objective truth, where only power can decide between competing claims. So with everyone trying to live their truth when it comes to God, Jesus, and the Bible, it's no surprise that statements like "Jesus is the only way to God" or "Jesus died for your sins" can be perceived as power grabs. Further, one of our current cultural zeitgeists, a popular ideology called critical theory, has reinforced the belief that truth claims are mere power plays.[3] In the most simplistic terms, critical theory functions like a worldview that understands and critiques power and oppression along the lines of race, ethnicity, class, gender, ability, sexuality, and other factors. It primarily sees the world through the lens of oppressed groups and their oppressors and attempts to recalibrate power in favor of the marginalized. When people adopt critical theory as the lens through which they see the world, God, and the Bible, they can make the false assumption that original sin is about keeping people under the church's power.

Here's how critical theory works in the deconstruction world. In the minds of many people today, Christianity (and evangelicalism in particular) is *assumed* to be shaped by oppressive ideologies like white supremacy, patriarchy, racism, homophobia, and Christian nationalism. For example, on an Instagram post by @eve_wasframed, the caption reads that "'hell' is actually completely made up by humans and has been used as a fear tactic to control people and coerce them into religion."[4] Notice how the writer assumes hell is "made up," then jumps immediately to explaining *why* it's "made up." She's attacking motives, not arguments. C. S. Lewis called this approach "bulverism,"[5] and it's rampant in the deconstruction explosion. Lewis wrote, "You must show *that* a man is wrong before you start explaining *why* he is wrong. The modern method is to assume without discussion *that* he is wrong and then distract his attention from this (the only real issue) by busily explaining how he became so silly."[6] Imagine a scientist saying, "The earth is round" and a flat-earther replying, "You're just saying that because you're a Western white man trying to control people." Of course, this response doesn't refute the scientist's claim. Rather, it assumes he's wrong and has nefarious motives for making the claim.

That's why it doesn't matter if a Christian points to a particular Scripture passage to explain the evidence for their belief. The deconstructionist sees this as merely protecting power and aims "to expose the will-to-power hiding inside various truth claims."[7] For example, deconstruction coach Angela J. Herrington clearly states her intention: "The only way to create an equitable religious community is to correct the imbalance of power that currently exists and that is threatening to those who benefit from the existing system."[8] She continues, "People are hurting right now and much of that harm is done by a church with doctrines rooted in colonialism, white supremacy, and gender bias."[9] Doctrines are viewed in terms of power, *not truth*, and thus deemed "toxic."

EVANGELICAL DECONSTRUCTION PROJECT

In recent years, a host of books have been published that appear to promote what has been referred to as the "evangelical deconstruction project." This idea began with self-described progressive evangelical David Gushee, who wrote the article "The Deconstruction of American Evangelicalism,"[10] challenging the idea that evangelicalism should be defined theologically. Rather, he argues that several younger scholars have more properly defined evangelicalism by its supposed characteristics and patterns of behavior. Books such as *The Making of Biblical Womanhood*, *White Evangelical Racism*, *Taking America Back for God*, *Jesus and John Wayne*, and *White Too Long* have also been associated with this project, with many of the authors tweeting their appreciation of Gushee's article.[11] The authors hold various views on biblical authority, and each takes on what they see as unjust systems within evangelicalism. To make their case, they tend to appeal primarily to sociology and history, rather than Scripture.

Gushee praises these books for pointing out the many ways

evangelicalism has failed to live up to its stated theological beliefs and has instead been used by the majority (primarily white Christian men) to maintain their power. For example, he summarizes the book *Worldview Theory, Whiteness, and the Future of Evangelical Faith* by Jacob Alan Cook this way:

> What white evangelicals have labeled "the Christian worldview" bears a striking resemblance to "whiteness," that is, white-centered and white-hegemonic ways of viewing and arranging the world and responding to human difference. In other words, all those worldview conferences and seminars really may have been about teaching us how to think like white people, not like Christian people.[12]

Is what evangelicals call the biblical worldview inherently racist? This is a serious charge. If true, we would agree with the authors affiliated with this "evangelical deconstruction project" that Christians should reject any theology that erroneously filters God's revelation through a particular cultural or ethnic bias. But the salient question is . . . is it true?

To discover the answer, we must look at *how* these authors are deconstructing what they call evangelical theology. Writing in the journal *Eikon*, Neil Shenvi describes their common methodology. Here's how the deconstruction project works in three simple steps.

Step one: Identify a problem in society.
Step two: Show how the church actively endorsed or passively allowed injustice.

Step three: Conclude that "hundreds of years of participation in white supremacy, patriarchy, and nationalism have warped 'white evangelical theology' such that it needs to be fundamentally reimagined."[13]

Shenvi calls this a "dangerous approach to theology via the disciplines of sociology and history" because it sows "the seeds of a deconstruction that goes far deeper than race, gender, and politics":

These authors' "deconstructive" approach to theology is necessarily a universal acid. Even if they weren't explicitly committed to challenging evangelical doctrine broadly, their methodological approach makes such an outcome inevitable.[14]

In other words, when examining evangelical positions, the primary question for these writers isn't "Is the belief true?" or even "What does the Bible teach?" but "Has this belief been used to oppress?" Philosopher John Searle describes the dangers of critiquing ideas disconnected from the truth. He writes, "What are the results of deconstruction supposed to be? Characteristically the deconstructionist does not attempt to prove or refute, to establish or confirm, and he is certainly not seeking the truth. On the contrary, . . . he seeks to undermine, or call in question, or overcome, or breach, or disclose complicities."[15] This form of deconstruction is about undermining perceived oppression, not falsifying truth claims.

Let's look at a specific example of this method using

The Making of Biblical Womanhood: How the Subjugation of Women Became Gospel Truth by Beth Allison Barr as a test case. Barr recounts the "second darkest story about my experiences inside complementarianism."[16] Her husband was fired from his position as youth pastor at their local church after challenging the leadership on their position of complementarianism, which she defines as "the theological view that women are divinely created as helpers and men are divinely created as leaders."[17] After serving in ministry at that particular church for fourteen years, the loss was palpable. Understandably, the whole experience affected their family in deep ways and caused anxiety and grief. According to Barr, the church mishandled certain aspects of the firing process by initially providing only one month of severance pay and not being forthright with the congregation as to why her husband was let go.[18] Her sense of loss was compounded by her experience years before as a younger single woman feeling stuck in an abusive relationship with a man who had internalized the teachings of the now disgraced Bill Gothard.[19] Despite these difficulties, Barr says, "Because my hope is in Jesus, I wasn't going to give up on his church."[20] Still, she writes that she realized she "had become complicit in a system that used the name of Jesus to oppress and harm women"[21] and was led to write "the historical truth about complementarianism"[22] in her book.

The Making of Biblical Womanhood repeatedly links complementarianism, as a theological belief, with abuse.[23] Barr makes this argument throughout her book, largely from a historical perspective. For example, speaking of inerrancy (the doctrine that the Bible is without error), Barr writes,

"The evangelical fight for inerrancy was inextricably linked with gender from the beginning. . . . Inerrancy wasn't important by itself in the late twentieth century; it became important because it provided a way to push women out of the pulpit."[24] Notice that she's saying the doctrine of inerrancy isn't about correctly understanding the nature of Scripture. It is *really* about controlling women.

Barr says that although complementarians assert they are holding to the plain meaning of Scripture, they are "really defending an interpretation that has been corrupted by our sinful human drive to dominate others and build hierarchies of power and oppression."[25] She rejects the complementarian view that God created men and women with different but complementary roles. Complementarianism—or biblical womanhood—is not only wrong, she claims, but damaging to women.

Granted, Barr expresses skepticism that what she experienced in complementarian churches "matched what the Bible taught."[26] Even so, in our view, she draws more on examples from culture and history while also engaging to some degree with biblical data. She evaluates teaching primarily based on the effect it has on people.[27] So with Barr's book in mind, let's revisit Shenvi's explanation of the methodology of the evangelical deconstruction project:

Step one: Identify a problem in society. When identifying patriarchy, Barr quotes historian Judith Bennett, who defines it as "a general system through which women have been and are subordinated to men."[28] It is also characterized by misogyny and the abuse of women as societal ills.

Step two: Show how the church actively endorsed or passively allowed injustice. This is where Barr spends much of her literary energy. She argues that the gender norms in the Bible were reflective of the surrounding culture rather than of divine decree, writing, "Patriarchy exists in the Bible because the Bible was written in a patriarchal world."[29] In other words, patriarchy is a cultural system adopted by the church and used as an oppressive tool against women. To make her point, she describes alleged missteps and abuses of complementarianism by Christians throughout Christian history, such as in the Bill Gothard scandal, her interpretation of the motives behind the ESV Bible translation, and modesty standards at Christian youth camps as evidence of the rotten fruit of complementarianism.

Step three: Conclude that hundreds of years of participation in white supremacy, patriarchy, and nationalism have warped "white evangelical theology" such that it needs to be fundamentally reimagined. Despite the fact that Scripture values hierarchy in the home and church (see Genesis 2:18; Mark 10:6-9; 1 Corinthians 11:3; Ephesians 5:21-33; Colossians 3:18-19; 1 Peter 3:1-7), Barr writes, "Complementarianism is patriarchy, and patriarchy is about power. Neither have ever been about Jesus."[30] She closes her book by citing the biblical stories of Mary sitting at the feet of Jesus and his conversation with the woman of Canaan (neither of whom were religious leaders). She writes, "Jesus set women free a long time ago. Isn't it finally time for evangelical Christians to do the same? Go, be free!"[31] Our analysis is that her argumentation is not based primarily on the Bible but upon historical abuses (real and perceived).

The extent to which women can participate in church leadership roles has been hotly debated among faithful Christians for millennia. The point of this case study is not to settle the correct biblical teaching on this topic. Rather, we're simply giving an example of the type of methodology used in evangelical deconstruction so we can illustrate its inability to discover true doctrines and rule out harmful, false ones.

As Christians, we should seek to reject false ideas. We ought to stand against abuse. But we will be unable to discern whether or not a teaching is abusive if we don't have a way to know what is correct in the first place. And we certainly cannot settle these theological disputes without an objective standard to appeal to. This requires the Bible. Deciding theological positions by what one perceives to be helpful vs. harmful, oppressive vs. liberating, or right vs. wrong is an invalid method for doing theology. If we simply follow some type of internal moral compass to determine which beliefs are "harmful," we might inadvertently reject truth in favor of our sensibilities. While neither of the authors of this book would fault someone for coming to an honest position on biblical grounds regarding the egalitarian vs. complementarian debate, we would fault someone for rejecting complementarianism simply because they didn't like where those Bible passages lead.

While we're on the topic of complementarianism, Kristen Kobes Du Mez also claims to see its origin using a similar method. In her book *Jesus and John Wayne: How White*

Evangelicals Corrupted a Faith and Fractured a Nation, she writes, "As evangelicals began to mobilize as a partisan political force, they did so by rallying to defend 'family values.' But family values politics was never about protecting the well-being of families generally. Fundamentally, evangelical 'family values' entailed the reassertion of patriarchal authority. At its most basic level, family values politics was about sex and power."[32] Notice that her critique focuses entirely on the motives she believes were behind the promotion of "family values" rather than a meaningful interaction with the Bible and these ideas themselves.

Andrew T. Walker, associate professor of Christian ethics and apologetics at Southern Baptist Theological Seminary, succinctly captures the problem in a couple of tweets. He says, "It is astonishing to me the incredulity of scholars who are unable (or unwilling) to understand that individuals might hold a good faith conviction due to honest biblical interpretation, and not out [of] some ulterior motive to protect one's power or privilege." He continues, "If a theological position is wrong, demonstrate the error exegetically, and not why it *must* be wrong because of the critic's precommitment to their own sociological constraints, or dare I say, 'worldview.' Who knew postmodernism would be this predictable and boring?"[33]

> Good theology is done by thinking deeply about God's revealed Word, not by assessing the Bible according to the standards of secular culture.

Where historians and authors often accurately *describe* the egregious history of the church, we stand with them. Christians ought to know their history so they aren't destined to repeat it. But these authors aren't merely describing history. They are prescribing theology. They are using history and sociology to inform our theological beliefs. But this is not how theology (the study of God) is to be done with integrity. Good theology is done by thinking deeply about God's revealed Word, not by assessing the Bible according to the standards of secular culture.

READING SCRIPTURE UPSTAIRS

How does an "upper-story" view of Scripture affect the way people interact with the Bible? Here's where two French philosophers come in. Michael Foucault, a social theorist and historian, saw truth claims as a mask for power-seeking: "'Truth' is linked in a circular relation with systems of power which produce and sustain it."[34] Jacques Derrida saw truth as a social construction, where meaning and knowledge are cultural creations and not objective truths. Let's turn now to Derrida's playbook. Writing in *The Post Card*, Derrida described how any written text is like a letter that never arrives at its destination.[35] Philosopher John Caputo applied this idea to religion:

> [Derrida] meant that even when it is not lost
> and even when it is understood, a text remains
> structurally and in principle capable of being
> understood *differently*—by different communities
> of readers at different times, in other times and
> places—so that it is always happening (*arriver*)
> but never arrives (*arriver*) decisively at just one

final destination . . . that would be authorized to pronounce its meaning once and for all.[36]

Leaving aside the irony that Caputo has no trouble definitely declaring what Derrida *meant*, this view undermines the authority of Scripture because one cannot submit to a text that has no particular meaning. Caputo goes on to apply Derrida's "postal principle" to Christianity. He writes, "The Christian tradition *itself* . . . is the history of taking the story of Jesus differently, again and again, over the course of the ages, in changing times and circumstances. It is everywhere itself and everywhere different. It keeps saying new things."[37] What kinds of "new things" is he talking about? Near the end of the book, Caputo uses the Bible's view of homosexual behavior as an example. He affirms that "Paul condemned what we today have constituted as 'homosexuality' and that if anyone ever asked Jesus about it . . . he would have said the same thing as Paul."[38]

Now watch what Caputo does next. While giving his own view on the matter, he explains that even though the Bible largely condemns the practice of homosexuality, he sides with the Greek culture of the time, which affirmed it. He goes on to comment that he has no problem saying the Jews and Christians were wrong on this point, just as the Bible (as Caputo understands it) is wrong on slavery and the oppression of women. He writes, "Indeed, by invoking the spirit of a certain Jesus, I would argue for a counterfactual conditional: were Jesus alive today and familiar with the pros and cons of the contemporary argument, his centeredness on love would have brought him down on the side of the rights of what we today call the 'homosexual' difference."[39] As justification for his deconstruction, Caputo cites how "Jesus systematically took the side of the outsider."[40]

First of all, Jesus *is* alive today. And the Scriptures are the revelation of a *living* God. Yet in response to the New Testament, Caputo turns not to the revealed Word of God, but to Derrida and Foucault. This is not uncommon in the evangelical deconstruction project. For example, when asked on Twitter how one can best analyze power and cultural systems so as not to be held captive by them,[41] Kristin Du Mez responded, "I should have a better answer but for me it wasn't one source but years spent reading social & cultural histories, histories of gender, Foucault, Gramsci, Adorno, Habermas, learning to be curious about how the [world] works."[42] We've already briefly discussed Foucault. Antonio Gramsci is known by many as the father of neo-Marxism, and Theodor W. Adorno was a leading member of the Frankfurt School, from which came critical theory.[43] Jürgen Habermas is a proponent of critical social theory.[44] These are not exactly the poster children for good theology. Yet self-described evangelicals are flocking to their ideas in droves.

In an interview on *The Deconstructionists* podcast, John Caputo explained, "Derrida is a philosopher who thinks that the world we live in—the set of meanings, the beliefs, and practices that we have accumulated—are contingent. They are revisable. They are reformable. They have been constructed in time and history and circumstance. And they didn't drop from the sky. They were laboriously constructed in history."[45]

What does it mean to say something is socially constructed? If something is socially constructed, then it has no *inherent* meaning—no meaning *in itself.* There are certainly some ideas that are socially constructed. For example, the idea that pink is for girls and blue is for boys is socially constructed. There is no objective standard outside of ourselves to determine which gender colors should be assigned to. But this doesn't mean that the categories of boy and girl are socially constructed. They are rooted in biology (objective), whereas colors are grounded in preference or opinion (subjective). Caputo believes religion is, like colors for genders, socially constructed. And since it's constructed, it can be deconstructed. He writes, "Whatever is constructed is deconstructible."[46]

The late progressive Christian author Rachel Held Evans builds upon the ideas of Jacques Derrida in her final work, *Wholehearted Faith,* which was completed after her death by her colleague Jeff Chu and her husband, Dan. Using Derrida's phrase "impoverishment by univocality," she advocates an approach to written texts that seeks to "amplify the richness of multiple perspectives."[47] She explains that according to Derrida, when we try to reduce a text to "one voice," we aren't able to fully grasp all it has to offer. She argues that to view the Bible as presenting a "'clear' and 'plain'" meaning is to "diminish its relevance to peoples across time and space and to fail to recognize that the Bible is anything but univocal."[48] She continues by saying we all have "masks" we impose upon God. We don't disagree with her there. All of us have biases, cultural backgrounds, spiritual environments we grew up in, and ways of thinking that might influence how we see God in an erroneous way. However, Evans articulates that "some of these masks ended up written down in Scripture."[49] She concludes that some masks are literary (not necessarily historical), and because of that, she writes, "I refuse to believe that God engaged in or commanded the violence that some Old Testament authors ascribe to God."[50]

Reader, don't miss the weight of this. It's one thing to claim that a person can have a false view of God. It's entirely another to propose that false views of God have been affirmed by the Bible. The Bible is the standard by which we determine if our view of God is correct or faulty. But a Derridean sleight of hand could lead someone to conclude that even the very Word of God is something that calls for a bit of deconstruction.

DIVINELY REVEALED, NOT SOCIALLY CONSTRUCTED

The gospel isn't socially constructed; it's divinely revealed. In his first letter to the Corinthian church, Paul lays it out: "I would remind you, brothers, of the gospel I preached to you, which you received, in which you stand, and by which you are being saved, if you hold fast to the word I preached to you—unless you believed in vain" (1 Corinthians 15:1-2). The gospel Paul preached "is not man's gospel" and he didn't "receive it from any man." Rather, he "received it through a revelation of Jesus Christ" (Galatians 1:11-12). That's why he could boldly proclaim: "Even if we or an angel from heaven should preach to you a gospel contrary to the one we preached to you, let him be accursed" (Galatians 1:8).

However, following Derrida's lead, Caputo thinks the

> The gospel isn't socially constructed; it's divinely revealed.

gospel is simply a construct. Speaking about Paul's warning against preaching another gospel, Caputo says there's "nothing to say that any one version of that text is normative."[51] To be fair, Caputo doesn't believe *any* text to be normative since, in his view, no authoritative standards exist. Furthermore, Derrida believed all written text is "recontextualizable."[52] So Paul wrote in a particular context, but his writing outlives its original context and can be recontextualized. In an academic paper titled "Who's Afraid of Postmodernism? A Response to the 'Biola School,'" philosopher James K. A. Smith says, "So we never get past texts and interpretations to things 'simply as they are' in any unmediated fashion . . . ; rather, we move from interpretation to interpretation. The entire world is a text. Thus, 'there is nothing outside of the text.'"[53] That last sentence—the idea that there is no objective "way things are" that would make any one interpretation of a text objectively true or false—is the key to understanding what's going on.

Let's stop for a moment and unpack some of the implications of this approach. First, think about what the gospel *is*. The word *gospel* means "good news." It's the message of salvation . . . delivered verbally. It's something communicated *with words*. It's what Jesus did when "he went throughout all Galilee, teaching in their synagogues and proclaiming the gospel of the kingdom and healing every disease and every affliction among the people" (Matthew 4:23). So deconstruction is a direct attack on the proclamation of the gospel. If you can't stop the gospel from being preached, you can certainly try to deconstruct the idea that meaning can be communicated with words. It's a brilliant plan, actually. Just slip in a little postmodernism, and there goes the gospel.

Derrida doesn't deny that the external reality exists, but "no interpretation of reality is (or can be known to be) *the* fact of the matter."[54] He completely contradicts the clear teaching of Scripture that "no prophecy of Scripture is a matter of one's own interpretation" (2 Peter 1:20, NASB). So which is it? Paul Franks and Richard Davis, both Tyndale University philosophy professors, provide your options: "This is one of those cases where you have to choose this day whom you will follow: either the Apostle Peter, who under the inspiration of the Spirit wrote 2 Peter 1:20, or the postmodern philosopher Jacques Derrida who, we may safely presume, wasn't thus inspired. For . . . Christians, the choice should be easy."[55]

But one can't even make that choice unless words have meaning. And if meaning can't be communicated with words, why would anyone read someone's philosophical opinions about words not having meaning? (Stop and think about that for a second. Or deconstruct that last sentence and make it mean whatever you want. You get the point.) That would be a waste of time. The serpent in the Garden of Eden asked Eve, "Did God really say?" Today, he is asking a different question: "Did God really *mean*?" Same deceiver; same goal.

9

FAITH

"Nobody should be able to tell you what your faith needs to look like because that's dependent on you and the work you do," said Caleb Luehmann, the husband of popular deconstructionist Jo Luehmann, in a video describing faith deconstruction.[1] In other words, if our beliefs are mere social constructs, why should we hold on to them if they don't work for us? Caleb continues,

> The moment you start to believe when somebody tells you, "This is what Christianity looks like, this is how you have to walk it out," you are then stepping into somebody else's identity and somebody else's shoes, and you're not being who you are. And later

on down the road, you're going to feel the trauma, and you're going to feel the pain, and be like, "Son of a gun, I have to freakin' deconstruct that."[2]

There's a lot to unpack here, but for now, notice that for Luehmann, each person defines the Christian faith *for themselves*. Faith is completely subjective. It's self-oriented, not truth-oriented. That's why no one gets to tell you what your faith should look like. It would be like someone marching into your home and telling you what your bedroom needs to look like. The bed goes here, the nightstands go there, the paint needs to be this color, the sheets need to be that color, and so on. Luehmann has moved faith to the realm of personal preference—the upper story, where you determine what's true for you.

Now contrast what Luehmann says with what the apostle Paul tells the church in Galatia: "You were running well. Who hindered you from obeying *the truth*? This persuasion is not from him who calls you. A little leaven leavens the whole lump. I have confidence in the Lord that *you will take no other view*, and the one who is troubling you will bear the penalty, whoever he is" (Galatians 5:7-10, emphasis added). The Christian converts in Galatia were being persuaded to accept circumcision as a means of justification. They were turning away from freedom in Christ and back to the law, "a yoke of slavery" (Galatians 5:1). In response, Paul doesn't say, "Just live your truth" or "It doesn't matter what your faith looks like." On the contrary, he tells the Galatians that they're being persuaded away from *the* truth, and they need to return to it. In other words, Paul has no trouble telling these Christians what their faith needs to look like because he is working from a different understanding of faith. For Paul, *your* faith can't be whatever you want it to be. Your faith needs to match up with *the* faith—what Paul takes to be objective reality.

When a person goes through deconstruction, something is being deconstructed. (Pretty profound, right?) So far, we've looked at what deconstruction is—the how. We showed how deconstruction is a postmodern process. Now we need to ask, what is being deconstructed? The answer may seem obvious: *faith*. In the biblical context, the word *faith* refers not only to "believing that" but also "believing in." The first is assent to certain beliefs (God exists, for example). The author of Hebrews says we must "believe that [God] exists and that he rewards those who earnestly seek him" (Hebrews 11:6, NIV). This is a necessary aspect of faith, but it's not sufficient. Something's still missing. After all, even the demons believe in God (James 2:19). The second aspect is an active reliance on, or trust in, what you believe is true. Both are necessary for genuine Christian faith.

Furthermore, there is a distinction between *your* faith and what we might call *the* faith. Every Christian believer has a personal faith in Jesus. As we just said, your Christian faith is a combination of "belief that" and "trust in." This entails a subjective element—it is dependent, in a certain sense, on the individual. As a result, there are different degrees of trust. Some Christians' faith is strong and sturdy, while others' faith is weak and fragile. For example, after speaking with a Roman centurion, Jesus "marveled," saying, "With no one in Israel have I found such faith" (Matthew 8:10). By contrast, just a few verses later, Matthew records Jesus getting into a boat with his disciples. When a storm threatens to capsize the boat, the disciples panic, and Jesus asks his disciples why they have such "little faith" (Matthew 8:26). This suggests that our personal faith is in flux. It changes over time. At times we might have more confident faith, and at other times we might have more uncertain faith.

A Christian's personal faith is distinct from *the* Christian faith. *The faith* is an objective reality—it is true no matter what we believe about it or how we feel about it. The Christian faith isn't private; it's public. That's why the apostle John says he's testifying to what he had "heard," "seen" with his eyes, and "touched" with his hands (1 John 1:1-3). The events surrounding the life, death, and resurrection of Jesus were objective, historical events that could be observed. And Paul tells Timothy that the details have been faithfully passed down: "What you have heard from me in the presence of many witnesses entrust to faithful men, who will be able to teach others also" (2 Timothy 2:2). Notice Paul passes the Christian faith to Timothy, who passes it to faithful men, who then pass it along to others still. In fact, Paul specifically tells Timothy to "continue in what you have learned and have firmly believed" (2 Timothy 3:14).

Imagine if Timothy had listened to the Luehmanns. Instead of learning from Paul, he might have said something like, "Nobody should be able to tell me what my faith needs to look like because that's dependent on me and the work I do. How dare you tell me what Christianity needs to look like or how to walk it out. Don't you realize you're stepping into my identity and my shoes, and not letting me be who I am? Son of a gun, I need to freakin' deconstruct." Doesn't sound right, does it? That's because the Christian faith *isn't* dependent on us. Our personal feelings, preferences, and beliefs don't change it. Jude tells his readers to "contend for *the* faith that was once for all delivered to the saints" (Jude 1:3, emphasis added). Paul says, "I have fought the good fight, I have finished the race, I have kept *the* faith" (2 Timothy 4:7, emphasis added). In other words, the Christian faith stands independent of any individual. It's like gravity, an objective feature of the world. Someone can deny gravity exists, yet he will fall to the ground if he jumps from the top of a building, no matter how strongly he believes he can fly.

So when someone is going through faith deconstruction, it's important to understand what they mean by faith—that is, the precise beliefs they are deconstructing—so we know exactly what it is that they're rejecting. After all, many people have a personal faith (that is, a belief system) that doesn't match an accurate "once for all delivered to the saints" faith. For example, a person can believe that God would never send anyone to hell, but that doesn't make that idea true. Someone else might have faith in a god who hates them and wants to send everyone to hell, but that doesn't make that belief true either. When we reject *false* beliefs, we're not rejecting Christianity, we're rejecting something else. Put another way, often in the deconstruction explosion, people mistake their own personal faith, which might be full of incorrect beliefs, with the authentic Christian faith.

WHY BREAKING UP (WITH YOUR FAITH) IS HARD TO DO

There's another important element of faith that needs to be addressed. Christian faith isn't merely propositional; it's relational. Some have described deconstruction as merely "dissecting" beliefs. In fact, I (Alisa) did that in my book *Another Gospel?* I wrote, "In the context of faith, deconstruction is the process of systematically dissecting and often rejecting the beliefs you grew up with.

Christian faith isn't merely propositional; it's relational.

Sometimes the Christian will deconstruct all the way into atheism. Some remain there, but others experience a reconstruction. But the type of faith they end up embracing almost never resembles the Christianity they formerly knew."[3]

However, there might be a better word to use than *dissecting*. As a former science teacher, I (Tim) looked forward to "Dissection Day." Depending on the grade level, students would dissect worms, frogs, or pigs. (Just thinking about it brings back the sweet smell of formaldehyde.) Dissecting a pig doesn't require much skill. We would give the students some simple instructions and a scalpel, then tell them to have fun.

However, there was always a small group of students who were worried about doing something wrong. "What's the worst that could happen?" I would ask them. (Alisa could say from experience that with one wrong move you could inadvertently squirt yourself in the eye with a frog's urinary bladder, scream from the shock, and then become the punchline of everyone's frog pee jokes for the rest of the day, but this is Tim's paragraph.) If you, for example, unwittingly nick the heart with your scalpel, there's no serious consequence, except maybe a lower grade. You're certainly not going to hurt the pig. It's already *dead*. In other words, when you dissect a pig, there's no danger to the pig. However, when you dissect your faith, the stakes are higher. There is a risk involved to both you and your relationship with Jesus. After all, you aren't dissecting something dead. You're dissecting something alive. In a way, deconstruction is more like vivisection than dissection. Vivisection is the practice of performing experimental surgery on a *living thing*.

What if my science classes had used *living* pigs? It's a morbid thought. But it demonstrates a point. Every time the scalpel touched the animal, there would have been a risk of severely injuring or even killing the pig. Clearly, vivisecting a pig is different from dissecting a pig. And just as vivisection can kill a pig, deconstruction can kill a faith. Be warned: Every time we put the scalpel of deconstruction to our faith, there is an inherent risk. While discussing the process of deconstruction on her YouTube channel *God Is Grey*, progressive Christian Brenda Marie Davies said, "Even [in] the process, *sometimes people do lose their faith*, and that's something I discuss too. For people that are considering deconstruction, *it is a risk that you run*, and I think it's worth acknowledging. I came out on the other side as a Christian—as a progressive Christian—so it really depends."[4] Davies recognizes a danger of deconstruction—the possibility of losing faith.

This leads to a related point some overlook. Christianity isn't merely a commitment to a set of propositions. It's a commitment to a *person*. Often, faith is treated as a set of propositions that can be dissected, examined, accepted, and, if need be, rejected. Of course, Christianity entails a set of beliefs, *but it's more than that*. It's a relationship with a person—Jesus.

Many different analogies have been used to explain deconstruction, such as a house that needs renovation or a sweater that is unraveling. For example, in her book, *The Most Beautiful Thing I've Seen: Opening Your Eyes to Wonder*, Lisa Gungor of the Liturgists described her deconstruction this way:

> Over the years, a thread comes loose and you try to
> just tuck it in alongside the others. You can cover the
> fraying up. You can pull the thread and think, *Oh, I
> don't need this one, because it is harmful to me; it's itchy
> and gets caught on corners.* It comes out easily. And
> the sweater stays together. Then you pull another,
> and another, and soon you find all the yarn is gone.
> You have deconstructed the entire thing. You are
> left naked.[5]

But these types of analogies all fall short because they fail to account for faith *as a relationship*. The biblical authors consistently speak of faith in terms of a loving relationship with God. Belief in Jesus is the entrance into "eternal life" (John 3:16). And Jesus, in a prayer, defines eternal life as knowing "you, the only true God, and Jesus Christ whom you have sent" (John 17:3). This isn't merely knowing *about* God. This is *knowing* God. It's relational, not just informational.

Moreover, when we put our faith in Jesus, we become "children of God" (John 1:12; see also Galatians 4:5-6). Romans 8:14-16 tells us that when we are led by the Spirit of God, we receive the "Spirit of adoption," and the "Spirit himself bears witness with our spirit that we are children of God." We aren't simply giving intellectual assent to a list of theological propositions. We are being adopted into a new family.

In this way, deconstructing faith is not just about dismantling particular beliefs and deciding to reject them or trade one worldview for another. The consequences mirror what might happen if someone were to rethink what they believed about their marriage, a scenario that would involve deeply felt consequences that would impact their spousal relationship. For example, imagine a husband who becomes suspicious of his wife's faithfulness. As a result, he begins following her to work, reading her emails and text messages, and constantly checking her whereabouts. What implications follow from rethinking *that* belief? Clearly, reevaluating the belief that your spouse is faithful is different from, say, taking a second look at the belief that your car gets 25 miles per gallon. Both examine a belief. But the former is tied to a relationship. Remember the sweater analogy? Deconstructing an inanimate object like a knitted cardigan is an entirely different thing from deconstructing your relationship with the person who made it and gave it to you.

All throughout Scripture, our relationship with God is compared to a marriage. From Yahweh declaring in the Old Testament that Israel had committed adultery by going after other gods, to Jesus and the church being called the Bridegroom and the bride, the Christian faith resembles a marriage covenant. This makes sense of why some decon-struction resembles divorce. Deconstruction often goes beyond merely examining beliefs and begins to resemble a bad breakup. Have you ever talked with a friend going through a nasty divorce? I (Alisa) have a close friend who recently went through a difficult divorce. Her husband once adored her and loved spending time with her. They traveled all over the world together and enjoyed years of ministry and companionship. But something happened. Over time, his positive beliefs about her were eroded and rejected. Now he can't stand her. He interprets every word she says and every move she makes through the lens of hatred. He assumes all her actions have the worst possible motives. He can't tolerate being in the same room with her. He hates her. His change of beliefs changed his relationship. That's because we don't marry a proposition. We marry a person.

This explains a lot of what is happening in the online deconstruction space. Divorce can get ugly. And so can deconstruction. Read the deconstruction stories for yourself. Follow the social media accounts. Many deconstructionists, like many people who have gone through a difficult divorce, are hurt, bitter, angry, irrational, and full of hate toward any-thing resembling their former relationship. Deconstruction doesn't just change your beliefs *about* Jesus. It changes your relationship *with* Jesus. There's a lot at stake.

Following a deconstructionist online can feel a lot like following someone on Instagram who's in the midst of a divorce. I had followed my friend's and her husband's accounts for years, and after a while, I began to observe changes in him. After the divorce, he started posting little hints of displeasure with his former wife. Then he began making little backhanded comments about her mothering and her faith. A few months later, he was bashing her church. Then it was Christianity in general. Then her again. He had deconstructed, and by the time I clicked "unfollow," the poison and toxicity being shouted from his Instagram account was nothing but propaganda. I knew this because I knew the whole story. But if the only information someone had came from his account, they would be getting only one very biased side of it.

There's nothing wrong with doubting, questioning, or pressing hard on what we believe. It is sometimes a necessary path to spiritual maturity. However, if we engage in this process based on our own personal feelings, we run the risk of walking away from eternal life. But if we engage in this process as seekers of truth, yielding our own personal preferences and feelings to the authority of God's Word, it's well worth the risk. Our relationship with Jesus is worth it.

JUST HAVE MORE FAITH?

If you were raised in a Christian home, you likely accepted a set of beliefs about Christianity *without even thinking about it*. These beliefs were received uncritically. What that means is, you didn't logically evaluate all the evidence for the beliefs before accepting them. You received these beliefs like you received gifts on your birthday. You just said thank you and moved on to the next one. Many Christians came to believe in God's existence because someone we trusted—namely, our parents—told us God exists. There's nothing wrong with that, as far as it goes. Most of our beliefs, at least initially, are handed to us from people we trust. Teachers, parents, coworkers, family, and friends all help us shape our view of the world. By the way, we trusted our parents for many *other* beliefs too. We trusted our parents when they said drinking and driving is deadly, or when they told us brushing our teeth prevents cavities. So believing what you've been told isn't necessarily a bad thing, but it has liabilities.

A few years ago, my wife asked me to kill a spider in the kitchen. After I (Tim) squished the eight-legged arthropod, she said, "Well, at least *we know* we don't have snakes."

Confused by what she'd just said, I asked what she meant.

She confidently declared, "If you have spiders in your house, then you don't have snakes."

Trying to hold back my laughter, I replied, "That doesn't make any sense. Why couldn't you have spiders *and* snakes?"

This was one of those moments when I could see the wheels turning. Then realizing how she had been duped, she said, "Well, when I was growing up, that's what my dad always told me whenever we found a spider in the house." At this point, we both burst out laughing over the fact that she'd fallen for it.

Lest you think *you* would never be misled by your parents, let's take a little quiz, shall we? How many of you grew up believing that sitting too close to the TV was bad for you, or that cracking your knuckles would give you arthritis, or that crossing your eyes would make them stay that way, or that swallowing your gum would cause it to stay in your stomach for seven years? This may come as a shock to some of you, but none of these beliefs is true. (Gum exits your digestive system the old-fashioned way, along with everything else.) Here's the point: We have all uncritically accepted beliefs, and some of those were *true* beliefs and some were *false* beliefs. This is why we need to understand *why* we believe the things we do. The reasons provide a foundation for the belief. This is especially important when it comes to our faith.

Some think the solution to experiencing doubt is to "just have more faith." Well, that's *partly* true. We want Christians to have more faith. But there's confusion about what that means. Many people—including professing Christians—don't know what biblical faith is. We see an example of this in a YouTuber's account of his transition from "fundamentalist" Christian to atheist. After giving some background on his religious upbringing and describing the tragic loss of his brother, Jake the Atheist makes some remarks that encapsulate a significant misunderstanding about faith. He describes how his Christian belief was intact until he started thinking about his faith. Specifically, Jake identifies his realization about the true nature of faith as "the biggest piece" of his deconversion to atheism. So what did he discover about faith? Defining the word, he says, "It's believing in something when you don't have all the evidence for it, or you don't know for certain."[6] Jake goes on to add, "Once I realized how much of my faith was based on faith, a flip switched in my brain and . . . I just knew that I didn't want to have to believe things on faith anymore."[7]

Sadly, it is rare to hear the word *faith* being used as the biblical authors intended. As a result, a common misunderstanding of faith is being propagated both inside and outside the church. In his influential book *Love Your God with All Your Mind*, Christian philosopher J. P. Moreland writes, "Faith is now understood as a blind act of will, a decision to believe something that is either independent of reason or that is a simple choice to believe while ignoring the paltry lack of evidence for what is believed."[8]

Is faith really a blind leap into the darkness of irrationality? Pudd'nhead Wilson, a fictional character created by Mark Twain, famously declared, "Faith is believing what you know ain't so."[9] According to that definition, if you know it, then you do not need faith. Faith is for people who want to believe something *in spite of* the evidence against it. Today, there are many propagating this false understanding of faith. Philosopher Peter Boghossian echoes this idea in his book *A Manual for Creating Atheists*. He says, "'Faith' is the word one uses when one does not have enough evidence to justify holding a belief, but when one just goes ahead and believes anyway."[10] Simply put, faith is "belief without evidence."[11] So belief in fairies, unicorns, and Santa Claus would all fall into this category.

If we want to properly understand the biblical concept of faith, we should consult the Bible itself. Unfortunately, many of those who criticize Christian faith have never bothered to open the Bible to see what it teaches on the topic. If they had, they would have come to a completely different conclusion. Moreland says, "Biblically, *faith is a power or skill to act in accordance with the nature of the kingdom of God, a trust in what we have reason to believe is true*. Understood in this way, we see that faith is built on reason. We should have good reasons for thinking that Christianity is true before we dedicate ourselves completely to it."[12] John Lennox, Oxford mathematician and author of *God's Undertaker*, emphatically states, "Faith is a response to evidence, not a rejoicing in the absence of evidence."[13] Moreland and Lennox affirm that faith and reason are *complementary*, not contradictory.

BIBLICAL FAITH

In his Gospel, Mark records how a group of friends brought a paralyzed man to see Jesus. Unfortunately, the house was too full, and they couldn't get in. Determined to get their physically disabled friend to Jesus, the friends lifted him onto the roof, created a hole, and lowered him down. Jesus' response was informative:

> When Jesus saw their faith, he said to the paralytic, "Son, your sins are forgiven." Now some of the scribes were sitting there, questioning in their hearts, "Why does this man speak like that? He is blaspheming! Who can forgive sins but God alone?" And immediately Jesus, perceiving in his spirit that they thus questioned within themselves, said to them, "Why do you question these things in your hearts? Which is easier, to say to the paralytic, 'Your sins are forgiven,' or to say, 'Rise, take up your bed and walk'? But that you may know that the Son of Man has authority on earth to forgive sins"—he said to the paralytic—"I say to you, rise, pick up your bed, and go home."
>
> MARK 2:5-11

Jesus recognized that anyone could *claim* to forgive sins since this is an invisible act that cannot be directly verified. Notice he didn't tell his audience to take a leap of faith and just believe he could forgive sin. Instead, Jesus provided his listeners with evidence so that they would *know* he had the authority to forgive sins. He provided physical evidence, a visible healing, to back up his claim, the invisible act of forgiving sins. This resulted in belief with evidence, not belief without evidence. Hebrews 2:4 even refers to miracles as "signs" and God's way of bearing witness to the salvation message that had been preached.

The most common verse used to define faith is found in the book of Hebrews. In chapter 11, the author writes, "Now faith is the *assurance* of things hoped for, the *conviction* of things not seen" (verse 1, emphasis added). Some people immediately focus on the terms "hoped for" and "not seen," and incorrectly conclude that faith is just wishful thinking. However, that is *not* what the verse says. Remember the context. Hebrews 11 gives a list of people who trusted God to faithfully fulfill his future promises (the things hoped for and not yet seen) *because they had good reason to*. Faith is the assurance of things hoped for, and assurance entails solid reasons to believe something. Think about the last time you were "assured" something was true. It was probably after you examined the reasons to be convinced of its truthfulness. We find assurance only when we have a sufficient amount of evidence.

An illustration might be helpful. When I (Tim) was a teenager, my dad offered to pick me up from a party. He said, "Tim, give me a call when you're done, and I'll come get you." The ride home was his future promise—the thing hoped for. Now I had assurance that he would pick me up later that night. Even though I hadn't received the ride home yet, I had faith it would happen. Was it just wishful thinking? No. I had assurance of the *future* promise—the thing hoped for—because I had evidence from *past* experience. In other words, I had good reason to trust that my dad would fulfill his promise to me. In the same way, Christians should have assurance of things hoped for and things unseen, like their future resurrection, because of the trustworthy evidence that has already been established through the resurrection of Jesus.

However, recognizing the evidence isn't what saves us. Saving faith is active trust based on that evidence. Imagine you are standing at the edge of Niagara Falls. While you are watching this magnificent waterfall, you notice a tightrope walker making his way from one side to the other, pushing a wheelbarrow full of rocks. You are mesmerized by his amazing ability, so you watch him do it over and over again. Then the tightrope walker sees that you have been observing him for some time and walks toward you. He asks, "Do you have faith I can do it again?" Given that you have seen him do it numerous times already, you reply, "Of course. I've seen you do it all day." Without hesitating, he dumps all the rocks out of the wheelbarrow and replies, "Okay, climb in." *That's* just like biblical faith. You *believe* based on evidence. But stepping into the wheelbarrow is *active trust*.

Saving faith is active trust based on the evidence.

So are faith and reason in conflict? It depends entirely on

how one defines faith. Faith as active trust based on evidence is certainly not at odds with reason. Reason *assesses* whether or not a belief is true and then faith trusts in *that belief* in light of those reasons. Apologist Greg Koukl summarizes, "So let's set the record straight. Faith is not the opposite of reason. The opposite of faith is unbelief. And reason is not the opposite of faith. The opposite of reason is irrationality. Do some Christians have irrational faith? Sure. Do some skeptics have unreasonable unbelief? You bet. It works both ways."[14] Certainly, there are Christians who practice a type of blind faith, but that does not mean that Christianity *advocates* blind faith. In fact, the concept of blind faith is completely foreign to the Bible.

That's not to say that everything about Christianity is equally clear. There are plenty of things that are beyond our understanding. As Os Guinness writes, "The rationality of faith goes hand in hand with the mystery of faith. . . . Mystery is beyond human reason, but it is not against reason."[15] When we refer to "having more faith," we're talking about an increased trust that is supported proportionally by increased evidence. We're referring to a stronger faith that results from a strong faith *foundation*.

THEOLOGICAL THIN ICE

Growing up in Canada, I (Tim) loved all things hockey. (Believe it or not, I even worked as a Zamboni driver at a hockey arena to pay my way through university.) When my friends and I weren't playing at the local rink, you could find us playing road hockey in the summer and pond hockey in the winter. For me, nothing beats pond hockey. There's something exhilarating about gliding across open ice while feeling the sun on your face and fresh air in your lungs. Of course, my mom didn't see it that way. All she saw was a dangerous game played on top of a (hopefully) frozen pond by a bunch of boys wearing no protective equipment other than razor-sharp skates, with long sticks and a hard rubber puck. This resulted in multiple trips to the emergency room over the years. I have a scar above my eye and another on my shin to prove it. But there was something scarier than stitches. My mom's worst nightmare was one of us falling through the ice. Because of this, we weren't allowed on the ice unless we checked the thickness first.

One time while we were taking the dog for a walk during early winter, our beloved cockapoo, Lady, who was off-leash, ventured out onto the ice of a small pond. Before anyone could get her attention and call her back, she broke through the ice. For a moment, she disappeared below the surface. When she popped back up, she was swimming for her life, *and there was nothing we could do to help*. After all, if the ice couldn't hold a twenty-five-pound dog, it wasn't going to hold us. We helplessly watched as she tried desperately to kick and claw her way out of the freezing water. We screamed, "Come on, Lady. You can do it! Don't give up! Keep going, girl!" Finally, after what seemed like forever, she managed to pull herself out.

Thin ice is dangerous. One minute you're standing on what you think is solid, the next minute you're fighting for your life. Unfortunately, many Christians are on spiritual thin ice. They don't have a faith capable of supporting them—especially when a crisis comes. If faith isn't strong enough, it won't hold up under the confusion of doubt, the weight of questions, the ache of suffering, or the injustice of spiritual abuse. Perhaps you feel like you're standing at the edge of a frozen pond, watching your loved one fall through the ice. You feel helpless—like there's nothing you can do about it. But there is hope. Behind every deconstruction is a very real person with a complex web of wounds, desires, triggers, foundations, and experiences. Each one is seen and loved by God.

10

DECONSTRUCTOR

One morning, I (Tim) was invited to speak at the three Sunday services at a church in southeast Texas. My topic was the nature of truth. I argued that truth exists and can be known. Unfortunately, this is not a popular message today. In fact, a group of young people walked out in the middle of my sermon and took to social media to condemn the church for hosting me. One guy who didn't even attend my talk posted my Instagram handle with a call to "bully" me. (Ironically, this was all in the name of tolerance.)

That evening turned out to be just as eventful. I was scheduled to do a two-hour Q and A session at the same church, with an emphasis on training parents and leaders of Gen Zers. During the Q and A, Frank sat in the front row with his arms crossed and a sour look on his face. Every few minutes he would shake his head from side to side while letting out an audible groan. It was obvious he didn't like what I had to say, and he wanted me and everyone in the church to know it. Frank's erratic behavior even caught the attention of a church security officer, who came and sat directly behind him. The congregation had been instructed to text their questions to the pastor anonymously so he could read them to me. Though I didn't know which question was Frank's, he made sure I (and everyone else) knew what he thought of my response to it. "You didn't answer my question!" he blurted out while jumping to his feet. Before I could respond, he stormed off toward the exit. Fortunately, church staff were able to intercept Frank and convince him to return before he made it to the parking lot.

Once the Q and A was over, Frank came to me and began to share his story. He recounted how he had been on a "quest for truth" for the last five years. Multiple times during our forty-minute conversation, he mentioned his willingness to "follow evidence wherever it leads." But the more we talked, the more I got the sense that Frank's "quest" wasn't about *truth*. For instance, Frank expressed his belief that faith requires Christians to believe without evidence. Attempting to correct his false understanding of biblical faith, I asked if he was married. My hope was that I could help him see the connection between biblical faith and what we commonly call trust.

"I'm divorced," he said.

Okay, that wasn't going to work. Taking a different tack, I asked, "Do you have any kids?"

"Yes, I have a son," he replied.

This was going to be my springboard to talking about a biblical definition of faith, which is active trust informed by evidence, not blind belief in spite of evidence.

"Do you trust your son?" I asked.

"No," he said.

Frank's response caught me by surprise. By this point, a large crowd of people had quietly gathered around us to listen to our discussion. I found out later that Frank's teenage son—the one he'd just told me he didn't trust—was the one who had invited him to the event. In fact, his son was sitting on the edge of the stage behind me with some of the youth group. This father's brutally honest answer caused one of the youth leaders, who knew the son, to burst into tears. I had just met Frank, but from our short conversation, I knew he *wasn't* the objective truth seeker he claimed to be. Frank was hurting.

After a little more back-and-forth, I decided to take a different approach. Rather than continue to try to convince him Christianity is true, I asked, "If Christianity were true, would you become a Christian?"

Frank immediately shot back, "No!"

Then something happened. Frank took a step back and paused to consider the implications of what he'd just said. If Frank was really willing to follow the truth wherever it led *and* Christianity is true, then shouldn't he become a Christian?

After a few moments of silence, he said, "Okay, fine. I'd become a Christian, but I wouldn't worship God."

Think about that statement for a second. A Christian is

a follower of Christ, and Christ said the *greatest* commandment is to "love the Lord your God with all your heart and
with all your soul and with all your mind" (Matthew 22:37).
Frank's qualification showed that his quest was about more
than merely following the evidence. He didn't just have an
evidence issue. He had a heart issue. Frank would follow the
evidence as long as it was *on his terms*. This highlights the
powerful influence that a whole host of factors, including
an individual's biases, relationships, past wounds, and pre-
suppositions, play in assessing spiritual things.

So far, we've examined the process of deconstruction (the
how) and the thing being deconstructed (the *what*). But our
analysis of deconstruction would be incomplete without looking at the person deconstructing—the *who*. Unfortunately,
this aspect of deconstruction is often given short shrift. On
the one hand, some assume all deconstructors are just "truth
suppressors." If someone is deconstructing, then they must be
in "rebellion against God." On the other hand, some assume
all deconstructors are "truth seekers." They see all those who
are deconstructing as sincere and objective seekers, following
the evidence wherever it may lead. Both of these characteriza-
tions are too simplistic. There's much more going on.

DECONSTRUCTORS AS IMAGE BEARERS

If we're going to understand deconstruction, we need to
begin with what we know about ourselves. There are some
things we know about *everyone* who has ever deconstructed
their faith. We know these things because they are true of
every human being. All deconstructors are made in the image

of God. This is what separates humanity from the rest of creation. Francis Schaeffer said, "Evangelicals have made a horrible mistake by often equating the fact that man is lost and under God's judgment with the idea that man is nothing—a zero." He continued, "There is something great about man."[1] In the Christian worldview, a person is *not* a zero. Men and women are infinitely valuable because they bear the image of their Maker. Therefore, we can confidently look every deconstructor in the eye and tell them they have intrinsic worth. This truth should inform our relationships. We ought to treat those deconstructing their faith with love and respect.

DECONSTRUCTORS AS SINNERS

There's something else we know about every deconstructor because it's true of all of us. We're not only God-imagers, but we're also lawbreakers—what the Bible calls sinners. This isn't meant to be an insult, though we know some take it that way. Rather, we're offering an accurate description of our standing before God. "All have sinned and fall short of the glory of God," the apostle Paul penned (Romans 3:23). The apostle John, one of Jesus' closest friends, agreed: "If we claim to be without sin, we deceive ourselves and the truth is not in us" (1 John 1:8, NIV). We sin because we have a sin nature that goes all the way back to Adam. "Sin entered the world through one man, and death through sin, and in this way death came to all people, because all sinned" (Romans 5:12, NIV).

According to Scripture, we're all sinners. This truth has

184 || THE DECONSTRUCTION OF CHRISTIANITY

implications for our daily lives. It affects our relationships, our desires, our emotions, and even our beliefs. In the New Testament, Paul is constantly reminding Christians to "put to death the deeds of your sinful nature" (Romans 8:13, NLT). He says, "Put to death therefore what is earthly in you: sexual immorality, impurity, passion, evil desire, and covetousness, which is idolatry" (Colossians 3:5).

Sin can play a role in deconstruction in two ways. First, deconstruction is often a *reaction to sin*. Every time someone deconstructs because of pastoral abuse, church hypocrisy, false teaching, broken relationships, or personal suffering, the root cause of the crisis is sin. Since Adam and Eve's rebellion, we live in a broken world marred by sin. This broken world produces broken people, relationships, and circumstances. Sin is why people suffer. Sin is why there is church abuse.

Second, deconstruction can be *motivated by sin*. This is where things get sticky. The idea that deconstruction is used as a license to sin is one that receives a lot of pushback in deconstruction circles. Some claim that it has almost become a cliché. But it's true. One deconstruction Instagram page asked their followers, "What misconception about deconstruction do you most commonly hear among your friends and family?"[2] Several comments reflected a general annoyance at being told sin is a root issue: "That people leave the church so that they can live sinful lives without conviction and guilt," wrote one commenter. Another Instagram page asked why people were deconstructing and one commenter sarcastically answered, "I just wanted to sin more."[3] On a different post, another deconstructionist wrote, "Yeah sex is great but have you ever experienced the pure joy of not believing in hell anymore."[4]

Sin can affect faith deconstruction in the same way it can affect faith construction or faith reconstruction. Our sin nature isn't something we can just put on the shelf until we want to "go out and do some sinning." Instead, it's *always* with us. It's there when we go to bed and when we wake up. It's there when we're reading the Bible, when we're debating theological issues, and when we're scrolling social media. It's a part of you and me. Because of our sin nature, "rethinking your faith" isn't a morally neutral enterprise. As theologian John Stott said, "In seeking God we have to be prepared not only to revise our ideas but to reform our lives."[5] This is easier said than done. Most people are quite comfortable living in sin. And we certainly don't like being judged for it. But that's precisely the problem. A sinner searching for God is like a fugitive searching for the police. Many don't *want* to find him. In *The Fact of Christ*, Presbyterian pastor Patrick Carnegie Simpson writes,

> We had thought intellectually to examine Him; we find that he is spiritually examining us. The roles are reversed between us. . . . We study Aristotle and are intellectually edified thereby; we study Jesus and are, in the profoundest way, spiritually disturbed. . . .
>
> We are constrained to take up some inward moral attitude of heart and will in relation to this Jesus. . . . A man may study Jesus with intellectual impartiality; he cannot do it with moral neutrality.[6]

So every deconstructor bears the image of God and the scars of the Fall. As apologist Greg Koukl puts it, "Even though man is beautiful, he is also broken."[7] As we discussed in chapter 8, if we really do have a sin nature and something in us is broken, the most loving thing we can do is point one another toward the cure.

DECONSTRUCTORS AS SEEKERS

Here's something that might sound surprising: *Everyone is a seeker.* At least, that's what the Bible says. While describing final judgment to the church in Rome, Paul says, "[God] will render to each one according to his works: to those who by patience in well-doing *seek for glory and honor and immortality*, he will give eternal life; but for those who are *self-seeking and do not obey the truth*, but obey unrighteousness, there will be wrath and fury" (Romans 2:6-8, emphasis added). Notice Paul puts people in two groups: *self*-seekers and *truth*-seekers. So the question isn't "Are you seeking?" The question is "What are you seeking?"

Self-seekers may give lip service to following truth, but they aren't really interested in it. A great example is described in Mark 15. As Jesus was hanging on the cross, "those who passed by derided him" (verse 29). The chief priests and the scribes "mocked him" and said to each other, "He saved others; he cannot save himself. Let the Christ, the King of Israel, come down now from the cross *that we may see and believe*" (Mark 15:31-32, emphasis added). These passages describe people who weren't sincere seekers. They were mockers. While demanding evidence from Jesus, they ridiculed him.

This type of sentiment is expressed all over social media. One deconstructionist, who identifies himself on Instagram as someone "helping people navigate deconstruction,"[8] regularly posts memes that mock Christianity. For example, one meme ends, "Jesus gave up his weekend for your sins." The deconstructionist comments, "No greater love has a man than this. . . . That he lay down his weekend for another."[9] In another short video, an angry man is seen walking around a backyard, slapping various people in the face, including women and small children. The caption reads, "What's your deconstruction got you wanting to slap the crap out of?" As he slaps each person, phrases like "Original Sin," "Eternal Conscious Torment," "Creepy Youth Pastors," "Purity Culture," "Honor your father and mother," and "I'm praying for you" flash one after another.[10]

The Mark 15 passage also describes a demand for evidence. While the chief priest and scribes were mocking Jesus, they said they would "believe" *if* they could "see" him come down from the cross. Of course, there is nothing wrong with wanting evidence for our beliefs—they should be based on good reasons. But the assumption was, if the religious leaders had been given some evidence, they would have believed. Interestingly, these religious leaders *had* been given plenty of evidence. They saw Jesus perform miracles and were often astounded by his teaching.

As we've discussed already, evidence plays an important part in biblical faith. But that evidence will be clearly seen only if one's motive is to seek honestly with the whole heart. Speaking through the prophet Jeremiah to the children of Israel, God says, "You will seek me and find me, when you seek me with all your heart" (Jeremiah 29:13). A similar idea is expressed through Moses: "You will seek the LORD your God and you will find him, if you search after him with all your heart and with all your soul" (Deuteronomy 4:29). The same promise is stated in the New Testament. For example, Jesus, the incarnate Son of God, repeats this truth by stating, "Ask, and it will be given to you; seek, and you will find; knock, and it will be opened to you. For everyone who asks receives, and the one who seeks finds, and to the one who knocks it will be opened" (Matthew 7:7-8).

There's a temptation to think that if we could just provide enough evidence, people would believe. It's as if people have an "evidence meter" in their heads, and when the device reaches a certain level, they believe in God. But this assumes that everyone is on an earnest truth quest, and it's not that simple. In reality, the heart behind people's seeking will play an important role in whether or not they discover truth.

God has provided enough evidence for those who seek truth but has left enough concealed for those who don't want to submit to truth.

Some seek after themselves while they "suppress the truth in unrighteousness" (Romans 1:18, NASB). Some seek after truth despite how they may feel about what they find. God has provided enough evidence for those who seek truth but has left enough concealed for those who don't want to submit to truth.

Philosopher Peter Kreeft sums it up this way: "If we had absolute proof instead of clues, then you could no more deny God than you could deny the sun. If we had no evidence at all, you could never get there. God gives us just enough evidence so that those who want him can have him."[11] Kreeft makes it clear that the evidence for God is *not* the primary issue. Instead, the issue lies with the desires of the human heart. To put it another way, the problem is not with God's failure to give evidence; the problem is with our failure to accept it. According to Kreeft, the evidence for God will have a different result depending on the *heart of the person* who sees it. Those who seek God with all their hearts will see the evidence and believe. Those who flee God with all their hearts will see the same evidence but will not believe. In other words, it's not an evidence issue; it's a heart issue.

DECONSTRUCTORS AS CAPTIVES

As we've seen so far, the Bible describes all humans—and so also all deconstructors—as imagers, sinners, and seekers. Each of these nouns denotes something significant about the person going through deconstruction. But there's another biblical description that's often overlooked. It's the concept of deconstructors as captives. Paul tells Timothy that some are "captured" by the devil "to do his will" (2 Timothy 2:25-26). The devil "captures" people by working hard to keep them from finding the truth. One scheme for accomplishing this is to propagate untruths. Paul says, "See to it that no one takes you captive by philosophy and empty deceit, according to human tradition, according to the elemental spirits of the world, and not according to Christ" (Colossians 2:8). We see false philosophies and empty ideas all over the deconstruction explosion.

There's another, more insidious scheme the devil employs

to keep people from the truth. It's the idea that you can never arrive at truth. This is inherent in the destruction process itself. Deconstruction, by its very nature, is a never-ending process. As we noted in chapter 8, John Caputo applies the ideas of postmodern philosopher Jacques Derrida to religion. Following Derrida, Caputo asserts that texts are never "'arriving' at a final, fixed, and finished destination." He then goes on to explain the implication: "We cannot simply 'derive' (*dériver*) direct instruction from it, but we must instead allow it a certain drift or free play (*dérive*), which allows that tradition to be creative and reinvent itself."[12] Interestingly, the apostle Paul warns against those who have "the appearance of godliness" but deny "its power." In fact, he says, "Avoid such people." Those who fall prey to their schemes include people who are "always learning and never able to *arrive at a knowledge of the truth*" (2 Timothy 3:5, 7, emphasis added). Today, many are being ensnared by a methodology that never arrives at truth. If truth isn't the goal because they don't believe it exists, then it can result in continual cynicism. Whether it's accepting untruth or rejecting truth, deconstructors are held captive by these erroneous ideas.

DECONSTRUCTORS AS REBELS

Pride is a major obstacle to finding God. As humans, we want to seek God on our terms, not his. But this cannot be done. We are finite creatures who cannot find God on our own. Thankfully, God has revealed himself to us. First, God speaks through what he has created. The psalmist sings, "The heavens declare the glory of God, and the sky above proclaims his handiwork" (Psalm 19:1). Second, God speaks through Scripture, which is "breathed out by God" (2 Timothy 3:16), as we explained in chapters 6 and 7.

But there is something within us that resists bowing before the Sovereign Lord. The psalmist writes, "In the pride of his face the wicked does not seek him" (Psalm 10:4). As creatures, we desire autonomy—freedom to rule our own lives. We want to be god. But if God exists, this presents a problem since he has the right to rule over our lives. Simply put, if God is God, then we are not.

We make a massive mistake when we think searching for God is like searching for our missing keys. It's more like searching for our King—the one who has authority over our lives. In many ways, we can be like King Herod, who told the wise men to "search diligently" for the newborn King so he could worship him (Matthew 2:8). Despite his claim, Herod didn't want to find Jesus to serve him. He wanted to find Jesus to "destroy him" (Matthew 2:13). That's because Herod saw Jesus as a challenge to his throne.

Jesus challenges our thrones too. We want to rule and reign. We want to be in charge. But Jesus confronts our pride and idolatry. He is King. He makes the rules. He's in charge. Jesus says, "*My* kingdom is not of this world" (John 18:36, emphasis added). Jesus has a Kingdom and he is the King. Jesus says, "If anyone would come after me, let him deny himself and take up his cross and follow me" (Matthew 16:24). We follow him. He doesn't follow us.

In the deconstruction explosion, however, submitting to an authority outside yourself is seen as authoritarian, controlling, and even cultish. One deconstructionist put it this way:

"Part of my deconstruction has included no longer allowing the opinions or expectations of others to determine my self worth, my choices, or my identity. I no longer look to anyone else to define me. Not God, not people. I am my own person."[13] When deconstruction separates a person from the revealed truth of who God is, they are left without access to complete knowledge about reality. Many deconstructors believe they are seeking after truth, but sadly, they are seeking only themselves. This disconnects them from any need to submit to God and his ways, which can create a temporary sense of freedom.

This leads us to one of the most common sentiments expressed in deconstruction stories . . . a sense of freedom and happiness after rejecting the faith. One deconstructionist wrote, "I think the most exciting thing about deconstruction is having the opportunity to decide what I believe for myself. No one is telling me what to believe anymore and that's freeing."[14] Another put it this way, "I recently realized that one of the biggest advantages to deconstructing your faith is that you don't have to ruthlessly and doggedly defend a theological narrative of the world that just doesn't work."[15] When Hillsong worship leader Marty Sampson announced that he was deconstructing, he wrote, "I'm genuinely losing my faith, and it doesn't bother me. Like, what bothers me now is nothing. I am so happy now, so at peace with the world. It's crazy."[16] Perhaps no one articulates this point better than atheist Rachael Slick, former Christian and daughter of well-known apologist Matt Slick: "Freedom is my God now, and I love this one a thousand times more than I ever loved the last one."[17]

It's not difficult to understand the sense of freedom that might be felt if one were to cast off the bounds of moral restraint or reject the rule and reign of an infinite Being. It could feel very much like freedom to change from a mindset of obedience to one of personal autonomy. The reality, however, is that in deconstruction, one trades being a servant of Christ for being a slave to sin. It can feel like freedom at first because we love our sin, but it's a path that leads to destruction: "Each person is tempted when he is lured and enticed by his own desire. Then desire when it has conceived gives birth to sin, and sin when it is fully grown brings forth death" (James 1:14-15). When our chief aim in life is to please ourselves and satisfy our cravings, destruction is inevitable.

Sadly, many people want freedom *from* obedience. The Bible offers freedom *within* obedience. It's talking about an entirely different freedom from the kind offered by deconstruction. Notice that when God put Adam and Eve in the Garden, he said they were "free" to eat from any tree but one (Genesis 2:16, NIV). Moreover, 2 Corinthians 3:17 tells us that "where the

Many people want freedom from obedience. The Bible offers freedom within obedience.

Spirit of the Lord is, there is freedom." Galatians 5:1 says, "It is for freedom that Christ has set us free. Stand firm, then, and do not let yourselves be burdened again by a yoke of slavery" (NIV).

In other words, while many deconstructors are rebelling against God, they are also captives of false ideas, false freedom, and sin. "There is a way that seems right to a man, but its end is the way to death" (Proverbs 14:12). Thanks to Jesus taking the penalty for our sin on himself, "everyone who believes is set *free from every sin*" (Acts 13:39, NIV, emphasis added). Christians have been released from the captivity of sin and are offered God's full forgiveness. Paul explains that when we are set free from sin, we aren't free to sin however we want—that would lead us back into bondage. He writes, "Now that you have been set free from sin and have become slaves of God, the benefit you reap leads to holiness, and the result is eternal life" (Romans 6:22, NIV). We actually become servants of another master. Where sin (an unforgiving and destructive master) once ruled over us, we are now ruled by Christ, our Maker and the source of life. The psalmist even connects following God's commands with true freedom: "I will walk about in freedom, for I have sought out your precepts" (Psalm 119:45, NIV). Christians are free from sin and are servants of Christ.

WE WILL ALL BOW

In his introduction to the 2001 edition of Francis Schaeffer's *He Is There and He Is Not Silent*, seminary professor and former Schaeffer student Jerram Barrs wrote that if we want to come to the truth, we have to surrender to God in three areas. He writes,

> To come to the truth men and women have to bow before God three times.
> We have to bow as creatures, acknowledging that God is God, and that we are not the source and

origin of our own life. Rather, we are dependent. Our hearts resist this.

We have to bow morally, acknowledging that we are sinners who have disobeyed God's commandments and who deserve His judgment. We are dependent on his mercy in Jesus Christ.

We have to bow in the area of knowledge. God is the source of truth and we are not. We are dependent on him in the area of understanding the world and even our own existence.[18]

The sobering reality is that whether or not we choose to bow to Christ in this life, we will all one day bow before him as Lord and King. Some will bow in thankfulness and true freedom, while others will bow in fear and trembling. As we pray for those in our lives who are in deconstruction, let us intercede on their behalf for mercy, for "As I live, says the Lord, every knee shall bow to me, and every tongue shall confess to God" (Romans 14:11).

PART 3

#HOPE

DAVE STOVALL TOURED THE COUNTRY with popular Christian bands Wavorly and Audio Adrenaline. He grew up in a conservative church that he describes as very "black and white." He writes, "I was taught that tattoos and alcohol were sinful, and that if you didn't believe God created the universe in seven consecutive twenty-four-hour days or that the Rapture would happen before the Tribulation, then you probably weren't truly saved." After reading and studying the Bible for himself, he realized these issues weren't so cut-and-dried. Later, after he read books by Rob Bell and listened to progressive Christian podcasts, his beliefs about the Bible changed. No longer did he see it as a divine book written to humans; instead, he saw it as a human book written about God.

"I began to question the faith I was handed, and I went down a path of eventually wondering if the God of the Bible was even real. This was a decade-long process of what we now know as deconstruction," Dave remembers. After abandoning biblical authority and embracing universalism, Dave felt "enlightened," and he began to share his new beliefs with others. He recalls, "I felt like a missionary. I had to help people who were stuck in evangelical Christianity, real judgmental people—I needed to help them think outside the box." He continues,

> This new path worked for me for a while, but then . . . I had kids. I was holding my baby boy with excitement about teaching him about life, but there was one nagging question: What was I going to teach him about God? Progressive Christianity had given me a lot of "I don't know" answers, but that wasn't enough anymore. So I prayed an earnest prayer and asked God to show me the truth. I didn't care if it led me away from Christianity; I had to know.
>
> To my surprise, God led me to a lead pastor of a Christian church who was fanatical about a thing called discipleship. He saw the teachability in me that I had prayed for. He began to form a friendship with me and started discipling me. He invited me to lunches after church, to join his home group, and to join his men's group. Throughout our conversations about God, I never once felt judged; I only ever felt genuine care and curiosity from him. We would talk on the way to hockey games about end-times theology. He would ask me to open up my Bible app and read certain passages out loud and then ask, "What is the author saying?" contrary to the progressive Christian question of "What does this verse mean to you?" We talked about how I should trust the words of the New Testament authors over

what twenty-first-century authors thought Jesus meant. We looked at how archaeological evidence lines up extremely well with the New Testament.

He gently led me back to a historical view of Scripture, and I ended up submitting myself to the lordship of Jesus through his Word once again. Peace came into my life and trickled down into my home. My wife began submitting to Jesus in Scripture again and found loads of healing and redemption for her scars. My kids have grown up in a completely different home than they would have, had my friend not had compassion for me and taken the time to disciple me. My kids know Jesus, and they're learning to pray and seek God when things get hard instead of learning to reinterpret Scripture to match the moral compass of culture. Praise God for disciple makers who take time to invest in people and lead them to (and sometimes back to) the real, historical Jesus.[1]

As Dave's story demonstrates, there is hope for our friends and loved ones in deconstruction. Though it's common for Christians to feel regret, fear, and guilt as they watch their loved ones walk away from the faith, in the upcoming chapters, we want to provide advice and hope for those of you who know someone in the midst of deconstruction. While this won't be a one-size-fits-all approach, we pray there might be something in the next three chapters that will help you thoughtfully and lovingly interact with those who are being swept up in this cultural phenomenon.

QUESTIONS

"Are mermaids real?"

That was the question my seven-year-old daughter, Jocelyn, asked me one sunny summer afternoon while I (Tim) was working on my laptop at the kitchen table. This was an easy one, I thought. "No, honey, mermaids aren't real."

Unsatisfied with my answer, she said, "But you don't know everything, Dad. Can you ask Siri just to be sure?"

Ouch. I thought I had a few more years before my omniscience was questioned. But I should have known better. Jocelyn has always been the kid who questions *everything*. She wants to know *what* things are, *where* things came from, and *how* things work. She's innately inquisitive. It's one of the things I love so much about her.

Hoping for some parental vindication, I pulled my phone out of my pocket and asked, "Siri, are mermaids real?"

Siri replied, "Not that I know of."

This wasn't the definitive answer I was looking for, but I hoped it would be enough to satisfy my daughter. Attempting to get back to work, I said, "See? Siri agrees with me. Mermaids aren't real."

"No," Jocelyn replied with one eyebrow raised. "Siri said she *doesn't know* if mermaids are real. Can you ask Siri to ask Google if mermaids are real? Google will know."

And there it is, folks. My seven-year-old was fact-checking me with Google. Now some of you might think that she was being disrespectful and that she shouldn't second-guess her father. But I wasn't angry with her. I was proud of her. That's because one of the lessons my wife and I taught her from an early age is "Just because somebody tells you something, that doesn't mean it is true."[1] This is actually the first lesson in *The Thinking Toolbox*, a book to help build your kids' reasoning skills. My sweet little girl was seeking truth the only way she knew how. (She hasn't yet learned that Google can help you find falsehoods too.) And it started with a question.

This story highlights a fact about each of us: We all want to know what's true (at least about some things). This is why we ask questions. It starts when we're young with questions about mermaids, but as we get older, we transition to bigger concerns: What will I do for a living? Who should I marry? Then there are *the* big questions of life: Why am I here? Is there purpose and meaning in life? Does God exist? Why is there so much evil in the world? What happens after death?

Over time, the answers we find shape our beliefs about the world—our worldview. But then something happens. We can begin to doubt some of those beliefs.

What if I'm wrong? Have you ever asked yourself that? There are times when we feel so confident about our convictions. But there are other times, if we're being honest, when we are anguished by uncertainty about our beliefs. After all, we're *finite* creatures. We don't know everything, as my daughter so astutely reminded me. Sometimes we get things wrong. And this can lead to questions and doubts about our faith.

MAKING ROOM FOR QUESTIONS

My daughter Jocelyn came to me with her question because she felt safe exploring the answer with me. However, many people don't feel the same way about the church. In fact, many believe their local faith community is not a safe place to express questions and doubts. In the article "Six Reasons Young Christians Leave the Church," the Barna Group reports that "nearly three out of every five young Christians (59%) disconnect either permanently or for an extended period of time from church life after age 15."[2] One of their findings deals directly with how the church addresses questions and doubts. They discovered that over one-third of the young people surveyed felt they were not able "to ask [their] most pressing life questions in church."[3] While this doesn't reflect every congregation, let's look at four reasons why the church can be perceived as an unsafe place to ask questions and express doubts.

No space for questions

The first problem is that some churches don't intentionally make room for questions. In most cases, this *isn't* because the church has nefarious motives. For better or worse, "church" is often very structured—everything from Sunday morning to midweek services to special programming is timed down to the minute. On Sunday, you show up. Sing a few songs. Listen to the sermon. Pass the plate. Listen to the announcements and benediction. Head home. Most churches don't have a Q and A slotted into the schedule. Unfortunately, this can unwittingly give the impression that questions are not allowed.

In a now-deleted Instagram post, former Hillsong worship leader Marty Sampson tells us why he left the faith: "This is a soapbox moment so here I go . . . How many preachers fall? Many. No one talks about it. How many miracles happen? Not many. No one talks about it. Why is the Bible full of contradictions? No one talks about it. How can God be love yet send four billion people to a place, all 'coz they don't believe? No one talks about it."[4] This is a bit mystifying to read because in many Christian circles, these questions *are talked about* all the time and have been discussed and written about exhaustively for millennia. Sadly, it appears Sampson wasn't part of a church community that *intentionally* addressed these important questions.

We want to suggest a solution. If your church doesn't have a Q and A time, it's time to start one. For many years, the late pastor Timothy Keller conducted a forty-minute Q and A session after every service. This allowed people to ask questions about the sermon as well as about Christianity in general. In an online article, Keller offered five reasons to host a Q and A after your worship service, explaining that it gives pastors immediate feedback on their sermon, gets people to press in beyond the worship service, provides a vehicle for evangelism, models how Christians should engage questions about faith, and keeps pastors connected to the questions their people are struggling with.[5] We would add a sixth: It creates a healthy milieu where questions can be expressed, discussed, and answered.

Vilified questions

Some deconstructors have said their churches approached questioning as if it were somehow bad or even sinful. This is a much more egregious error. For example, in a discussion with me (Alisa) on the *Unbelievable?* radio show, Christian music artist Lisa Gungor described how her deconstruction started with the idea that questions were sinful. She said, "There were some things I started questioning a little bit, but then I was told you don't question. If you question the Bible, if you question the teacher or the pastor, then you are, in essence, sinning. So I kind of shut down any kind of question that I had."[6] For Gungor, confessing her doubts was akin to confessing her sins. Tragically, this bad teaching has caused some to carry their questions alone.

In the book *God in the Dark*, social critic Os Guinness tells the story of a peasant who beat his donkey.[7] The donkey had bales of firewood strapped to its back and was forced to carry the load up a long, steep path on a hot day. Over time, the donkey slowed from exhaustion. Enraged, the merciless peasant began to whip the donkey harder and harder. Finally, the weight and the wounds took their toll, and the donkey dropped to the ground in defeat. That's when the peasant beat the donkey to death. Commenting on the illustration, Guinness says, "The injustice is that the donkey is beaten until it collapses and then it is beaten *for collapsing*."[8]

Some Christians erroneously treat faith like that donkey. We force it to carry questions and doubts it cannot handle, and when it eventually collapses under the strain, we condemn it for not being strong enough. This is partly because many Christians are confused about what faith actually is. Faith is not a blind leap in the dark, and it's not concrete certainty. As we explained in chapter 9, when the Bible talks about faith, it's usually talking about an active type of trust. And it's not a trust that is threatened by questions or even by doubts. Faith and doubt are not opposites.

Asking questions isn't bad. Suppressing questions is. In his book *You Lost Me*, Barna CEO David Kinnaman says, "I believe *unexpressed* doubt is one of the most powerful destroyers of faith."[9] This conclusion also finds support from a three-year longitudinal study launched by the Fuller Youth Institute. Summarizing their findings, researchers Kara Powell and Steven Argue state,

> According to our study . . . over 70 percent of
> churchgoing high schoolers report having serious
> doubts about faith. Sadly, less than half of those
> young people shared their doubts and struggles with
> an adult or friend. Yet these students' opportunities
> to express and explore their doubts were actually

correlated with greater faith maturity. In other
words, it's not doubt that's toxic to faith; it's silence.[10]

Strictly speaking, doubts and questions are *not* the problem. In fact, when honest doubts are carefully explored, this
can lead to strong faith formation. However, when doubts
are carelessly ignored or suppressed, this can lead to faith
destruction. Sadly, this is what the online world is witnessing
in the deconstruction movement.

Bad answers

Up to this point, we've seen how ignoring and suppressing
questions about faith can create an unsafe environment. But
the problem is not merely with how we engage questions. It's
also with how we *answer* questions.

This leads to the third reason why some think church
is not a safe place to express questions and doubts: Some
churches give bad answers.
Thoughtful questions demand
thoughtful answers. When we
respond with half-baked or
pat answers, we communicate

> Thoughtful questions demand
> thoughtful answers. Bad answers
> shut down sincere questions.

that we're not taking the questions seriously—or even worse,
that we simply don't have any good answers. Bad answers
shut down sincere questions.

This is nothing new. Friedrich Schleiermacher, for
example, was a German theologian in the early 1800s. As
the son of an army chaplain and the grandson of a pastor,
Friedrich was brought up with a deep devotion to the Bible
and a personal commitment to Christ. However, he began to

doubt what he'd been taught, and those doubts snowballed when he went to university. While away at school, he wrote a letter to his father suggesting that his teachers didn't really engage with or give good answers for the doubts many students were experiencing. Of course, he didn't tell his father that the doubts were really his own. It was one of those "asking for a friend" situations. His father didn't pick up on that and dismissed his son's concerns by telling him he'd read the skeptical literature and considered it nonsense that wasn't worth looking into. There's no doubt his father meant well, but the "nothing to see here; keep moving along" approach pushed Friedrich away. He continued to rethink his beliefs for six months before stunning his father with a letter. He wrote:

> Faith is the regalia of the Godhead, you say. Alas! dearest father, if you believe that without this faith no one can attain to salvation in the next world, nor to tranquility in this—and such, I know, is your belief—oh! then pray to God to grant it to me, for to me it is now lost. I cannot believe that he who called himself the Son of Man was the true, eternal God; I cannot believe that his death was a vicarious atonement.[11]

Today, Friedrich Schleiermacher is remembered by many as the father of modern liberal theology.

Some answers aren't really answers at all. Many people in deconstruction describe asking legitimate questions, only to be told, "God's ways are higher than our ways." While the sentiment is technically true, it can be used as a cop-out. Rather than wrestle with the question, some Christians run from it. Granted, not everyone can answer *every* question. Sometimes the best response is "I don't know." Yet for some, this appeal to "God's higher ways" can reveal an unwillingness to search for God's *available* answers.

In 2014, evangelist Ray Comfort made headlines with his answer to evolution. Holding a banana in his right hand, he boldly declared, "Behold, the atheists' nightmare!" Comfort went on to describe some of the banana's user-friendly design features, including how "the banana and the hand are perfectly made, one for the other," how "God has made it with a nonslip surface" for holding, how "God has placed a tab at the top" for opening, and how it has "just the right shape for the human mouth."[12]

What Comfort didn't realize at the time was that the banana he was holding is an example of artificial selection, a mechanism by which humans select beneficial traits of a particular plant or animal and then engineer future varieties to develop these traits over time. We see this in everything from toy poodles to seedless watermelons to tangelos (a hybrid of a tangerine and a grapefruit). In this case, the modern banana was cultivated by humans to have just the right shape, size, and seedless goodness. Moreover, artificially selected bananas hardly resemble their ancient banana ancestors. So what Comfort intended as an argument for God's intelligent design was really explained by human intervention. Fortunately, Comfort and his organization Living Waters recognized the mistake. He was a good sport about the banana debacle, even making jokes about it himself. But sadly, the "banana argument" (and others like it) contributes to the false idea that Christians don't have good responses to tough challenges.

Giving no answer is better than giving a bad answer. Augustine made this powerful point in his *Confessions*. In reference to the question "What was God doing before he made heaven and earth?" Augustine imagined retorting with a snappy comeback: "He was preparing Hell for people who pry into mysteries." That's what others had done in an attempt to evade the question. But he cautioned against that, saying:

> It is one thing to make fun of the questioner and another to find the answer. So I shall refrain from giving this reply. For in matters of which I am ignorant I would rather admit the fact than gain credit by giving the wrong answer and making a laughing-stock of a man who asks a serious question.[13]

Translation: Augustine, one of the most profound theologians and influential thinkers of Western civilization, basically answered a tough query with "I don't know." We would be wise to follow Augustine's example lest we bring ridicule to the one asking the question and disrepute to the one answering it.

During a Q and A time following one of my (Tim's) talks, a Christian woman sitting in the second row asked me, "Why didn't God prevent my daughter from getting into a recent car accident?" My response began with three words: "I don't know." Now, I had more to say about the problem of pain in general. But the truth is, I don't know why God permits particular incidents of pain and suffering in certain individual lives and yet intervenes in the lives of others. God has not given that specific information to me. *Only God knows.* That may not be a very *satisfying* response. But it is an *honest* one.

I (Alisa) recall a Q and A session at a conference where I was speaking during a particularly busy season of ministry. I was the only speaker, so there was no one to punt to, should I encounter a question about bacterial flagellum or epistemic contextualism (insert grimace emoji). I was seated on the floor level in an oversized cushioned chair when I was asked how to interpret an obscure passage in Revelation. My mind raced to remember the Bible classes I audited in seminary, but I had nothing. Not a clue. In that moment, I remembered the time I emailed a professor a question about a particular passage, and he responded simply, "I'm not sure. Let me see what I can dig up for you." I was stunned. A seminary professor with a PhD didn't know the answer to my question, and he wasn't afraid to admit it. I was impressed with his humility. I was also compelled to trust him when he claimed he *did* know the answer to a question. That's because I knew he wouldn't just make something up on the spot to save face. So when I was asked about the passage in Revelation, I did what had been modeled for me. I simply said, "I don't know off the top of my head, and I wouldn't want to comment on it without looking at the passage in context and thinking it through." A woman came up to me after the session and pointed out how refreshing it was that I didn't try to make up an answer. Sadly, she believed that many pastors and speakers she knew would have. I'm not sure I agree with her on that, but it demonstrates the lack of trust many carry that can be a potential inroad to deconstruction.

Unaccepted answers

When asked difficult questions, church leaders are sometimes quite well-equipped to answer them, but the answers they give aren't ones the questioner wants to hear. It's not that the answers aren't true; it's that the answers aren't *accepted*. For example, this often happens when people ask questions about God's wrath. There are aspects of God's nature that make people uncomfortable, and for many, his divine anger is at the top of the list. The problem is, there are more than six hundred references to wrath in Scripture that can't be ignored, glossed over, or denied.[14]

The doctrine of God's wrath against the wicked is clearly taught throughout the Bible. Listen to how the prophet Nahum describes God's fury with Nineveh:

> The LORD is a jealous and avenging God;
>   the LORD is avenging and wrathful;
> the LORD takes vengeance on his adversaries
>   and keeps wrath for his enemies.
> The LORD is slow to anger and great in power,
>   and the LORD will by no means clear the guilty. . . .
> Who can stand before his indignation?
>   Who can endure the heat of his anger?
> His wrath is poured out like fire,
>   and the rocks are broken into pieces by him.

The LORD is good,
    a stronghold in the day of trouble;
he knows those who take refuge in him.
    But with an overflowing flood
he will make a complete end of the adversaries,
    and will pursue his enemies into darkness.

NAHUM 1:2-3, 6-8

We cited this lengthy passage for a reason. Most people are happy to quote verses like "The LORD is slow to anger" (verse 3) and "The LORD is good, a stronghold in the day of trouble" (verse 7), yet they ignore verses like "The LORD is avenging and wrathful" (verse 2) and "His wrath is poured out like fire" (verse 6). They want to take the former but leave the latter. However, this minor prophet won't allow it. God's goodness and wrath are inseparably interwoven *within the same text.*

Many people have the mistaken impression that in the Bible, the character of God is split—the God of the Old Testament is angry and wrathful, and the God of the New Testament is gracious and merciful. This simply isn't true. Not only do Nahum's own words allude to God's goodness and mercy (verse 7), but Nahum's audience was well aware of God's goodness. How do we know? Nahum is writing about the Ninevites. These are the same Ninevites to whom God sent Jonah. These are the same people who had repented and received mercy from God. Moreover, in response to God sparing the Ninevites, Jonah declared, "I knew that you are a gracious God and merciful, slow to anger and abounding in steadfast love, and relenting from disaster" (Jonah 4:2). Over a century had passed since Jonah's oracle, and the Ninevites had turned back to their wicked ways. Now the Ninevites, who had previously received God's mercy, were going to receive God's wrath. The tragic history of the Ninevites displays two aspects of God's nature, and both are *equally true*. God is gracious and merciful. But he is also avenging and wrathful. Sound theology never pits one against the other.[15]

Unfortunately, some professing Christians aren't interested in answers that contradict their personal preferences. Questions about salvation, sexuality, gender, and abortion all have answers that aren't theologically complicated.[16] But they *are* controversial in our contemporary culture. Sadly, they are sometimes controversial in Christian culture as well. In an attempt to bring "nuance" into discussions surrounding these types of hot-button issues, many Christian influencers end up obfuscating rather than nuancing. Some things are just not that complex. When people claim their questions are "unanswered" because they do not *accept* the biblical responses they've been given, the church cannot compromise its convictions. That's true even if the questioners consider the environment to be "unsafe" as a result.

DON'T BE AFRAID OF QUESTIONS

Regardless of how people respond to the answers we give, we need not fear questions. In fact, the church has a rich history of asking questions. For Christians who are made in the image of God, the desire to know is *God-given*. We were created to question. In fact, God asks questions. This is odd if you think about it. Why would an all-knowing God ask questions? It can't be because he doesn't know something. That answer won't work. When God asks questions, it's not for his benefit; it's for *ours*. Think about the very first thing God tasked Adam with in Genesis 2, even before Eve was created. After instructing Adam on which trees he could and could not eat from, God brought every animal to Adam "to see what he would call them" (verse 19). The very first thing Adam had to do was answer the question, *What should I call it?* Over and over. The text hints at why God had Adam do this: "Then the LORD God said, 'It is not good that the man should be alone; I will make him a helper fit for him'" (verse 18). It wasn't until Adam had named all the animals that the passage declares: "For Adam there was not found a helper fit for him" (verse 20). Of course, God knew all along that Eve would be Adam's perfect counterpart, but there seems to be a sense in which God wanted Adam to fully realize this too. After a fruitless search for a "helper fit for him," God created woman out of man, prompting Adam to break out into the first poem in the history of mankind:

> This at last is bone of my bones
>   and flesh of my flesh;
> she shall be called Woman,
>   because she was taken out of Man.
>
> GENESIS 2:23

After spending tireless time and energy encountering all manner of birds, livestock, and beasts of the field, it's no wonder Adam was so impressed with God's creation of Eve!

God certainly used a repetitive question to help Adam come to this conclusion.

Philosopher and mathematician Blaise Pascal pointed out that questions help people come to conclusions on their own, which can lead to changed minds. He wrote, "People are generally better persuaded by the reasons which they themselves discovered than by those which have come into the mind of others."[17]

Answers or exits?

It's often said that behind every question is a questioner. This self-evident truth has serious implications. Let's say you walk into a doctor's office after a biopsy of an underarm lump. You ask the doctor, "Is it cancer?" Now imagine the doctor simply answers yes in a stoic and calculated manner. If you are the patient, you will be shocked and even angered at her coldness and lack of compassion. However, if you are an intern who is learning to tell the difference between benign and malignant tumors, you will think it's a perfectly appropriate response from your attending physician. Notice it's the same question, yet each questioner has a different *reason* for asking the question.

What does this have to do with deconstruction? Virtually every deconstruction testimony talks about "unanswered questions." That's part of the story . . . but it's not the whole story. That's because it fails to account for the reason the person is asking the question. Broadly speaking, there are two kinds of questioners. There are questioners looking for *answers*, and there are questioners looking for *exits*; that is, they're looking for reasons to abandon historic Christianity.

Let's first look at those who are asking sincere questions and searching for truth. Their questions come with different degrees of importance. Why is the sky blue? Why does a pencil look bent in water? The answers to these questions might be interesting, though they have little bearing on everyday life. But questions about our deeply held beliefs are different. That's because the answers have consequences. They have the power to build up our beliefs, and they have the power to destroy our convictions.

In John 3, we read about a Pharisee named Nicodemus who seeks out Jesus at night to ask a question. Some speculate that he comes at night because he is afraid or ashamed to be seen publicly with Jesus. However, Nicodemus recognizes that Jesus is "a teacher come from God" (verse 2). After all, he has seen Jesus perform signs to substantiate his claims. Nicodemus reasons, "No one can do these signs . . . unless God is with him" (verse 2). He follows the evidence because he's looking for answers. This is where Jesus makes a profound proclamation. "Truly, truly, I say to you, unless one is born again he cannot see the kingdom of God" (verse 3). This strange statement prompts Nicodemus to ask a question: "How can a man be born when he is old? Can he enter a second time into his mother's womb and be born?" (verse 4). Obviously Nicodemus doesn't fully grasp what Jesus is talking about. He's not talking about a physical rebirth. He's talking about a spiritual rebirth. Even after Jesus describes the nature of being born again, Nicodemus asks, "How can these things be?" (verse 9).

Interestingly, the next time Nicodemus shows up in John's Gospel, he is defending Jesus' right to a fair hearing before being judged (John 7:50-51). The chief priests and Pharisees have sent officers to arrest Jesus. When they come back empty-handed, the Pharisees are furious. That's because they have *prejudged* Jesus. Nicodemus, on the other hand, is looking for truth.

Nicodemus shows up again at Jesus' burial (spoiler alert!). John says, "Nicodemus also, who earlier had come to Jesus by night, came bringing a mixture of myrrh and aloes, about seventy-five pounds in weight" (John 19:39), reminding his readers that though Nicodemus previously came to Jesus privately, he now seems to be showing his allegiance to Jesus publicly. Nicodemus and Joseph of Arimathea, a "disciple of Jesus" (John 19:38) and fellow member of the Sanhedrin, bind Jesus' body in linen cloth with the spices and lay it in a tomb. Though we can't say for sure, Nicodemus's final recorded act in John's Gospel may be a demonstration of his declaration of faith. Regardless, Nicodemus appears to honestly seek after truth.

So some questioners are looking for answers. But some questioners are *looking for exits*. The goal isn't truth; it's something else. Sometimes questions are asked to make the Christian position look foolish in order to justify a person's rejection of the whole system. For example, the Pharisees and Herodians join forces to trap Jesus, saying, "Teacher, we know that you are true and do not care about anyone's opinion. For you are not swayed by appearances, but truly teach the way of God. Is it lawful to pay taxes to Caesar, or not?" (Mark 12:13-14). Although this might sound like a sincere question, it isn't. Jesus sees right through their hypocrisy and calls them out. He replies, "Why put me to the test?" (verse 15). Their question was meant to test, not to find truth.

Immediately following his interaction with the Pharisees and Herodians, Jesus is confronted by the Sadducees. In this case, the Sadducees attempt to trap Jesus with a question about marriage in the resurrection.

> Sadducees came to him, who say that there is no resurrection. And they asked him a question, saying, "Teacher, Moses wrote for us that if a man's brother dies and leaves a wife, but leaves no child, the man must take the widow and raise up offspring for his brother. There were seven brothers; the first took a wife, and when he died left no offspring. And the second took her, and died, leaving no offspring. And the third likewise. And the seven left no offspring. Last of all the woman also died. In the resurrection, when they rise again, *whose wife will she be*? For the seven had her as wife."
>
> MARK 12:18-23, EMPHASIS ADDED

Again, does this sound like a sincere question? It sounds more like a clever riddle than a genuine inquiry. For starters, the Sadducees are asking about the resurrection when they don't actually believe in a resurrection. The question just comes across as disingenuous. Though there's nothing wrong with asking about someone else's beliefs, in this context, it's a giant red flag.

Some people ask questions seeking exits, not answers.

While we can't see the heart, some people ask questions seeking exits, not answers. We hear questions like this all the time. "Who made God?" might be a sincere question from my six-year-old, but wielded by an Oxford University biologist, it comes across as insincere. Not all questions are equal. Some are genuine. Some aren't.

How to doubt well

In today's skeptical culture, it's not a matter of *if* doubts come, but *when* they come. So we need to teach Christians to doubt well. The Bible can be of great help because it is a book full of doubters. Moses, Habakkuk, Job, David, Zechariah, Peter (pre-Pentecost), and Thomas all doubted. When you doubt, know you are in good company. Let's look to John the Baptist to learn how to doubt well.

Most people don't immediately associate John the Baptist with doubt. After all, John has some serious religious credentials. Think about it. He's the son of a priest, a prophet of God, and Jesus' cousin. Still not impressed? Remember, this is the same John, who, at one time, leaped in his mother's womb at the sound of the pregnant Mary's voice (Luke 1:41). This is the same John who confidently declared, "Behold, the Lamb of God who takes away the sin of the world!" (John 1:29). This is the same John who baptized Jesus and heard the voice from heaven say, "This is my beloved Son, with whom I am well pleased" (Matthew 3:17). All of this makes John's doubt so intriguing.

If you don't know the story, John the Baptist was arrested and thrown into prison. While awaiting a probable execution, he began to waver, going from proclaiming the Messiah to doubting him. Consequently, John the Baptist had a question for Jesus. "When John heard in prison about the deeds of the Christ, he sent word by his disciples and said to him, 'Are you the one who is to come, or shall we look for another?'" (Matthew 11:2-3). There's a lot we can learn from how John handled his doubts—whether we ourselves have questions or want to help someone we care about who does.

First, John expressed his question. We're not told what caused John to doubt. Maybe his suffering caused his uncertainties to rise to the surface since doubt often comes through trials. Maybe it was a false expectation about how God should act in his situation. Maybe it was fear or confusion in his circumstances. We just don't know. Here's what we *do* know: John didn't keep his doubts to himself.

We should follow John's example and articulate our questions. We shouldn't *suppress* our doubts or the doubts of others but rather *express* them. Expose them to the light. Doubts that are left hidden, ignored, and unanswered can drive one to despair or deconstruction. Sometimes friends and family members may be ashamed to admit they have doubts. We may feel the same way, especially if we've been a Christian for a long time or we're in a position of leadership in the church. Take heart! If the prophet John the Baptist can raise his doubts, so can we. John could have let pride get in the way. He could have protected his reputation, but instead he modeled great humility in questioning the very sentiment he had so boldly declared early in his ministry— Jesus as Messiah.

Second, John questioned in community. The text says John sent word to Jesus "by his disciples" (Matthew 11:2). Notice how John shared his uncertainty with his disciples—his inner circle. There's a lesson here. Never doubt alone. Find solid people in your life with whom you can share your deepest doubts. Who is your inner circle? Who are the people you can trust with your questions? This is where discipleship comes in. In the deconstruction communities we find online, the instinct of deconstructors to disconnect from their church communities is strong. Often, they deconstruct together, away from mature Christians who can help guide them toward truth. Who we choose to be in community with is of utmost importance.

There is another side to this. Not only should we share our doubts with others, but we should also be the kind of people others share their doubts with. This isn't easy. When people question or doubt our deeply held beliefs, we can feel threatened and get defensive. This has even caused some Christians to verbally attack those who doubt. Jude, the half-brother of Jesus, offers an important corrective. He tells us to "have mercy on those who doubt" (Jude 1:22). That's a command, not a suggestion. Mercifully, John's friends provided a safe community to express doubt. *Are you a safe place—someone with whom your friends and family can share their questions and doubts?*

Third, John understood his question and its implications. In other words, John knew what he was questioning and what he was not questioning. Notice what John's question presumes. When he asks *if* Jesus is the Messiah, he's assuming there is a God who will send the Messiah; there is authoritative Scripture that promises the Messiah; and there is one who will come as the Messiah. John's doubt didn't lead him to throw out his entire faith. He understood the implications of his doubt.

Fourth, John sought an answer to his question. Pay attention to Jesus' response to John's doubt. Jesus said, "Go and tell John what you hear and see: the blind receive their sight and the lame walk, lepers are cleansed and the deaf hear, and the dead are raised up, and the poor have good news preached to them" (Matthew 11:4-5). Jesus *didn't* tell John to look inside his heart for some subjective feeling. He *didn't* tell John to ignore his doubts and just blindly believe. Rather, Jesus pointed to objective evidence to substantiate who he is. What evidence? The blind see. The lame walk. The deaf hear. In sum, Jesus told John to believe based on the works he was doing. He gave evidence to back up his claim.

Not every question gets a neat-and-tidy answer. That's because Christianity isn't tidy. There are formidable objections, difficult concepts, and troubling texts. There will always be some unanswered questions. That's not unique to Christianity, by the way. *Every* worldview has unanswered questions. The real question is, which worldview *best* explains reality? We think it's the Christian worldview.

John got his question answered, but we might not. God doesn't always give us an answer. Even in John's circumstance, he must have had *other* questions. For example, if Jesus was the Messiah, why was John stuck in prison? Shouldn't the Messiah be setting the captives free? Shouldn't the Messiah be burning up the chaff with unquenchable fire (Matthew 3:12)? Though John got an answer, we don't know if all of his doubts were resolved before he died in prison.

The final lesson we can learn from Jesus' interaction with

John the Baptist is this: Jesus can handle our doubts. Jesus' comforting response to John is telling of his general approach to doubters. Jesus never scolded John for asking questions. He never second-guessed John's spirituality or called him a "bad" Christian. He didn't simply tell John to have more faith. On the contrary, Jesus said to others, "Truly, I say to you, among those born of women there has arisen no one greater than John the Baptist" (Matthew 11:11). Remember, Jesus paid John this complement *after* John had wavered in his belief.

John the Baptist's story lays out a helpful strategy for addressing big theological questions. Don't ask people to ignore or suppress their questions. Instead, be the kind of person to whom people can express their questions. Do your best to understand their doubts while encouraging these friends and family members to keep them in their proper perspective. Help them frame their doubts as questions, and then search for good answers.

Not all doubts are equal. There are some doubts that stand up against tough scrutiny. As a result, these doubts require us to change our beliefs. However, there are other doubts that collapse under the weight of the evidence. This is what happened to John's doubt. Jesus gave John good evidence to doubt his doubts.

When we start creating environments that intentionally make room for questions and doubts, we will begin to see Christians grow deeper in their knowledge and love of God.

12
ADVICE

My friend Heather was in the throes of deconstruction after a painful experience of spiritual abuse at a local church. One night I (Alisa) met with Heather and her husband for dinner, where they brought up some difficult questions regarding biblical reliability. Heather had been reading some skeptical scholarship and had become convinced that the church canonized the Bible as a way of exerting control and power over people—in particular, women—with the motive of manipulating them into submission. It wasn't difficult to understand *why* she was thinking this way. Her pastor of many years had been controlling and manipulative, with a history of breaking off relationships with anyone who challenged his authority or simply asked the wrong questions.

The conversation was emotionally charged, and several times throughout the evening, Heather erupted into deep sobs and angry tears. I decided that instead of offering a string of answers, it would be more compassionate and fruitful to simply listen. It felt insensitive to interrupt her lament with logical arguments that could make her feel as if I was challenging her to a debate. My heart broke for her. She had survived an abusive father, and now here she was again, facing the same type of mistreatment from someone who was supposed to be loving her, teaching her, and pointing her to Jesus.

After dinner, I walked the couple to their car and hugged them goodbye. In an unexpected statement that felt both nonchalant and biting, Heather burst out, "Well, if you'd had any answers, we would have taken them!" The implication was that the reason I didn't offer answers was that I had none. Here I was, an apologist with a book deal, a blog, and a podcast, and when faced with truly tough questions, I had come up with a big fat goose egg. My heart sank. I had let Heather down. After that, her deconstruction hit a momentum that led her to quickly denounce organized religion.

For a couple of years, I carried a deep sense of failure until I realized that Heather's deconstruction is not on me. Before that evening, we had emailed back and forth many times, and I'd answered similar questions and sent her a plethora of good resources to help her study these topics for herself. In retrospect, I think my choice to listen instead of speak was probably the right call. She didn't need more answers in that moment. She needed to know that she was loved and that someone cared about what she had been through. But for argument's sake, let's say I *did* totally blow it by failing to offer answers to the significant questions and challenges she brought up over dinner. Her deconstruction still isn't on me. I am not Heather's savior. I am not Jesus. I am not the Holy Spirit. My failures, the gaps in my intellectual knowledge, and my inability to communicate clearly are not the reasons she deconstructed.

Perhaps as you're reading this book you're feeling an avalanche of emotions regarding your friends and loved ones who are in deconstruction. Maybe you feel guilt and shame over your failures. Maybe you feel that if you had just done more, said more, or been a better example, this wouldn't be happening. We want to help you with that. In this chapter, we'll talk through some practical steps you can take as you walk with a loved one through this painful process.

STEP ONE: PRAY

Now might be a good time to remind ourselves of the rich and valuable truth found in Philippians 4:4-9:

> Rejoice in the Lord always; again I will say, rejoice. Let your reasonableness be known to everyone. The Lord is at hand; do not be anxious about anything, but in everything by prayer and supplication with thanksgiving let your requests be made known to God. And the peace of God, which surpasses all understanding, will guard your hearts and your minds in Christ Jesus.
> Finally, brothers, whatever is true, whatever

is honorable, whatever is just, whatever is pure, whatever is lovely, whatever is commendable, if there is any excellence, if there is anything worthy of praise, think about these things. What you have learned and received and heard and seen in me— practice these things, and the God of peace will be with you.

We are reminded to always rejoice. *Always.* That's difficult to do when we are anxious about the spiritual lives of our loved ones. So what does the Bible instruct us to do? Make our requests known to God with thanksgiving in our hearts. Then he promises to give us his peace, which goes beyond anything we could ever understand. Isn't it wonderful that when we feel worried or stressed, we are instructed to abandon anxiety and go to God in prayer? He promises to be with us, to hear us, to consider our requests, and to grant us peace that surpasses a mind spinning with questions and confusion. We will offer a specific prayer you can pray over your deconstructing friend or loved one in chapter 13.

STEP TWO: STAY CALM AND STAY IN THEIR LIFE

As we learned in chapter 5, people often find themselves in deconstruction after a crisis or a series of crises, which can be complex and layered. It can be tempting to try to fix their theology over a coffee date or to react emotionally, especially if the one who is deconstructing is lashing out with accusations against the church, impugning your beliefs, or even mocking Christianity. Maybe they are deconstructing quietly and haven't openly shared their struggles but are simply exhibiting signs of deconstruction. If you have a loved one who is even talking with you about their deconstruction, be very thankful. That is huge! The most important thing you can do is to stay calm. Take a deep breath. Don't freak out. Don't jump in to try to "fix" them. Whether or not they are open about their deconstruction, it's likely a fragile situation, and you don't want to react argumentatively or fearfully. It's important to keep in mind that their deconstruction didn't happen overnight, and it most likely won't be resolved overnight. Your goal should be to keep the lines of communication open. You might say something like, "Thank you for being so open and honest with me. This was probably very difficult for you, and I want you to know that I appreciate you coming to me, knowing my beliefs. I love you and I'm here for you."

When you are in step two, you have permission to *not* try to persuade them toward right theology. You may have a very fragile window of opportunity to simply stay in their life. They probably already know what you believe. After all, they may have grown up in your home or in your church. Some families and friends will be in step two for a long time. It might take weeks, months, or even years for the deconstructing person to come to a place where they are ready to hear your point of view. Use this time to understand the faith crisis your loved one is facing. Maybe there has been spiritual abuse. Maybe there is deep confusion over Christian hypocrisy. Maybe they are suffering and feel God is absent. This would be a good time to live out Romans 12:15, which instructs the Christian to "weep with those who weep." Give them space to process what is happening.

However, in many cases, the one in deconstruction has already concluded that Christian theology is toxic or that the church is not a safe place. It's common for deconstructors to shut out the environment of the faith tradition they grew up in and deconstruct online with others who are on a similar journey. While you're in step two, try to establish yourself as a safe person for them to talk to. This will require immense patience and consistent graciousness. But you must set realistic expectations. There's a chance they will never see you as "safe" simply because your beliefs are morally repugnant to them. In fact, there may be someone who is hiding their deconstruction from you for this very reason. Whether you know or simply suspect that a loved one is in deconstruction, the best thing you can do is live out the beauty of the gospel consistently and without compromise. Let them see the fruit of the Spirit overflowing from your life. In Galatians 5, Paul unpacks what it means to walk by the Spirit, which is the opposite of walking by the flesh. Walking in the flesh will manifest in all sorts of sexual immorality, fits of anger, dissension, and strife (verses 19-21). But a true Christian will bear the fruit of "love, joy, peace, patience, kindness, goodness, faithfulness, gentleness, self-control" (verses 22-23). Model the beautiful fruit the gospel has produced in your life. Maybe you haven't always been the best example of these

> *Whether you know or simply suspect that a loved one is in deconstruction, the best thing you can do is live out the beauty of the gospel consistently and without compromise.*

things. In that case, model repentance! Let your life demonstrate what humility and grace look like when worked out in a biblical manner.

Many in the deconstruction movement believe Christians are fearful, simpleminded, and reactionary. Be the opposite. Break the stereotype. Pray and ask God to help you fully and unconditionally love those in your life who are in deconstruction. Ask the Lord to help you demonstrate the fruit of peace and joy as you live out the beauty of the gospel in front of them. You may be in step two for years before the relationship is ready to move into step three. For others of you, step two will move quickly and naturally into step three or even overlap.

STEP THREE: DO SOME TRIAGE

In a hospital, triage is the process of assessing the urgency and significance of someone's injuries before deciding which wounds to treat first and in what order. Similarly, when someone is in deconstruction, there can be several different variables to consider.

What is your relationship (friend/parent/spouse)?
Do you have a close enough relationship that a
    conversation would be welcome?
How old is the person who is deconstructing?
What do they mean by deconstruction?
Have they been hurt by the church?
Are they struggling with their sexuality?
Have they concluded that biblical ethics are oppressive?

Are they confused about certain passages of Scripture in the Old Testament?

This would be a good time to do some digging so that when the person is ready, the issues can be addressed in order of urgency.

For example, imagine a scenario in which sexual abuse by a youth pastor causes a young woman to not only question what the youth pastor taught her about Jesus, but also to wrestle with how a good God could allow such an evil to occur in the first place. Church does not feel like a safe place to her, and her immediate needs call for practical help such as alerting the authorities, getting her good counseling, and protecting her and others from further harm. This isn't the time to bring out intellectual arguments for God's existence and goodness. She needs to see that goodness lived out in the lives of the Christians around her. She needs to experience genuine Christians loving her, caring for her, protecting her, and holding her abuser accountable.

Imagine another scenario in which a young couple wants to move in together before they are married and can't understand why the church would be so old-fashioned as to not bless their plans. They begin to question the biblical sexual ethic, which leads them to reinterpret the Bible's commands regarding sexual relationships. This leads them to reassess the Scriptures on several other topics. Before they know it, they are "Christian" in name, but they've thrown out the exclusivity of the gospel and have aligned their ethics with the popular ideas of culture. In this case, the couple needs to be lovingly confronted by the Christians around them and invited to repent and turn to Christ in submission to his Word. As you can see, these are two very different situations that require very specific courses of action.

The first step in the deconstruction triage is to figure out what someone even means by *deconstruction*. Here's a hypothetical scenario: Johnny comes home from youth camp and announces to his Christian parents that he is in deconstruction. His parents say, "Thanks for sharing that with us. What do you mean by deconstruction?" Turns out, Johnny heard from some friends that deconstruction is a way of making sure you believe what is true. For him, it's a healthy process of thinking through what he's been taught and making his faith his own. In that case, the parents would be wise to see this as a wonderful opportunity to actively disciple their son, teach him discernment, and help him think critically about his beliefs. It would also be a teaching moment to gently nudge him in the direction of analyzing the word *deconstruction*. They could show him what most people mean when they use that word and how it almost always ends in a move away from essential Christian beliefs. They could compliment him on his desire to make his faith his own and encourage him to use a more biblical word like *discernment* or *reformation* to describe the process.

Here's a very different hypothetical scenario: Ruth and David grew up in church together. Both were actively involved in youth group and never really questioned what they believed. They married right after high school. A few years and two kids into their marriage, David determined that the Christian sexual ethic was oppressive to his LGBTQ+ friends. Months turned into years as he quietly wrestled with his beliefs. He gave little clues here and there with offhand comments and jokes, but he didn't tell Ruth how his beliefs had changed. Even so, she perceived his shift in beliefs and began digging deeper into what and why she believed. Her views also changed, but in the opposite direction. She felt more confident in the reliability of the Bible, which caused her to trust the entire Bible as the authoritative Word of God. His views on what the Bible says about sexuality changed, which caused him to question the validity and authority of the rest of the Bible. This led him to rethink the very definition of Christianity. Over time, he came to embrace a more progressive type of Christianity and finally told Ruth he was deconstructing.

At this point, Ruth would be wise to stay calm and thank David for letting her know what was going on with him. In many ways, David's deconstruction had been and would be just as painful for Ruth as it had been for him. What once united them as a couple could now potentially divide them, destroy their marriage, and affect the spiritual lives of their kids. If that happened, Ruth would have to walk the challenging road of living out her Christian beliefs with kindness and without compromise. She would need to seek out the support and community of strong believers around her. She would have to actively disciple her kids, knowing she no longer had the support of her husband, who would likely be attempting to undermine their faith in the authority of Scripture. She would have to struggle through living the reality of 1 Peter 3:1: "Wives, in the same way submit yourselves to your husbands so that, if any of them do not believe the word, they may be won over without words by the behavior of their wives" (NIV). Because of the nature of the marriage relationship, Ruth might have more of an open door to reason with her husband than a parent of an adult child would have. But it would also introduce a new set of complex and difficult questions that would require godly discernment, wisdom, and courage.

STEP FOUR: SET BOUNDARIES (AND RESPECT THEIRS)

Each deconstruction is different, which means the advice we give here will need to be considered, adapted, and accepted or even rejected depending on certain variables. (This is why the triage step is so important.) Setting healthy boundaries will be an important part of protecting the relationship while safeguarding yourself against undue anxiety and stress. As in the triage step, there are some questions to ask to help analyze what types of boundaries you might need to put in place.

How close is your relationship with the person in
  deconstruction?
Is this a family relationship or one that is more casual?
Are you bringing up issues of faith every time you see
  this person?
Should you back off a bit?
Should you speak up more?
Are you being a good listener?
What has the person's response been?
Is your own faith eroding because of their influence?
How is this affecting others in your family or circle of
  friends?

Is the loved one asking you to affirm something that is
not true?

Have they asked you not to bring up spiritual issues?

Have *they* drawn a boundary with you, letting you know
they are not open to discussing matters of faith?

As you can see, the questions are almost endless. Here are
a couple of scenarios to consider.

John and Rick have been best friends since elementary
school. They grew up in the same church and attended the
same youth group, even going on the same mission trips and
summer-camp excursions. Now Rick is about three months
into his first semester at college. Between what he is reading
in his evolutionary biology class and his history of religion
class, Rick has begun to question everything he was ever
taught about God. Combine that with the moral liberties he
sees his fellow classmates indulging in, and he begins to wonder if Christianity is really just a toxic authoritarian system
put in place to control the voting bloc and restrict people's
sex lives. Before you know it, Rick is in deconstruction and
tells John he has become an agnostic. This is the first time
John has been meaningfully confronted with intellectual and
moral arguments against the faith he grew up with. As Rick
shares his process over a period of a few months, John feels
like he can barely keep up with the laundry list of historical,
philosophical, and scientific claims against Christianity.

By the time Rick brings up a new issue, John has barely
skimmed the surface of the last one. John is beginning to feel
overwhelmed by all the information and is concerned that
his own faith might be headed toward deconstruction. In this

case, it's okay for John to press the pause button with Rick. A good boundary for John might be to say, "Rick, I appreciate that you're thinking these things through. I want to think through them also. But I need some time. I still haven't been able to investigate for myself all the issues you brought up last time we spoke. I need you to wait a couple of months before bringing up another argument." This way, John isn't closing the door on the conversation, and he isn't shutting Rick out of his life. He is simply drawing a boundary, putting spiritual conversations on hold until he can catch his breath and do some of his own research.

In another scenario, Charles and Jennifer are Christians with four young children. They are active members in their church community, along with their niece Laura. Over the past couple of years, Laura has stopped attending church and has been posting memes on social media that mock Christian teaching about sexuality. She posts diatribes accusing the church of oppressing LGBTQ+ people and has started dressing in a more masculine way. She is now living as a man and goes by Landon. Laura/Landon will be coming to Charles and Jennifer's house for the first time in a year and has made it clear that this new identity must be affirmed or there will be no relationship going forward. In this case, it might be wise for Charles and Jennifer to talk with Laura/Landon and reason some things through before the visit. They might say something like, "Please hear our hearts and try to understand where we're coming from. We would never want to do anything to hurt

Every deconstruction is unique, and each relationship dynamic requires wisdom.

you or ostracize you. We love you. We want you to be part of our family. But can you understand the difficult position this puts us in, especially with how we explain this to the kids? You are asking us to use pronouns that go against our conscience. You are asking us to guide our children to do the same. We respect your right to live as you choose. Can you respect our right not to affirm something we don't believe is right? Is there a way we can remain in relationship without using these pronouns?"

It's possible that Laura/Landon will not understand and will end the relationship. That is a sad reality, but when we draw healthy boundaries, sometimes these types of situations will occur. Charles and Jennifer can respect this boundary by giving Laura/Landon space. The family can continue to show love through prayer and a readiness to reestablish contact.

While in step four, pray and ask the Lord to give you guidance and wisdom to know which boundaries to draw, which ones to respect, and how to walk through each relationship with grace and love.

Every deconstruction is unique, and each relationship dynamic requires wisdom. Thankfully, wisdom is one of those things God promises to give to those who simply ask: "If any of you lacks wisdom, let him ask God, who gives generously to all without reproach, and it will be given him" (James 1:5). As you move through each of these steps with your loved one, ask God for wisdom and surround yourself with wise and godly Christians who can support you and pray for you.

I 3

SATURDAY

WE SHOULDN'T BE WRITING A BOOK about deconstruction—
at least not the kind that discourages it.

ALISA

I should be standing hand in hand with the mass exodus of
exvangelicals flocking to social media to share their deconversion stories and placing the hashtag #deconstruction promi-
nently in their bios. I *should* be one of them.

I used to be a Christian pop star. It feels silly to write that
down, but among my many vocations such as professional
cheerleading instructor, restaurant hostess, softball coach,
youth center director, juice bar operator, Starbucks barista,
worship leader, cookie entrepreneur, and makeup artist (I

once applied powder to Steven Curtis Chapman's nose at a TBN gig, so that counts, right?), the time I spent as a contemporary Christian music artist is my biggest claim to fame. As one-third of the teen pop group ZOEgirl, I toured the country and experienced just about every type of commercial Christianity you could imagine during the early 2000s. I also encountered the good, the bad, and the downright ugly in the church.

My memories are filled with sales conventions where showrooms with dozens of fold-out tables were lined up in rows, covered with branded tablecloths, and arrayed with all manner of "Jesus junk," as we called it. Gum, mints, jewelry, mini-figurines, refrigerator magnets, coffee-table books, plush toys, T-shirts, bookmarks, and just about every other type of trinket you can think of were stamped with Bible verses and engraved with crosses and doves. I always felt the tension when we were escorted to a signing table or meet-and-greet booth where people would wait in line to meet us, only to be shuffled through like a herd of cattle. "One item per person, please! We can't stop for photographs, so just take them as you walk by," our handlers would announce to the line of CCM fans eagerly awaiting their big moment.

We are Christians. This doesn't seem right. We should be different from the world, I thought as I took my place behind a signing table after a concert one night early in our career. I had just protested to one of the higher-ups, "I don't want to do this. It feels wrong. We should be glorifying Jesus, not sitting behind barriers signing autographs." He reassured me that if we didn't do it, the people would think we were stuck-up and would be angry that they didn't get what they came for. After all, "So-and-So (famous artist) does it," and "The Such and Such (famous band) do it." So I did it. For almost a decade. It never felt right. (To this day, I'm always happy to sign a book if someone asks, but I generally avoid sitting behind a table to have people walk by in a hurried manner.)

Along with the shallowness of some commercial aspects of evangelical Christianity, I experienced the ugly. One of the final tours ZOEgirl participated in was a heavily marketed and well-funded event produced by a globally recognized women's ministry and promoted to middle school and high school–aged girls. Every word was scripted, the imaging was finely tuned, and the marketing was precisely branded. As it was presented to us, the goal would be to end each conference with a gospel presentation inviting these young girls to surrender their lives to Jesus. That sounded great, but as the conference got off the ground, I became uncomfortable with some of the messaging.

My discomfort grew into disgust when one of the visiting bigwigs said to me, "We've been researching this product for a long time. We're really excited." Did he actually refer to an event that culminates in a gospel presentation as a *product*? Yes, he did. But make no mistake; I never heard the gospel preached. The message I picked up sounded more like "Make Jesus your BFF today, and God will like totally help you in your life." It was painful. I was sitting next to one of the highest-paid and most well-known female Christian artists of the time when this "gospel" was presented for the first time. She looked at me and sharply whispered, "What?! *That* is not the gospel. What are they doing? No way. This is not okay." After the show, she promptly marched backstage and gave someone a talking-to. I noticed that the next time the gospel was presented, the speaker actually mentioned repentance and salvation. I suppose when the biggest name on your program balks, you'll make some changes. Even preach the gospel.

My bandmate Chrissy was asked to share her testimony (scripted, of course), and during a certain part of her story, her wedding picture was flashed onto the jumbotron. The photo showed her bright blue eyes sparkling into the camera, while her blonde hair contrasted with her husband's rich brown Samoan skin. When the tour made its way to the deep South, one of the people in charge came into our dressing room and let us know they wouldn't be showing the wedding picture that night because they didn't want to "offend" anyone.

If events and attitudes like this are what people think Christianity is, it's no wonder they are leaving the faith in droves. If I had thought *this* was Christianity, I'd have wanted nothing to do with it either. I'm so thankful that I had been given the real gospel and knew authentic Christians from all sorts of cultural, ethnic, and denominational backgrounds. Otherwise that experience alone could have thrown me into deconstruction right then and there. But I knew better. This was big business dressed up as Christianity; it wasn't *genuine* Christianity. My faith crisis wouldn't come until a couple of years later.

There are some things they don't tell you about what it's like to be a touring Christian artist. When you're plucky, ambitious, and young, you imagine how satisfying and fulfilling it will be to reach multiple thousands of people for

Christ with your music. I don't want to sell that part short. In many ways, it was satisfying. But mostly, being in the CCM industry makes you cynical, hard, and jaded—unless you fight wholeheartedly against those traits. I toured with CCM artists who did that well. They would wake up early, complete a workout, and do their Bible study before hitting a local coffee shop early enough to make it back in time for a sound check. They had pastors on their tour buses and strict rules regarding expected behavior from their staff.

I (insert nervous laughter) was not (wince) one of those people. Every tour, I started out with good intentions. For about two whole days I would wake up by 10 a.m. (cut me a break—I was twenty-five, and midmorning was practically the crack of dawn for a flaky artist), study my Bible and the massive *Strong's Concordance* I brought on the tour bus, and spend some time in prayer and reflection for the day. But by the end of the tour, I was going to bed at 6 a.m. and rolling out of my bunk just in time for our 3 p.m. sound check. When the tour would come back to Nashville for a few days off, I would spend most of the time by myself in my small apartment bingeing on video games or movies. Some of that time was spent pondering and recovering from nasty notes that would be passed to our tour manager about how our pants were too tight or how we "looked too sexy to be Christian artists." I didn't mean to look sexy. Sometimes the pants were tight because I ate too much after-show pizza and couldn't afford another pair.

I became depressed. Like really depressed. By the end, I was barely functioning. Every mom who passed through the autograph line with helpful tips like "Girls, you better stay strong and not fall. My daughter looks up to you" put bricks on my back that no mere mortal could bear. It's hard to admit all this because I truly loved looking into the eyes of every little ZOEgirl fan who looked up to me. I loved them. They were the reason I kept going for so long. But if you combine depression, the tension of celebrity, the shallowness of so much of the commercial Christian world, the full realization of your own brokenness, and some bad church experiences, you are ripe for deconstruction.

Still, I never thought I would ever doubt *my* faith. But after ZOEgirl came off the road and life settled down, my husband and I began attending a local church in Middle Tennessee. I went to a small and exclusive study group at the invitation of the pastor, and in a whirlwind of unexpected events, I ended up tiptoeing to the edge of agnosticism. I chronicle this journey in *Another Gospel?: A Lifelong Christian Seeks Truth in Response to Progressive Christianity*. In that book, I use the word *deconstruction* to describe my experience. It was the best word I had at the time. But after researching and writing this book, I no longer use that word to characterize what I walked through. Now that I've witnessed a word turning into a hashtag that exploded into a movement that is not about lining up one's beliefs with what corresponds to reality, I realize that isn't what happened to me. I didn't want to orient my beliefs around my personal opinion of what was good, helpful, or liberating. I wanted to know what was true, and it took years of questioning and studying to start figuring it out. As soon as I would crack the lid off one question, a dozen more would erupt and overshadow the one I had just asked. It wasn't a deconstruction in the way we see it manifest today, but it was the most disorienting, painful, and isolating experience of my life. It left me walking with a limp, a little more skeptical than I'd once been. But as I wrote in the book, "I'd rather walk with a limp on solid ground than run with strong legs on breaking ice."[1]

Even though I've seen her dark side, I love the church. I love Jesus' bride. I will not abandon her. As Christians, we are one big family—the body of Christ—but families can be complicated. We all have that annoying uncle who makes us stress-eat mashed potatoes at Thanksgiving. But we love him, God help us, even when he waxes on about how entitled young people are today. I love my brothers and sisters in Christ. Even the obnoxious-uncle ones. But I admit I'm still a little uncomfortable walking into church. She and I have a complicated relationship. I still tend to sit in the back and watch from afar. I still have a way to go. But that is why I wanted to write *this* book. I've been to the other side, and I hope to encourage you that if someone you love is in deconstruction, *there is hope.* God grabbed hold of me in the darkest night of doubt, even when I couldn't feel him, touch him, or experience him. Even when I thought he didn't exist, he was always there, walking me here—to you. That same God can do the same for your friend or loved one. That is my prayer.

> *God grabbed hold of me in the darkest night of doubt. Even when I thought he didn't exist, he was always there, walking me here—to you. He can do the same for your friend or loved one.*

TIM

I shouldn't be writing a book about deconstruction either—because unlike Alisa, I've never experienced a life-altering crisis of faith or a deconstruction. Serious questions? Sure. Agonizing doubts? You bet. But I wouldn't describe my experience as deconstruction.

I was blessed to grow up in a loving Christian home. We attended a small Free Methodist church in the country, where the parsonage and church were surrounded by farmland on all sides. If the wind was blowing, you would likely catch a whiff of manure. We lived in town about twenty-five minutes away, so this wasn't a church we went to out of convenience. We probably passed a half dozen churches to get there. But this was the church my mom had attended her whole life and where my dad became a Christian. We had history there.

Everyone in the church was really close. This church wasn't *like* family. It *was* family—literally. Nearly a third of the congregation was made up of my aunts, uncles, and cousins. And the rest treated us like family. I have many fond memories of potlucks, hayrides, caroling, candlelight Christmas Eve services, testimony times, Sunday school picnics, and the annual Christmas programs, where I usually played the lead role.

My family didn't have much as I was growing up. When my parents couldn't afford the down payment on our first house, the bank wouldn't give them a loan—but a couple in the church did. There were Christmases when money was tight, and the people in this church helped put gifts under our tree. I get choked up now even thinking about it. These were beautiful people who showed me the beauty of Christ.

Despite my mostly good church experience growing up, my faith was tested in 2000. Our beloved pastor revealed he'd been having an affair with a woman he was counseling. Just a year before, I'd lost my grandma after her long battle with severe arthritis. She was only sixty-six years old. I watched her go from hosting dozens of people each week at the family farm to being confined to a chair all day. While my grandma's death brought devastating grief, I was comforted by the hope of her future resurrection. My pastor's infidelity was different. I felt betrayed, angry, and bewildered. How could a pastor—a "man of God"—do something like this?

I still have lots of questions. As long as there is mystery, there will be unanswered questions. But as long as there is a risen Savior, there is hope.

I still have lots of questions. Christianity isn't tidy, and neither is the church. As long as there is a church, there will be church hurt. As long as there is a cursed creation, there will be suffering. As long as there is mystery, there will be unanswered questions. But as long as there is a risen Savior, there is *hope*. And that's what I want to leave you with. I want to share a story of hope.

On the morning of March 1, 2018, I got a call I'll never forget. "Your grandpa's kidneys aren't functioning properly, and it's not looking good," my mom told me over the phone. I knew my grandpa's health wasn't great, but this news still came as a shock. My wife and I packed our three daughters in our SUV and headed to the hospital.

On the way, we began prepping my daughters with the reality that this might be the last time they would ever see their great-grandpa. Attempting to encourage us, my six-year-old daughter said, "Don't worry, we will see him again in heaven." Her words brought me to tears. But rather than offering support, they produced overwhelming sorrow. You see, my grandpa had not believed in Jesus to receive eternal life (John 3:16), and time was running out.

When we got to the hospital, we were surprised to find all of my extended family in the lobby. We were told that doctors weren't letting anyone in to see Grandpa because they were running tests. As a result, all thirty family members were forced to wait in a cramped lobby. After sitting there for over an hour, we were told my grandpa needed some additional tests that would take another hour or so. Our young girls were getting antsy and hungry, so we decided to take them home.

After a quick bite to eat at home, I picked up my eldest sister, and we headed back to the hospital. I had to fly out the next morning for a student apologetics conference in Dallas, so this would likely be my last opportunity to speak to my grandpa.

That night, God worked in two surprising ways. First, when we got back to the hospital, the lobby was empty. That could mean only one thing: My family—my grandma, aunts, uncles, cousins, parents, and siblings—were all crammed into that little hospital room. My heart sank. You see, that morning after hanging up the phone with my mom, I had prayed that God would give me courage to communicate the gospel to my grandpa one last time. But the prospect of doing that in a room full of my extended family seemed scary, even for a professional speaker. When my sister and I inquired about what room my grandpa was in, the nurses promptly informed us that he had tested positive for tuberculosis and that no one was allowed in his room. The reason my family wasn't in the lobby was because they'd all left for dinner. Since this was possibly my last opportunity to talk to my grandpa, I wasn't leaving without seeing him. So after some persuading, the hospital staff agreed to let us in his room as long as we wore what looked like hazmat suits—medical gowns, gloves, goggles, masks, and face shields.

In our time together, we reminisced about sitting in Grandpa's living room watching *America's Funniest Home Videos* and helping him make his famous homemade pizza. We reminded him that he'd introduced us to fried bologna on our annual camping trip. After my sister and I each shared our fondest memories, we talked about the gospel—how Jesus died for our sins so that we could have eternal life. Quite surprisingly, my grandpa received it with joy. If I'm honest, I couldn't believe what I was hearing. When I was growing up, my grandpa had no interest in Christianity. Any attempt to talk about spiritual things was quickly shut down. Sharing the gospel seemed like a lost cause. Frankly, the closest he came to showing religious devotion was in his love for the Toronto Maple Leafs.

It isn't supposed to be this easy, I thought to myself as our conversation came to a close. After all, he didn't raise any objections. He didn't change the subject. He simply believed. After praying with my grandpa, my sister and I left his hospital room overwhelmed by God's goodness. God had answered my prayer in two ways: He providentially orchestrated the opportunity to share the gospel. Then he saved my grandpa.

A day that started out hope*less* ended hope*ful*. God did "far more abundantly than all that we ask or think" (Ephesians 3:20).

The next morning, I boarded my flight to Dallas, and as I sat waiting for takeoff, I got a text from my mom: "Your grandpa passed away in his sleep."

We pray this true story offers you some hope. Your loved one's story isn't over yet. My grandpa put his trust in Jesus to forgive his sins and give him eternal life *just a few hours before his death*. You may think your situation is impossible, but that's where God does his best work.

LIVING IN THE SATURDAY

After Jesus was betrayed by Judas and arrested in Gethsemane, Mark records, "And they all left him and fled" (Mark 14:50). All of Jesus' closest friends abandoned him. They were all gone—including Peter. Earlier in Jesus' ministry, when many people were turning away from him, Jesus asked Peter if he was going to leave too. Peter replied, "Lord, to whom shall we go? You have the words of eternal life" (John 6:68). Remember, Peter was adamant that he would "never fall away," telling Jesus, "Even if I must die with you, I will not deny you!" (Matthew 26:33, 35). That's a confident confession. Yet, when push came to shove and the pressure was on, Peter did deny Jesus. Three times. "But he [Peter] began to invoke a curse on himself and to swear, 'I do not know this man of whom you speak'" (Mark 14:71). By Friday night, Peter's world was turned upside down. His leader was dead. His expectations about the Kingdom of God had been crushed. His faith in Jesus had been rocked. That was Friday.

Of course, we know what happened on Sunday. Speaking to the women at the tomb, an angel brought the good news: "He has risen; he is not here" (Mark 16:6). And then the angel continued, "But go, tell his disciples and Peter that he is going before you to Galilee. There you will see him, just as he told you" (verse 7). Sunday brought hope and healing. That was Sunday.

But what about Saturday? We aren't told much about Saturday, so we can only speculate. Have you ever wondered what was going through Peter's mind? Did he start "deconstructing" his beliefs? Did he feel guilty for denying Jesus? Did he question some of the miracles Jesus had done? Maybe he looked back and tried to find a natural explanation for what he had experienced. Maybe he questioned Jesus' identity and teaching. After all, how could the real Messiah be crucified?

Perhaps you have loved ones who have experienced a crisis of faith and are living in a "Saturday." Like Peter, they may have unanswered questions, they may be suffering, they may be feeling abandoned and alone, they may be uncertain about what they've been taught. But here's what we know about Peter: Although all hope seemed lost on Saturday, Sunday was around the corner. And Sunday brought hope and led him to a stronger, lasting faith. If it can happen for Peter, then it can happen for you or your loved one too.

IFFY PRAYER

The Gospel of Mark records a story about a desperate dad who comes to Jesus in a last-ditch effort to get his son healed. The boy has a demon that's destroying his life. The father first seeks out Jesus' disciples, but they aren't able to help. Then he comes to Jesus and pleads, "But if you can do anything, have compassion on us and help us" (Mark 9:22). Notice the uncertainty of the father's request: "if you can." You might feel like this hopeless parent. Maybe Jesus' followers have let *you* down. Maybe you've tried everything, but your loved one's situation hasn't changed. Maybe the only faith you can muster up begins with a big "if." That's okay because Jesus doesn't turn away from iffy prayers. Responding to this father, Jesus says, "'If you can'! All things are possible for one who believes" (Mark 9:23). Commenting on this passage, author and pastor John Ortberg writes, "This man has iffy faith and prays an iffy prayer. When Jesus points this out, a response comes out of this man's mouth so fast that it is like an eruption, because this is exactly his quandary. His hope dangles by a slender *if.* Immediately the boy's father exclaims, 'I do believe; help me overcome my unbelief!' (Mark 9:24)."[2]

And Jesus heals the boy. Many of you feel like that father. You believe, but you also need help because of your unbelief. The task seems too desperate, too hopeless, too impossible. But all things are possible with God, even if your faith is small and struggling.

Some have called this father's plea the Doubter's Prayer. We'd like to close this book by offering a Deconstructor's

Prayer; that is, a prayer you can pray for those who are going through deconstruction.

Father in heaven, you are worthy of all praise,
honor, and glory. You are all-powerful, all-good, and
all-loving. You know the end from the beginning.
You know what lies deep in the heart and mind of
_____, who is in deconstruction. You know
the causes, the confusion, and the circumstances that
have led them to doubt the reality of your Word, your
plan, and your gospel. I ask you to lead them to Truth
and heal all wounds. I ask that you use me in this
process and give me wisdom to know what to say and
when to say it. Shine your light on me and convict me if
I have sinned against my loved one that I might repent
and model that repentance to them. I trust you with my
loved one and ask that you save them. Help me to trust
you with this relationship, knowing that you work all
things together for good for those who love you and are
called according to your purpose. May the beauty of the
gospel be on display in my life that it might be beautiful
to all who see.

In Jesus' name, amen.

Acknowledgments

We (Alisa and Tim) would like to thank the many people who gave of their time, energy, and intellectual prowess to help make this project the best it can be. Dave Wolcott, for the valuable research and encouragement throughout the writing process. Bec Andrew and Sharon Core, for helping with research. Amy Hall and Greg Koukl, for going through every line of the manuscript and offering such valuable feedback and editing suggestions. All who read sections of the book and offered valuable feedback (their assistance does not necessarily imply endorsement of the entire book or its conclusions): Neil Shenvi, Carl Trueman, Nancy Pearcey, Doug Groothuis. Your insights and corrections were invaluable. A special thanks to those who allowed us to share their stories. Our agent, Bill Jensen, for your constant encouragement, spiritual guidance, and advocacy. This would not have happened without you! Ron Beers, Jon Farrar, Kim Miller, Annette Hayward, Cassidy Gage, Katie Dodillet, and the rest of our remarkable team at Tyndale, we are deeply thankful for your belief in and support of this book, along with your relentless attention to detail, editing excellence, promotion, and PR.

I (Alisa) would like to thank my husband, Mike, and our kids for your constant support, encouragement, and prayer. Tim, we did it! Thanks for giving your energy and brilliance to this project.

I (Tim) am thankful to my wonderful colleagues at Stand to Reason, who constantly challenge me to think more deeply about my Christian convictions. You are an incredible team who have played a major role in shaping me into an ambassador for Christ.

I want to thank Alisa for replying to that original text message that launched this whole project. Your hunger for the truth and your heart for the lost inspire me. I couldn't ask for a better coauthor and guide through the wild world of book publishing.

I'm especially grateful to "my girls," Julianna, Jocelyn, and Alison. My desire to see you stand firm in the faith served as my motivation for this book.

Finally and foremost, this book wouldn't be possible without my wife, Stacey. Writing a book is hard work. There were times when it took its toll. As a result, there were missed family meals and bedtime stories, stressful days and restless nights, and, if I'm honest, times when I wanted to give up. Yet, through it all, you gave me endless patience, abundant grace, and constant encouragement. You are more than I deserve.

Notes

CHAPTER 1: EXPLOSION

1. Michael Foust, "Skillet's John Cooper: It's Time to 'Declare War' on the Deconstruction Movement," ChristianHeadlines.com, February 10, 2022, https://www.christianheadlines.com/contributors/michael-foust/skillets-john-cooper-its-time-to-declare-war-on-the-deconstruction-movement.html. See also Tyler Huckabee, "Skillet's John Cooper: It's Time to 'Declare War against This Deconstruction Christian Movement,'" *Relevant*, February 9, 2022, https://relevantmagazine.com/current/skillets-john-cooper-its-time-to-declare-war-against-this-deconstruction-christian-movement/.

2. Jesse T. Jackson, "John Cooper Responds to Ex-Christian Jon Steingard's Question regarding Declaring War on Deconstruction Movement," ChurchLeaders, February 11, 2022, https://churchleaders.com/news/417092-former-christian-jon-steingard-responds-john-cooper-for-declaring-war-on-deconstruction-movement-skillets-frontman-responds.html.

3. Huckabee, "Skillet's John Cooper"; James Walden and Greg Willson, "What Would Jesus Deconstruct?," TGC website for The Gospel Coalition, February 14, 2022, https://www.thegospelcoalition.org/article/what-would-jesus-deconstruct/; Josh Shepherd, "Christian Rocker John Cooper 'Declares War' on Deconstruction, Provokes Controversy," Roys Report, February 11, 2022, https://julieroys.com/christian-rocker-john-cooper-declares-war-deconstruction-provokes-controversy/; Phil Vischer, "Episode 497: The Progressive Christian Checklist and Ending Online Worship with Tish Harrison Warren," *Holy Post* (blog), February 24, 2022, https://www.holypost.com/post/episode-497-the-progressive-christian-checklist-ending-online-worship-with-tish-harrison-warren.

4. Huckabee, "Skillet's John Cooper."

5. Jackson, "John Cooper Responds."

6. Greg oo Warfare: Truth Encounters," *Stand to Reason* (blog), June 7, 2013, https://www.str.org/w/spiritual-warfare-truth-encounters.

7. Carol Kuruvilla, "Evangelical Songwriter Says He's No Longer Christian in Emotional Instagram Post," *HuffPost*, August 26, 2019, https://www.huffpost.com/entry/marty-sampson-hillsong-christianity-doubt_n_5d605421e4b02cc97c8d8724.

8. "Rhett's Spiritual Deconstruction," *Ear Biscuits* (podcast), February 3, 2020; YouTube video uploaded February 9, 2020, 1:44:50, https://www.youtube.com/watch?v=1qbna6t1bzw&t=85s.

9. Erik Strandness, "Autopsy of a Deconstruction: Jon Steingard and the Foundations of Faith," Patheos, September 10, 2020, https://www.patheos.com/blogs/unbelievable/2020/09/autopsy-of-a-deconstruction-jon-steingard-and-the-foundations-of-faith/.

10. Jeannie Ortega Law, "DC Talk's Kevin Max Says He's an 'Exvangelical': 'Deconstructing' and 'Progressing,'" Christian Post, May 18, 2021, https://www.christianpost.com/news/dc-talks-kevin-max-reveals-hes-an-exvangelical.html.

11. Law, "DC Talk's Kevin Max." See also Gabriel Jones, "Kevin Max Returns!," *Decent Christian Talk* (podcast), December 9, 2020, https://www.youtube.com/watch?v=Rvm2ZOowcNM&t=2s.

12. Richard Rohr, *The Universal Christ: How a Forgotten Reality Can Change Everything We See, Hope For, and Believe* (New York: Convergent, 2019), 18.

13. Leah MarieAnn Klett, "Former Desiring God Writer Paul Maxwell Announces He's No Longer Christian," Christian Post, April 9, 2021, https://www.christianpost.com/news/author-paul-maxwell-announces-he-is-no-longer-a-christian.html.

14. Checked on March 9, 2023.

15. The concept of deconstruction as "an explosion" came from a deconstructionist during a private Zoom meeting.

16. Josh Harris (@harrisjosh), Instagram photo, July 26, 2019, https://www.instagram.com/p/B0ZBrNLH2sl/.

17. A. J. Swoboda, *After Doubt: How to Question Your Faith without Losing It* (Grand Rapids, MI: Brazos Press, 2021), 7.

18. Swoboda, *After Doubt*, 7.

19. "Deconstruction: The Way of Jesus and the Ideologies of the World," Bridgetown Church, YouTube video, 13:54, February 23, 2021, https://www.youtube.com/watch?v=iXniowEdmUQ.

20. Lecrae (@lecrae), Twitter, September 14, 2022, 9:31 a.m., https://twitter.com/lecrae/status/1570057594516955136.

21. Lecrae (@lecrae), Twitter, September 14, 2022, 9:31 a.m., https://twitter.com/lecrae/status/1570057596144320515.

22. Lecrae (@lecrae), Twitter, September 14, 2022, 9:31 a.m., https://twitter
    .com/lecrae/status/1570057596144320515.

23. Lecrae (@lecrae), Twitter, September 14, 2022, 9:31 a.m., https://twitter
    .com/lecrae/status/1570057592595963904.

24. Andrew Kerbs (@deconstruct_everything), Instagram, September 27,
    2022, https://www.instagram.com/p/CjB9cD-Omo8/.

25. Phil Drysdale (@phildrysdale), Instagram meme with post, October 11,
    2022, https://www.instagram.com/p/CjlGQLkMhBO/.

26. David Hayward (@nakedpastor), "My 10 Warnings about the So Called
    Deconstruction Movement," TikTok video, 2:44, December 31, 2021,
    https://www.tiktok.com/@nakedpastor/video/7047917477136813317.

27. Kurtis Vanderpool, "The Age of Deconstruction and Future of the
    Church," *Relevant*, April 7, 2021, https://relevantmagazine.com/faith
    /the-age-of-deconstruction-and-future-of-the-church/.

28. "Teachings of Presidents of the Church: Joseph Smith," chapter 2: "God
    the Eternal Father," website of the Church of Jesus Christ of Latter-Day
    Saints, accessed January 11, 2023, https://www.churchofjesuschrist
    .org/study/manual/teachings-joseph-smith/chapter-2.

29. "Doctrine and Covenants 130," instruction 22, website of the Church
    of Jesus Christ of Latter-Day Saints, accessed January 11, 2023, https://
    www.churchofjesuschrist.org/study/scriptures/dc-testament/dc/130?lang
    =eng&id=22#p22.

30. "Gospel Principles," chapter 47: "Exaltation," website of the Church of
    Jesus Christ of Latter-Day Saints, accessed January 11, 2023, https://
    www.churchofjesuschrist.org/study/manual/gospel-principles/chapter-47
    -exaltation.

31. Amy K. Hall, "Is It Possible Some Mormons Are Saved?," *Stand to Reason*
    (blog), April 3, 2020, https://www.str.org/w/is-it-possible-some-mormons
    -are-saved-?p_l_back_url=%2Fsearch%3Fq%3Dmormon%2Bjesus.

32. "Philosophy: Jacques Derrida," The School of Life, YouTube video, 9:41,
    September 2, 2016, https://www.youtube.com/watch?v=H0tnHr2dqTs.

33. Helen Pluckrose and James Lindsay, *Cynical Theories: How Activist
    Scholarship Made Everything about Race, Gender, and Identity—and Why
    This Harms Everybody* (Durham, NC: Pitchstone Publishing, 2020), 40.

34. Melissa Stewart (@lissajostewart on TikTok), 1:15:17 (quote starts at
    36:06), February 10, 2022, https://podcasts.google.co/feed/aHR0cHM
    6Ly9mZWVkcy5tZWdhcGhvbmUuZm0vQkNFUDM5NDI1MzYzNTg
    /episode/ODU5MjQwNGMtOGE4My0xMWVjLTk3YTAtMjdiN
    2EwZWIyODgx.

35. David Hayward (@nakedpastor), TikTok video, 0:58, February 25, 2023,
    https://www.tiktok.com/@nakedpastor/video/7221937107852430597.

36. Derek Webb (@DerekWebb), Instagram, February 20, 2023,
    www.instagram.com/p/Co6KpW3ui7i/.

37. Julia (@thatlouddeconstructingone), Instagram, November 4, 2021, https://www.instagram.com/p/CV4EnDSrMQZ/.

38. Natasha Crain, *Faithfully Different: Regaining Biblical Clarity in a Secular Culture* (Eugene, OR: Harvest House, 2022), 113.

CHAPTER 2: EXVANGELICAL

1. Eve (@eve_wasframed), TikTok video, 0:07, October 18, 2022, https://www.tiktok.com/@eve_wasframed/video/7155825175823519018.

2. Abraham Piper (@moreabrahampiper), TikTok video, 1:14, October 14, 2022, https://www.tiktok.com/@moreabrahampiper/video/7154426767363853614.

3. Kitt (@firestrong14), Twitter, November 19, 2022, 10:21 a.m., https://twitter.com/firestrong14/status/1594003019036753922.

4. Mamatried (@erynjohnston), Twitter, November 17, 2022, 2:05 p.m., https://twitter.com/erynjohnston/status/1593334614818422784.

5. "Deconstructing My Religion," CBS News video, 26:54, December 1, 2018, https://www.cbsnews.com/video/deconstructing-my-religion/#x.

6. Bradley Onishi, "The Rise of #Exvangelical," Religion and Politics, April 9, 2019, https://religionandpolitics.org/2019/04/09/the-rise-of-exvangelical/; Blake Chastain, "Evangelicals: You're Still Not Really Listening to What Exvangelicals Are Saying," Religion News Service, August 28, 2021, https://religionnews.com/2021/08/28/evangelicals-youre-still-not-really-listening-to-what-exvangelicals-are-saying/.

7. Carl Trueman, *The Real Scandal of the Evangelical Mind* (Chicago: Moody, 2011), 12.

8. See David W. Bebbington, *Evangelicalism in Modern Britain: A History from the 1730s to the 1980s* (London: Routledge, 1989), 2–3.

9. "The State of Theology," statements 7, 3, and 31, respectively, accessed January 11, 2023, https://thestateoftheology.com/.

10. Trueman, *Real Scandal of the Evangelical Mind*, 12.

11. Blake Chastain, "'Exvangelical'—A Working Definition," *Exvangelical* (blog), March 2, 2019, https://www.exvangelicalpodcast.com/blog/exvangelical-a-working-definition/.

12. Chastain, "'Exvangelical'—A Working Definition."

13. *Merriam-Webster*, s.v. "literal (*adj.*)," accessed January 11, 2023, https://www.merriam-webster.com/dictionary/literal.

14. Chastain, "'Exvangelical'—A Working Definition."

15. Hillary Morgan Ferrer with Amy Davison, *Mama Bear Apologetics Guide to Sexuality: Empowering Your Kids to Understand and Live Out God's Design* (Eugene, OR: Harvest House, 2021), 29.

16. Chastain, "'Exvangelical'—A Working Definition."

17. Dictionary.com, s.v. "nationalism (*n.*)," accessed January 11, 2023, https://www.dictionary.com/browse/nationalism.

18. "Christians against Christian Nationalism" statement, Christians against Christian Nationalism website, accessed January 11, 2023, https://www.christiansagainstchristiannationalism.org/statement.

19. Emily Judd, "The Threat of White Christian Nationalism Explored in New YDS Podcast," Yale Divinity School News, September 13, 2021, https://divinity.yale.edu/news/threat-white-christian-nationalism-explored-new-yds-podcast.

20. Douglas R. Groothuis, *Fire in the Streets: How You Can Confidently Respond to Incendiary Cultural Topics* (Washington, DC: Salem Books, 2022), xiv.

21. Kurtis Vanderpool, "The Age of Deconstruction and Future of the Church," *Relevant*, April 7, 2021, https://relevantmagazine.com/faith/the-age-of-deconstruction-and-future-of-the-church/.

CHAPTER 3: RERUN

1. Martin B. Copenhaver, *Jesus Is the Question: The 307 Questions Jesus Asked and the 3 He Answered* (Nashville, TN: Abingdon Press, 2014).

2. Quoted in Carly Mayberry, "Josh Harris Launches Course on Deconstructing Faith, but Some Theologians Question His Motives," *Newsweek*, August 13, 2021, https://www.newsweek.com/josh-harris-launches-course-deconstructing-faith-some-theologians-question-his-motives-1619263.

3. Some might protest that Jesus is the primary revelation of what God is like. Of course, that's true. But everything we know about Jesus comes from God's Word.

4. "The State of Theology," statements 4, 15, 31, and 7, respectively, accessed January 11, 2023, https://thestateoftheology.com/.

5. Genesis 9; 12; 15; Exodus 19; 24; 2 Samuel 7; Jeremiah 31:31-34; and Luke 22:14-23.

6. James Strong, *Strong's Concordance*, s.v. "echō," https://biblehub.com/greek/2192.htm.

7. James Strong, *Strong's Concordance*, s.v. "tēreō," https://biblehub.com/greek/5083.htm.

8. Douglas K. Stuart, *Exodus: An Exegetical and Theological Exposition of Holy Scripture*, vol. 2 of *The New American Commentary* (Nashville, TN: B&H, 2006), 555.

9. Introduction to Thomas Jefferson, *The Jefferson Bible: The Life and Morals of Jesus of Nazareth*, accessed April 22, 2023, https://thejeffersonbible.com.

10. This is referred to as "expressive individualism." See Carl R. Trueman, *The Rise and Triumph of the Modern Self: Cultural Amnesia, Expressive Individualism, and the Road to Sexual Revolution* (Wheaton, IL: Crossway, 2020).

11. "Rhett's Spiritual Deconstruction," *Ear Biscuits* (podcast), February 3, 2020, video, 1:44:50, https://www.youtube.com/watch?v=1qbna6t1bzw.

12. "Link's Spiritual Deconstruction," *Ear Biscuits* (podcast), February 10, 2020, video, 1:37:49, https://www.youtube.com/watch?v=w1AZhlyoD9s.

CHAPTER 4: FALLOUT

1. Please note we're not saying experiencing the physical death of a loved one is *exactly the same* as experiencing the spiritual deconstruction of a loved one.
2. "The Phases of Deconstruction," accessed January 11, 2023, https://cdn.shopify.com/s/files/1/0542/0733/files/Deconstruction_Free_Guide_-_NakedPastor.com.pdf?v=1630575130&utm_source=Deconstruction. Emphasis added.
3. Derek Webb (@derekwebb), Twitter, October 10, 2017, 10:34 a.m., https://twitter.com/derekwebb/status/917775398460710914.
4. "Goodbye, For Now," track 13 on the album *Fingers Crossed*, produced, written, recorded, and performed by Derek Webb, released September 29, 2017, https://genius.com/Derek-webb-goodbye-for-now-annotated.
5. For more, see Alisa's book *Another Gospel?: A Lifelong Christian Seeks Truth in Response to Progressive Christianity* (Carol Stream, IL: Tyndale Elevate, 2020).
6. "Deconstruction Doesn't Mean You're Losing Your Faith," *Relevant*, December 1, 2021, https://relevantmagazine.com/faith/how-to-deconstruct-your-faith-without-losing-it/.
7. Angela J. Herrington, "Book Review: *Gaslighted by God* by Tiffany Yecke Brooks, PhD," AngelaJHerrington.com, accessed April 11, 2023, https://angelajherrington.com/book-review-gaslighted-by-god-by-tiffany-yecke-brooks-phd/.
8. Herrington, "Book Review: *Gaslighted by God*."
9. Elizabeth Dias, "Nashville Evangelical Church Comes Out for Marriage Equality," *Time*, January 29, 2015, https://time.com/3687368/gracepointe-church-nashville-marriage-equality/.
10. Everybody Church, "Stan Mitchell's Story (Part 3 of 3)," Facebook video 44:57 (quote starts at 10:43), August 11, 2019, https://www.facebook.com/everybodychurch/videos/646974352473924.
11. Everybody Church, "Stan Mitchell's Story (Part 3 of 3)," (quote starts at 11:09).
12. Phil Drysdale, "WTF Is Progressive Christianity?" *God Is Grey*, YouTube video, 1:14:39 (quote starts at 23:47), August 31, 2020, https://www.youtube.com/watch?v=6YEmqJBK3Ec.
13. Phil Drysdale (@phildrysdale), Instagram, May 13, 2022, https://www.instagram.com/p/Cdf-lTfF28l/.
14. Phil Drysdale (@phildrysdale), Instagram, May 10, 2022, https://www.instagram.com/p/CdYTyhmsVXK/.

CHAPTER 5: CRISIS

1. Chelsea Cole, "An Inside Look at Earthquake-Proof Buildings: Features, Designs, and Materials," Buildertrend, November 19, 2021, updated January 19, 2023, https://buildertrend.com/blog/extreme-building -earthquakes/.

2. Drew said this to me (Tim) in an interview on stage at the Reality Student Apologetics Conference in Seattle. This was recorded, though the video is not public.

3. Keith Giles, "The 6 Pillars of Religious Deconstruction," Patheos, August 27, 2019, https://www.patheos.com/blogs/keithgiles/2019/08/the-6-pillars -of-religious-deconstruction/.

4. Emily Strohm, "Jinger Duggar Vuolo on Growing Up under 'Cult-Like' Religious Beliefs: 'I Was Terrified of the Outside World,'" January 18, 2023, *People*, https://people.com/tv/jinger-duggar-vuolo-on-growing-up -following-cult-like-religious-beliefs/.

5. Jinger Duggar Vuolo, *Becoming Free Indeed: My Story of Disentangling Faith from Fear* (Nashville: W Publishing, 2023), 93.

6. Vuolo, *Becoming Free Indeed*, 9.

7. Ripley the Drifter (@RipleyDrifter), Twitter, October 15, 2022, 5:58 a.m., https://twitter.com/RipleyDrifter/status/1581238189255450624. Also, scroll through posts at https://twitter.com/search?q=Trump%20 %23exvangelical&src=typed_query&f=live.

8. Eve (@eve_wasframed), Instagram, October 19, 2022, https:// www.instagram.com/p/Cj5vJ07OvP3/.

9. Amy Davison, "What Went Wrong with the 90's 'Purity Culture'?," *Mama Bear Apologetics* (blog), accessed January 12, 2023, https:// mamabearapologetics.com/what-went-wrong-90s-pc/.

10. Terry Gross, "Memoirist: Evangelical Purity Movement Sees Women's Bodies as a 'Threat,'" NPR, September 18, 2018, https://www.npr .org/2018/09/18/648737143/memoirist-evangelical-purity-movement -sees-womens-bodies-as-a-threat.

11. Linda Kay Klein, *Pure: Inside the Evangelical Movement That Shamed a Generation of Young Women and How I Broke Free* (New York: Touchstone, 2018). See the description at https://lindakayklein.com/pure/.

12. Dan Kimball, "Deconstructing and Losing Faith by Reading the Bible," Christian Post, January 17, 2022, https://www.christianpost.com/voices /deconstructing-and-losing-faith-by-reading-the-bible.html.

13. Phil Drysdale (@phildrysdale), Instagram, accessed January 12, 2023, https://www.instagram.com/p/CifYSbusy9M/.

14. James Strong, *Strong's Concordance*, s.v. "olah," https://biblehub.com/hebrew /5930.htm.

15. Irreverent Reverend (@TheAmberPicota), Twitter, June 25, 2021, 7:31 a.m., https://twitter.com/TheAmberPicota/status/1408402522944032771.

16. Anna Skates, "The Trouble with Easter: How to (and Not to) Talk to Kids

about Easter," *Patheos*, April 12, 2017, https://www.patheos.com/blogs/unfundamentalistparenting/2017/04/trouble-easter-not-talk-kids-easter/.

17. ALLI⁷ i heart elon (@damnairport), Twitter, June 26, 2021, 12:14 a.m., https://twitter.com/damnairport/status/1408654984791666689.

18. Deconstruction Resources (@exfundamentalist), Instagram, October 23, 2022, https://www.instagram.com/p/CkEpvGWPaUo/, accessed March 8, 2023.

19. Deconstruction Resources (@exfundamentalist), Instagram, October 23, 2022, https://www.instagram.com/p/CkEpvGWPaUo/, accessed March 8, 2023.

20. Amatullah Shaw, "People Who've Experienced Religious Abuse Are Sharing Their Stories, and This Needs to Be Talked about Way More Often," *BuzzFeed*, October 27, 2021, https://www.buzzfeed.com/amatullahshaw/spiritual-abuse-survivors-stories.

21. Deconstruction Girl (@deconstructiongirl), Instagram, October 16, 2022, https://www.instagram.com/p/Cjx0RkmuVIE/.

22. Jo Luehmann, "Abusive Theology (Penal Substitutionary Atonement)," Facebook video, 1:00, March 2, 2021, https://www.facebook.com/watch/?v=903687307033184.

23. Greg Stier (@gregstier), Twitter, October 30, 2022, 7:46 a.m., https://twitter.com/gregstier/status/1586701041239674880.

24. Greg Stier is an evangelist, author, speaker, and founder of Dare 2 Share Ministries: https://www.dare2share.org/about/.

25. Greg Stier (@gregstier), Twitter, October 30, 2022, 7:46 a.m., https://twitter.com/gregstier/status/1586701041239674880.

CHAPTER 6: UPPER STORY

1. You can find this promo trailer at https://www.facebook.com/watch/?v=280688270481999.

2. Janice Lagata (@godhasnotgiven), Instagram video, 1:28, July 20, 2021, https://www.instagram.com/p/CRjyN3dnd6A/.

3. Douglas Groothuis, *Christian Apologetics: A Comprehensive Case for Biblical Faith* (Downers Grove, IL: IVP Academic, 2011), 117.

4. I learned this technique from my mentor and friend Greg Koukl.

5. Groothuis, *Christian Apologetics*, 124. Italics in the original.

6. Greg Koukl, "The Primal Heresy," *Stand to Reason* (blog), March 1, 2021, https://www.str.org/w/the-primal-heresy.

7. Nancy Pearcey, *Total Truth: Liberating Christianity from Its Cultural Captivity* (Wheaton, IL: Crossway, 2004, 2005), 233.

8. Pearcey, *Total Truth*, 21.

9. This is what Pearcey referred to as the "fact/value split." See Pearcey, *Total Truth*, 21.

10. Francis A. Schaeffer, *The God Who Is There* (Downers Grove, IL: InterVarsity Press, 1968), 96.

11. Pearcey, *Total Truth*, 21.

12. Pearcey, *Total Truth*, 119.

13. J. Warner Wallace, "I'm Not a Christian Because It Works for Me," *Cold-Case Christianity with J. Warner and Jimmy Wallace* (blog), May 10, 2019, https://coldcasechristianity.com/writings/im-not-a-christian-because-it-works-for-me/.

14. Lewis wrote, "I am trying here to prevent anyone saying the really foolish thing that people often say about Him: 'I'm ready to accept Jesus as a great moral teacher, but I don't accept His claim to be God.' That is the one thing we must not say. A man who was merely a man and said the sort of things Jesus said would not be a great moral teacher. He would either be a lunatic—on a level with the man who says he is a poached egg—or else he would be the Devil of Hell. You must make your choice. Either this man was, and is, the Son of God: or else a madman or something worse. You can shut Him up for a fool, you can spit at Him and kill Him as a demon; or you can fall at His feet and call Him Lord and God. But let us not come with any patronising nonsense about His being a great human teacher. He has not left that open to us. He did not intend to." C. S. Lewis, *Mere Christianity* in *C. S. Lewis Signature Classics* (New York: HarperCollins, 1952, 2002), 50–51.

15. Koukl, "Primal Heresy."

16. Koukl, "Primal Heresy."

17. Koukl, "Primal Heresy."

18. *Encyclopaedia Britannica Online*, s.v. "orthodoxy," accessed January 12, 2023, https://www.britannica.com/dictionary/orthodoxy.

19. *Encyclopaedia Britannica Online*, s.v. "heresy," accessed January 12, 2023, https://www.britannica.com/dictionary/heresy.

20. Heather Plett, quoted on Deconstructing Mamas (@deconstructingmamas), Facebook, September 25, 2022, https://www.facebook.com/deconstructing mamas/posts/pfbid02bFnifJTksoJnKq45Aq3Xh8eLGnkoPe1rA8M3We 7ZVkt5uPMXJZmayS1ectP6KF1xl.

21. Esther Joy Goetz, quoted on Deconstructing Mamas (@deconstructingmamas), Facebook, October 9, 2022, https://www.facebook.com/deconstructingmamas /photos/188245027035442.

22. Jo Luehmann, "Our Journey of Faith Deconstruction," YouTube video, 23:16 (quote starts at 3:53), March 19, 2019, https://www.youtube .com/watch?v=Vl8b3YeePZA.

23. Ericka Andersen, "Deconstructing? There's a Coach for That," Religion News Service, May 12, 2022, https://religionnews.com/2022/05/12 /deconstructing-theres-a-coach-for-that/.

24. Katie Blake, "I'm Katie, a Belief Artisan," Katie Blake website, https:// drkatieblake.com/about.

25. Katie Blake, "What Is a Belief Artisan? Learning to Be Creative with

Your Beliefs," Katie Blake website, accessed January 12, 2023, https://drkatieblake.com/blog/2022/8/4/what-it-means-to-be-a-belief-artisan.

26. Francis Beckwith, "What's Upstairs," review of *Total Truth: Liberating Christianity from Its Cultural Captivity* by Nancy Pearcey, *First Things*, November 2004, https://www.firstthings.com/article/2004/11/total-truth -liberating-christianity-from-its-cultural-captivity.

27. "Find Your Way," emphasis in the original, Our Bible App, accessed January 12, 2023, https://www.ourbibleapp.com.

28. Andersen, "Deconstructing? There's a Coach for That."

29. "About Our Bible App," Our Bible App, accessed March 8, 2023, https://www.ourbibleapp.com/mission.

30. "Deconstruction Coaching," Kurtis Vanderpool Life Coaching website, accessed January 12, 2023, https://kurtisvanderpool.com/deconstruction -coaching/.

31. David Hayward (@nakedpastor), Twitter video, 0:26, June 7, 2022, 11:09 a.m., https://twitter.com/nakedpastor/status/1534205802000547842.

32. David Hayward (@nakedpastor), TikTok video, 0:58, February 25, 2023, https://www.tiktok.com/@nakedpastor/video/7204152138124233990.

33. Pearcey, *Total Truth*, 20. Italics in the original.

34. Angela J. Herrington, quoted on Deconstructing Mamas (@deconstructingmamas), Facebook, October 22, 2022, https://www.facebook.com/deconstructingmamas/photos/190903750102903.

35. Chris Kratzer, Facebook, June 17, 2022, https://www.facebook .com/CreatedForConversation/, accessed March 9, 2023.

36. Chris Kratzer, Facebook, September 21, 2022, https://www.facebook .com/chris.kratzer/posts/pfbid02ppYCPKaArHVs6gHB4HtndcmW 7FXCti7T3BEYDC7PdZ2Dwwe4E1cBBVcZceQj4VQtl.

37. John Wenham, *Christ and the Bible*, 3rd ed. (Eugene, OR: Wipf and Stock, 2009).

CHAPTER 7: REFORMATION

1. Vi La Bianca (@AuthorConfusion), Twitter, March 13, 2022, 9:09 a.m., https://twitter.com/AuthorConfusion/status/1503010444759506944.

2. Thomas C. Brickhouse and Nicholas D. Smith, *Plato's Socrates* (New York: Oxford University Press, 1994), 14.

3. Andre Henry, "Deconstruction Is a Valid Christian Practice. Ask Martin Luther," Religion News Service, January 5, 2022, https://religionnews .com/2022/01/05/deconstruction-is-a-valid-christian-practice-ask -martin-luther/.

4. Henry, "Deconstruction Is a Valid Christian Practice."

5. Derek Webb (@derekwebb), Twitter, July 4, 2022, 3:31 p.m., https://twitter.com/derekwebb/status/1544056295707246595.

6. Michael Horton, "Reformed and Always Reforming," in *Always Reformed:*

Essays in Honor of W. Robert Godfrey, ed. R. Scott Clark and Joel E. Kim (Escondido, CA: Westminster Seminary California, 2012), 116–134.

7. Michael Horton (@MichaelHorton_), Twitter, August 1, 2015, 3:54 p.m., https://twitter.com/MichaelHorton_/status/627583159870230528.

8. Kevin DeYoung, "Semper Reformanda," The Gospel Coalition (blog), October 27, 2016, https://www.thegospelcoalition.org/blogs/kevin-deyoung/semper-reformanda/.

9. DeYoung, "Semper Reformanda."

10. "The Airing of Grief and Unbelief (Beliefs x Authenticity) with Derek Webb," *Listen Now: The Life After Podcast*, 88:12 (quote starts at 77:30), March 23, 2018, https://www.stitcher.com/show/the-life-after/episode/the-airing-of-grief-and-unbelief-beliefs-x-authenticity-with-derek-webb-53823682.

11. Dianne Modestini, "History of the Salvator Mundi," Salvator Mundi Revisited website, accessed January 12, 2023, https://salvatormundirevisited.com/History-of-the-Salvator-Mundi.

12. See "Salvator Mundi Revisited," https://salvatormundirevisited.com/Pentimenti. Despite this finding, there is still debate over whether this painting is original.

13. There's even a fascinating documentary called *The Lost Leonardo*, released in 2021 by Sony Pictures Classics.

14. Martin Bailey, "Major Museum Casts Fresh Doubt over the Authenticity of $450M 'Salvator Mundi,'" CNN, November 16, 2021, https://www.cnn.com/style/article/salvator-mundi-prado-museum/index.html.

15. Katya Kazakina, "That Missing $450 Million da Vinci Painting Is Reportedly on Saudi Crown Prince MBS' Yacht," *Time*, June 10, 2019, https://time.com/5604018/missing-da-vinci-painting-mbs-yacht/.

16. "Woman Who Ruined Spanish Fresco 'Had Permission' from Priest," BBC News, August 23, 2012, https://www.bbc.com/news/av/world-europe-19358072.

17. Laura Allsop, "Living Up to Leonardo: The Terrifying Task of Restoring a da Vinci," CNN, November 10, 2011, https://www.cnn.com/2011/11/10/living/restoring-leonardo-da-vinci.

18. Deconstruction Girl (@deconstructgirl), Instagram, February 4, 2022, https://www.instagram.com/p/CZkmaKSLH_t/.

19. This challenge is simple to refute when one understands the true nature of Jesus' sacrifice on the cross. For more, see William Lane Craig, *Atonement and the Death of Christ: An Exegetical, Historical, and Philosophical Exploration* (Waco, TX: Baylor University Press, 2020).

20. William Lane Craig, *Reasonable Faith: Christian Truth and Apologetics*, 3rd ed. (Wheaton, IL: Crossway, 2008), 15.

21. Francis A. Schaeffer, *The God Who Is There* (Downers Grove, IL: InterVarsity Press, 1968), 137–143.

22. Alister E. McGrath, *Mere Apologetics: How to Help Seekers and Skeptics Find Faith* (Grand Rapids, MI: Baker Books, 2012), 23.

23. Here we summarize an argument articulated by Steven B. Cowan and Terry L. Wilder, eds., *In Defense of the Bible: A Comprehensive Apologetic for the Authority of Scripture* (Nashville, TN: Broadman and Holman, 2013), 443.

24. Cowan and Wilder, *In Defense of the Bible*, 446.

25. Cowan and Wilder, *In Defense of the Bible*, 444.

26. Craig, *Reasonable Faith*, 300.

27. See also N. T. Wright, *The Resurrection of the Son of God* (Minneapolis, MN: Fortress Press, 2003); Michael R. Licona, *The Resurrection of Jesus: A New Historiographical Approach* (Downers Grove, IL: InterVarsity Press, 2010); and Gary R. Habermas and Michael R. Licona, *The Case for the Resurrection of Jesus* (Grand Rapids, MI: Kregel, 2004).

28. For a defense of each, see William Lane Craig's book *Reasonable Faith*.

29. Craig, *Reasonable Faith*, 399.

30. Cowan and Wilder, *In Defense of the Bible*, 447.

31. John Wenham, *Christ and the Bible* (Eugene, OR: Wipf and Stock, 2009), 28.

32. Craig L. Blomberg, *The Historical Reliability of John's Gospel: Issues and Commentary* (Downers Grove, IL: IVP Academic, 2001), 214.

33. Michael J. Kruger, "'When They Read the Old Covenant': Canonical Clues in 2 Cor 3:14," *Canon Fodder* (blog), December 3, 2012, https:// www.michaeljkruger.com/when-they-read-the-old-covenant-canonical -clues-in-2-cor-314/.

34. Cowan and Wilder, *In Defense of the Bible*, 462.

CHAPTER 8: TOXIC

1. Shaley: Cult Slayer (@shaysserendipity), TikTok video, 0:27, https:// www.tiktok.com/@shaysserendipity/video/7144443432449166638.

2. Greg Koukl, "Freedom Fading," *Stand to Reason* (blog), May 1, 2021, https://www.str.org/w/freedom-fading.

3. It would be beyond the scope of this book to fully explain critical theory here, but for an expanded treatment of critical theory and Christianity, see Neil Shenvi and Patrick Sawyer, "Engaging Critical Theory and the Social Justice Movement," Ratio Christi, June 5, 2019, https://ratiochristi .org/engaging-critical-theory-and-the-social-justice-movement/.

4. eve_wasframed (@evewasframed), TikTok, January 17, 2023, https://www.instagram.com/p/CnhdRUfK7ej/.

5. C. S. Lewis, "Bulverism," in *God in the Dock*, ed. Walter Hooper (Grand Rapids, MI: Eerdmans, 1970), 271.

6. C. S. Lewis, *God in the Dock*, 273. Italics in the original.

7. Jonathan Leeman, "Editor's Note: Defending Sound Doctrine against

the Deconstruction of American Evangelicalism," 9Marks, November 16, 2021, https://www.9marks.org/article/editors-note-defending-sound -doctrine-against-the-deconstruction-of-american-evangelicalism/.

8. Angela J. Herrington, "Why Faith Deconstruction Won't Go Away (and Why That's Good)," accessed January 12, 2023, https://angelajherrington .com/why-faith-deconstruction-wont-go-away-and-why-thats-good/.

9. Herrington, "Why Faith Deconstruction Won't Go Away."

10. David Gushee, "The Deconstruction of American Evangelicalism," Baptist News Global, October 11, 2021, https://baptistnews.com/article /the-deconstruction-of-american-evangelicalism/#.Y225dS-B2L0.

11. Neil Shenvi (@NeilShenvi), Twitter, December 1, 2021, 6:40 a.m., https://twitter.com/NeilShenvi/status/1466024473207918594.

12. Gushee, "Deconstruction of American Evangelicalism."

13. Neil Shenvi, "Sociology as Theology: The Deconstruction of Power in (Post) Evangelical Scholarship," Council on Biblical Manhood and Womanhood, November 21, 2021, https://cbmw.org/2021/11/21/sociology-as-theology -the-deconstruction-of-power-in-postevangelical-scholarship/.

14. Shenvi, "Sociology as Theology."

15. John R. Searle, "The Word Turned Upside Down," *New York Review of Books*, October 27, 1983, https://www.nybooks.com/articles/1983/10/27 /the-word-turned-upside-down/.

16. Beth Allison Barr, *The Making of Biblical Womanhood: How the Subjugation of Women Became Gospel Truth* (Grand Rapids, MI: Brazos, 2021), 201.

17. Barr, *Making of Biblical Womanhood*, 5.

18. Barr, *Making of Biblical Womanhood*, 2–3.

19. Barr, *Making of Biblical Womanhood*, 201–204.

20. Barr, *Making of Biblical Womanhood*, 9.

21. Barr, *Making of Biblical Womanhood*, 6.

22. Barr, *Making of Biblical Womanhood*, 201.

23. Barr, *Making of Biblical Womanhood*, 207.

24. Barr, *Making of Biblical Womanhood*, 191.

25. Barr, *Making of Biblical Womanhood*, 7.

26. Barr, *Making of Biblical Womanhood*, 5.

27. For a thorough critique, see Kevin DeYoung, "*The Making of Biblical Womanhood*: A Review," *Themelios* 46, no. 2, accessed January 12, 2023, https://www.thegospelcoalition.org/themelios/article/the-making-of -biblical-womanhood-a-review/.

28. Barr, *Making of Biblical Womanhood*, 14.

29. Barr, *Making of Biblical Womanhood*, 36.

30. Barr, *Making of Biblical Womanhood*, 218.

31. Barr, *Making of Biblical Womanhood*, 218.

32. Kristin Kobes Du Mez, *Jesus and John Wayne: How White Evangelicals Corrupted a Faith and Fractured a Nation* (New York: Liveright, 2020), 88.

33. Andrew T. Walker (@andrewtwalk), Twitter, October 12, 2021, 2:14 p.m., https://twitter.com/andrewtwalk/status/1448004251519787012.

34. Michael Foucault, "Truth and Power" in *Power/Knowledge: Selected Interviews and Other Writings 1972–1977*, ed. Colin Gordon (New York: Pantheon Books, 1980), 133.

35. Jacques Derrida, *The Post Card: From Socrates to Freud and Beyond*, trans. Alan Bass (Chicago: University of Chicago Press, 1987).

36. John D. Caputo, *What Would Jesus Deconstruct?: The Good News of Postmodernism for the Church* (Grand Rapids, MI: Baker Academic, 2007), 47. Italics in the original.

37. Caputo, *What Would Jesus Deconstruct?*, 48. Italics in the original.

38. Caputo, *What Would Jesus Deconstruct?*, 108–109.

39. Caputo, *What Would Jesus Deconstruct?*, 109.

40. Caputo, *What Would Jesus Deconstruct?*, 109.

41. Ryan Ashton (@ryanllashton), Twitter, December 2021, 11:39 a.m., https://twitter.com/ryanllashton/status/1476971307388616705.

42. Kristin Du Mez (@kkdumez), Twitter, December 31, 2021, 11:53 a.m., https://twitter.com/kkdumez/status/1476974873377443844.

43. Russell, Haggar, "Gramsci and Neo-Marxism: An Introduction," Earlham Sociology and Political Pages, accessed April 19, 2023, https://earlhamsociologypages.uk/gramscineomarxism/; Andrew Fagan, "Theodor W. Adorno," Internet Encyclopedia of Philosophy, accessed April 19, 2023, https://iep.utm.edu/adorno/.

44. Martin Beck Matustik, "Philosophy and Social Theory of Jürgen Habermas," *Encyclopaedia Britannica*, accessed April 19, 2023, https://www.britannica.com/biography/Jurgen-Habermas/Philosophy-and-social-theory.

45. "Ep 18—John D. Caputo 'Derrida/Deconstruction/Weak Theology,'" *The Deconstructionists* podcast, July 6, 2016, 1:17:56 (quote starts at 13:57), https://podcasts.apple.com/us/podcast/ep-18-john-d-caputo-derrida-deconstruction-weak-theology/id1080170463?i=1000371979152.

46. Caputo, *What Would Jesus Deconstruct?*, 35.

47. Rachel Held Evans and Jeff Chu, *Wholehearted Faith* (New York: HarperCollins, 2021), 124.

48. Evans and Chu, *Wholehearted Faith*, 124.

49. Evans and Chu, *Wholehearted Faith*, 124.

50. Evans and Chu, *Wholehearted Faith*, 125.

51. "Ep 18—John D. Caputo—Derrida/Deconstruction/Weak Theology," (quote starts at 56:19).

52. "Ep 18—John D. Caputo—Derrida/Deconstruction/Weak Theology," (quote starts at 55:47).

53. James K. A. Smith, "Who's Afraid of Postmodernism? A Response to the 'Biola School,'" chapter 11 in *Christianity and the Postmodern Turn:*

Six Views, ed. Myron B. Penner (Grand Rapids, MI: Brazos Press, 2005), 225.

54. Richard Brian Davis and W. Paul Franks, "Against a Postmodern Pentecostal Epistemology," *Philosophia Christi* 15, no. 2 (2013), 387.

55. Davis and Franks, "Against a Postmodern Pentecostal Epistemology," 388.

CHAPTER 9: FAITH

1. Jo Luehmann, "Our Journey of Faith Deconstruction," YouTube video, 23:06 (quote starts at 21:19), March 19, 2019, https://www.youtube.com/watch?v=Vl8b3YeePZA.

2. Luehmann, "Our Journey of Faith Deconstruction," (quote starts at 21:52).

3. Alisa Childers, *Another Gospel?: A Lifelong Christian Seeks Truth in Response to Progressive Christianity* (Carol Stream, IL: Tyndale Elevate, 2020), 24.

4. "WTF Is Progressive Christianity?," *God Is Grey*, YouTube video, 1:14:39 (quote starts at 1:16), https://www.youtube.com/watch?v=6YEmqJBK3Ec, emphasis added.

5. Lisa Gungor, *The Most Beautiful Thing I've Seen: Opening Your Eyes to Wonder* (Grand Rapids, MI: Zondervan, 2018), 95. Italics in the original.

6. "My Deconversion Story," Jake the Atheist, YouTube video, 11:47 (quote starts at 8:20), https://www.youtube.com/watch?v=4p-PdYjpGj8.

7. "My Deconversion Story," Jake the Atheist (quote starts at 9:39).

8. J. P. Moreland, *Love Your God with All Your Mind: The Role of Reason in the Life of the Soul*, 2nd ed. (Colorado Springs, CO: NavPress, 2012), 19.

9. Mark Twain, "Pudd'nhead Wilson's New Calendar" in *Following the Equator* (1897), ch. 12, http://www.online-literature.com/twain/following-the-equator/12/.

10. Peter Boghossian, *A Manual for Creating Atheists* (Durham, NC: Pitchstone, 2013), 23.

11. Boghossian, *Manual for Creating Atheists*, 23.

12. Moreland, *Love Your God with All Your Mind*, 19, emphasis in original.

13. John C. Lennox, *God's Undertaker: Has Science Buried God?* (Oxford, UK: Lion Hudson, 2007), 15.

14. Gregory Koukl, "Is Faith Irrational?" in Sean McDowell and Jonathan Morrow, *Is God Just a Human Invention?: And Seventeen Other Questions Raised by the New Atheists* (Grand Rapids, MI: Kregel, 2010), 30.

15. Os Guinness, *God in the Dark: The Assurance of Faith beyond a Shadow of a Doubt* (Wheaton, IL: Crossway, 1996), 80.

CHAPTER 10: DECONSTRUCTOR

1. Francis A. Schaeffer, *He Is There and He Is Not Silent* (Carol Stream, IL: Tyndale House, 1972), 3.

2. The Deconstruction Network (@thedeconstructionnetwork), Instagram, October 26, 2022, https://www.instagram.com/p/CkLlv8stzj0/.

3. Phil Drysdale (@phildrysdale), Instagram, September 22, 2021, https://www.instagram.com/p/CUIHEUQsfOi/.

4. Deconstruction Girl (@deconstructiongirl), Instagram, October 24, 2022, https://www.instagram.com/p/CkGuOPyuodD/.

5. John Stott, *Basic Christianity*, 3rd ed. (Grand Rapids, MI: Eerdmans, 2008), 8.

6. Patrick Carnegie Simpson, *The Fact of Christ: A Series of Lectures*, 2nd ed. (London: Hodder and Stoughton, 1901), 39–40.

7. Gregory Koukl, *The Story of Reality: How the World Began, How It Ends, and Everything Important That Happens in Between* (Grand Rapids, MI: Zondervan, 2017), 75.

8. Phil Drysdale (@phildrysdale), Instagram, accessed January 13, 2023, https://www.instagram.com/phildrysdale/.

9. Phil Drysdale (@phildrysdale), Instagram, October 27, 2021, https://www.instagram.com/p/CViAzeMM7bD/.

10. Phil Drysdale (@phildrysdale), Instagram video, July 28, 2022, https://www.instagram.com/p/CgjvG2GFrRc/.

11. Peter Kreeft, quoted in Lee Strobel, *The Case for Faith: A Journalist Investigates the Toughest Objections to Christianity* (Grand Rapids, MI: Zondervan, 2000), 33.

12. John D. Caputo, *What Would Jesus Deconstruct?: The Good News of Postmodernism for the Church* (Grand Rapids, MI: Baker Academic, 2007), 57. Italics in the original.

13. Julia (@thatlouddeconstructingone), Instagram, September 8, 2021, https://www.instagram.com/p/CTkFcDOLAKa/.

14. Mel (@runofthemel), Twitter, March 4, 2021, https://twitter.com/runofthemel/status/1367497596177182730.

15. Josh (@thelocalheretic), TikTok video, 2:55, October 23, 2022, https://www.tiktok.com/@thelocalheretic/video/7157800566364589358.

16. Leah MarieAnn Klett, "Hillsong Writer: 'I'm Genuinely Losing My Faith,'" Christian Post, August 12, 2019, https://www.christianpost.com/news/hillsong-writer-reveals-hes-no-longer-a-christian-im-genuinely-losing-my-faith.html.

17. Hemant Mehta, "The Atheist Daughter of a Notable Christian Apologist Shares Her Story," guest post by Rachael Slick, Patheos, July 15, 2013, https://friendlyatheist.patheos.com/2013/07/15/the-atheist-daughter-of-a-notable-christian-apologist-shares-her-story/.

18. Francis A. Schaeffer, *He Is There and He Is Not Silent*, rev. ed. (Carol Stream, IL: Tyndale House, 2001), xxiv–xxv.

PART 3: #HOPE

1. Dave's story was taken with his permission from a personal email with the author and this podcast interview: Alisa Childers, "Faith after Deconstruction: Audio Adrenaline's Dave Stovall Shares What Brought Him Back," YouTube video, 55:47, March 28, 2021, https://www.youtube .com/watch?v=an__eC8pE0Y.

CHAPTER 11: QUESTIONS

1. Nathaniel Bluedorn and Hans Bluedorn, *The Thinking Toolbox: Thirty-Five Lessons That Will Build Your Reasoning Skills* (Muscatine, IA: Christian Logic, 2005), 16.

2. "Six Reasons Young Christians Leave Church," Barna Research: Millennials and Generations, September 27, 2011, https://www.barna .com/research/six-reasons-young-christians-leave-church/.

3. "Six Reasons Young Christians Leave Church."

4. "Hillsong Songwriter Marty Sampson Says He's Losing His Christian Faith," *Relevant*, August 12, 2019, https://relevantmagazine.com/culture /hillsong-songwriter-marty-sampson-says-hes-losing-his-christian-faith/.

5. Tim Keller, "5 Reasons to Host a Q&A after Your Worship Service," The Gospel Coalition, July 27, 2016, https://www.thegospelcoalition .org/article/5-reasons-to-host-qa-after-worship-service/.

6. "Deconstruction, Doubt and Finding Faith Again—Lisa Gungor and Alisa Childers," Premier Unbelievable? (@PremierUnbelievable), YouTube video, 1:10:50 (quote starts at 4:59), September 18, 2019, https://www.youtube.com/watch?v=So9NJ72_IiI.

7. Os Guinness, *God in the Dark: The Assurance of Faith Beyond a Shadow of Doubt* (Wheaton, IL: Crossway, 1996), 21.

8. Guinness, *God in the Dark*, 22.

9. David Kinnaman with Aly Hawkins, *You Lost Me: Why Young Christians Are Leaving Church . . . and Rethinking Faith* (Grand Rapids, MI: Baker Books, 2011), 192. Italics in the original.

10. Kara Powell and Steven Argue, "The Biggest Hindrance to Your Kids' Faith Isn't Doubt. It's Silence," *Christianity Today*, February 21, 2019, https://www.christianitytoday.com/ct/2019/february-web-only/doubt -parenting-biggest-hindrance-kids-faith-is-silence.html.

11. B. A. Gerrish, *A Prince of the Church: Schleiermacher and the Beginnings of Modern Theology* (Philadelphia: Fortress Press, 1984), 25.

12. "Ray Comfort's 2006 Hysterical Banana Argument Demonstrates What Creationists Mean by 'Proof,'" HuffPost, February 24, 2014, https:// www.huffpost.com/entry/ray-comforts-banana-argument_n_4847082.

13. Saint Augustine, *Confessions*, trans. R. S. Pine-Coffin (Baltimore: Penguin, 1961), 262.

14. Gavin Ortlund, "4 Problems with Downplaying God's Wrath," The

Gospel Coalition, January 5, 2018, https://www.thegospelcoalition
.org/article/4-problems-downplaying-divine-wrath/.

15. It also won't do to simply attribute this to Nahum's own interpretation of God. The apostle Peter says, "No prophecy of Scripture comes from someone's own interpretation. For no prophecy was ever produced by the will of man, but men spoke from God as they were carried along by the Holy Spirit" (2 Peter 1:20-21).

16. Greg Koukl, "Faithfulness Is Not Theologically Complicated," *Stand to Reason* (blog), September 1, 2019, https://www.str.org/w/faithfulness
-is-not-theologically-complicated-1.

17. Blaise Pascal, *The Living Thoughts of Pascal*, presented by François Mauriac, ed. Alfred O. Mendel (Philadelphia: David McKay, 1940), 117–118.

CHAPTER 13: SATURDAY

1. Alisa Childers, *Another Gospel?: A Lifelong Christian Seeks Truth in Response to Progressive Christianity* (Carol Stream, IL: Tyndale Elevate, 2020), 235.

2. John Ortberg, *Faith and Doubt* (Grand Rapids, MI: Zondervan, 2008), 79. Italics in the original.

About the Authors

Alisa Childers is a wife, a mom, an author, and a speaker. She was a member of the award-winning CCM recording group ZOEgirl. She is a popular speaker at apologetics and Christian worldview conferences. She is the author of *Another Gospel?* and *Live Your Truth and Other Lies.* She has been published at The Gospel Coalition, Crosswalk, the Stream, For Every Mom, *Decision* magazine, and The Christian Post. You can connect with Alisa online at alisachilders.com.

Tim Barnett is a husband, a father, an author, and a social media content creator. He is a speaker and apologist for Stand to Reason (STR). In addition, his online presence on *Red Pen Logic with Mr. B* helps people assess bad thinking by using good thinking, reaching millions of people every month through multiple social media platforms. Tim resides in the greater Toronto area with his wife, Stacey. They have three daughters and a Morkipoo.

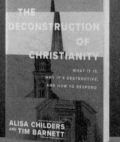

RECLAIM THE TIMELESS TRUTHS
OF HISTORIC CHRISTIAN BELIEFS

Another Gospel?—In a culture of endless questions, you need solid answers. If you have encountered the ideas of progressive Christianity and aren't sure how to respond, Alisa's journey will show you how to determine—and rest in—what's unmistakably true.

Another Gospel? DVD Experience—In this six-session series, Alisa will teach you how to use discernment, think logically, and make biblically based observations. This DVD experience includes in-depth interviews with *Cold-Case Christianity* author J. Warner Wallace and popular *Waddo You Meme??* YouTube apologist Jon McCray. Also available via streaming.

Another Gospel? Participant's Guide—This six-session workbook is designed for use with the companion *Another Gospel? DVD Experience*. This is a great resource for anyone wanting to explore the nuanced topic of progressive Christianity in a group or individually.